D. Ash

Mexican Americans

ETHNIC GROUPS IN COMPARATIVE
PERSPECTIVE • General Editor
PETER I. ROSE *Smith College*

Random House, New York

Mexican Americans

Ellwyn R. Stoddard
University of Texas at El Paso

Library of Congress Cataloging in Publication Data

Stoddard, Ellwyn R   1927-
Mexican Americans.

(Ethnic groups in comparative perspective)
Bibliography: p.
1. Mexican Americans. I. Title.
E184.M5S73   301.45 16 872073   73-3163

Manufactured in the United States of America.

First Edition

98765

Sincerely dedicated
    to all Mexican Americans, Chicanos, or any other names
    by which they are known,
            who inspired this volume

◉ Foreword

"Nation of nations" or "*Herrenvolk* democracy"? Melting pot or seething caldron? How does one describe the ethnic character of the United States?

The conventional wisdom, reflected in traditional texts on American history and society, tells of the odyssey of one group of newcomers after another who came to these shores: some of their own free will and others in the chains of bondage; some to escape religious persecution, others fleeing from political oppression, and many seeking their fortunes. "Rich and poor," goes the story, "mighty and meek, white and black, Jew and Gentile, Protestant and Catholic, Irishman and Italian and Pole . . . a motley array who, together, make up the Great American Nation."

Although many a school child can recite the litany, even he knows that it has a rather hollow ring. For most people there are at least three kinds of Americans: whatever one happens to be, the members of the dominant group (viewed differently depending where one stands in the status hierarchy), and everybody else. And, if one happens to see himself as a member of the dominant group, the number of alternatives may be reduced to two: they and we.

For a variety of reasons writers of textbooks and teachers of American history have tended to overlook or underplay this essential fact of American life. While acknowledging the pluralistic character of the social structure and celebrating the extent to which "our differences make us strong," they rarely convey the true meaning of membership in an ethnic group. And none know this better than those whose life experiences belie the notion of tolerance for all. Recently, a common plea has arisen from various quarters: "Give us equal time."

In response to such demands there have been attempts to

alter the rather lopsided image of American history and of the American people. Historians and social scientists have begun to respond to the call for a more accurate and meaningful view of race and ethnicity in America. Many have sought to "redress the balance," as they say, by upgrading the status of one group or another and rewriting their history to parallel that of the dominant group. One finds new volumes that appear to make the same strategic errors as those they wish to complement, i.e., placing emphasis on great events and prominent figures while avoiding in-depth descriptions of patterns of social organization, cultural traditions, and everyday activities.

Fortunately, there have been some other approaches tried recently, most notably studies seeking to reassess the entire ethnic experience not by playing the mirroring game (we have a hero, you have a hero; we have a holiday, you have a holiday; everybody has . . .) but by getting to the core of the social and economic and political realities of existence for the various peoples who came (or were brought) and stayed. The work of the latter scholars is far more important and, by its very nature, far more difficult. It involves new ways of looking, new prospectives. It encourages the examination of history and biography, of episode and event, as before. But it also requires careful study of culture and community and character, the examination of everyday life.

Those who have and use such an imagination (C. Wright Mills called it "the sociological imagination") must possess a willingness to challenge the old homilies, to get away from stereotypes and deal with real people, and to relate that which is revealed with both detachment and compassion.

For a student to truly understand the nature of group life in the United States and the relevance of race, religion, and nationality as meaningful social categories (and critical social variables), he should receive two kinds of messages: those which help him to know, and others which help him to understand. This means that, if truly successful, writers of articles and books on the Irish in America, or the Jews, or the black experience, should be able to evoke in their readers some sense of empathy, some visceral response to what it means to read a sign IRISH NEED NOT APPLY, or to hear the echo of "Sheeney,

Sheeney, Sheeney" ricochet off the walls between two old-law tenements, or to know what it is to be called "boy" by some and "brother" by others.

In planning the series it was decided that all books should follow a relatively common format which would include chapters on social history, descriptions of social organization of the various communities and their differing cultural characteristics, relations with others and with the wider society, and a conclusion to tie the early chapters together.

The very best qualified historians and social scientists would be invited to join in the venture, those not only informed but committed to the approach sketched earlier. Each author would be given the freedom to work within the framework in his own way and in his own literary style so that each volume would be a unique contribution to the overall project—and each could stand alone.

ABOUT THIS BOOK

One of our largest minorities, a people whose homeland is closest of all to the United States (in fact, some of it is now *in* the United States), is hardly known by most of our countrymen. When the average American thinks of Mexican Americans, images of mustachioed desperadoes or sombreroed peons or dark-shawled señoras fill his mind's eye. The stereotypes are not only offensive to those so caricatured, they are often far off target. The fact is that most of us know more about peoples who came from across the seas than about those who came from across the Rio Grande—or, along with other native Americans, were already here.

Careful study of the culture and character of Mexican Americans shows great variety, though, to be sure, certain unifying threads tend to bind members of what some call "La Raza" together. There is the Indian strain and, of course, the Spanish —which is manifest most clearly in certain traditions and in their language. And, like so many other ethnic groups who become "hyphenates" (joining what they were with where they now find themselves), Mexican Americans have also been quite heavily influenced—some would say confused—by the manners and mores, the aspirations and the values, of members of the dominant Anglo society.

The differences that exist show up when one moves from one southwestern region to another, from one class level to another, from one generation to another. These factors separately and in combination account for a certain amount of conflict and contradiction within the larger Mexican American context and, especially, for different solutions to problems that have been endemic since the Treaty of Guadalupe Hidalgo.

The sociologist who attempts to study so vast a grouping (well over 6 million in number, making it the second largest nonwhite minority in the nation) must ask a number of questions. How do these people see themselves? Each other? How do they deal with their past, including their relationship to the Catholic Church and its missions? What does it mean to be called "Chicano," that corruption of "Mexicano" which seems to be viewed with pride by some and scorn by others? Who, if anyone, can speak for this group that is not really a community? Who should? What relationship exists between Mexican Americans and others who are often the victims of ignorance and/or the target of prejudice? What should it be?

These questions and many others are difficult to answer. An attempt is made to do so in the pages to follow. This book, *Mexican Americans*, is the fifth to appear in the ethnic series. The present author, like the others, begins in the beginning. Professor Stoddard considers the Hispanization of the native Mexicans, the story of annexation, and the various attempts that have been made to Anglicize the immigrants from south of the border; he deals with the problems of identity, the clash of values, educational programming and social mobility, community organization. On close examination one finds a comprehensive and, at various points, controversial treatment of a very complicated subject.

Utah-born and educated (through the Master's level), Ellwyn Stoddard's first professional contacts with Mexican Americans came as a result of research he conducted for his Michigan State University Ph.D. dissertation, "Catastrophe and Crisis in a Flooded Border Community." That early research on a natural disaster ultimately led him into the study of potential disasters in social relationships.

In addition to his concern with the border and its many problems, Professor Stoddard has investigated and reported on a number of interesting issues including community development in several midwestern towns, policemen and "blue-coat crime," and role strain and alienation in military intelligence. In his many research reports, articles, and essays, Professor Stoddard has demonstrated an intensity of commitment, a catholicity of interest, and a willingness to try to move beyond the myths to get at the facts. This volume is no exception. It is a thorough study covering a wide range of topics that, together, give the reader not only a portrait of Mexican Americans by an outsider who came to know, to interpret, and to write their history, but also a sociological account that is both sensitive and sound.

Mexican Americans now takes its place alongside the other volumes in this series on Ethnic Groups in Comparative Perspective. Its author, Ellwyn Stoddard, takes his place along with other important commentators on American ethnic groups.

Peter I. Rose

Northampton, Massachusetts

◉ Preface

The story of the Mexican American people can be told from two perspectives. It can be told by a Mexican American, who reveals his inner feelings of joy, privation, and satisfaction at being identified with that ethnic group, or by an external observer who is not Mexican American by birth and who relies on both Mexican American writings and other accounts to give the most accurate picture possible of the heterogeneity of the Mexican American social structure. There is a need for each type of book, and whereas this book is of the latter type, it does not replace ethnically based work—nor is this its purpose.

Many individuals have made direct and indirect contributions to this volume that merit my gratitude and appreciation. Peter I. Rose, this series' editor, took a chance with an Anglo-surnamed scholar in recommending this volume for publication. Moreover, his criticisms of the initial manuscript were very helpful. Ilene Haimowitz and her associates contributed to its readability through their painstaking editorial work. And my fellow scholars, by their professional contributions over the years, have supplied me with the raw materials from which to make this integrated synthesis. Also, thanks to Mexican American and Chicano friends and colleagues who provided criticisms of former drafts from which valuable insights were gained for improving this book. But my own deep personal debt of gratitude must be extended to all Spanish-speaking persons who have touched my life—from the warm people of Argentina, who, more than a quarter-century ago, allowed me to catch a glimpse of their world, to my current friends and associates throughout the Southwest, who have shared with me their rich heritage and have, in so doing, enriched my own.

E. R. Stoddard

El Paso, 1973

◎ Contents

Mexican Americans

Chapter 1 ◉ Introduction

Of the more than 9 million persons of Spanish descent reported in the United States in 1970, more than 6 million are of Mexican or Spanish American background.[1] The only larger minority group within the United States of America is the black population, which numbers some 22 million.

Mexican Americans are principally located in five southwestern states. They constitute one out of every three persons in New Mexico, one out of every six persons in Arizona and Texas, and one out of every ten persons in California and Colorado (Manuel, 1965:24). One of every three Spanish-speaking persons in the Southwest lives in one of its four urban centers—Los Angeles, San Antonio, San Francisco, or El Paso. A numerical and cultural force to be reckoned with, they cannot be ignored as they have been in the past. Moreover, this ethnic bloc will no longer allow distorted accounts of their cultural heritage to be disseminated without reacting overtly to correct them. A private interview with a prominent Mexican educator illustrates well this reaction.

Anglo history always begins with the premise that nothing of importance happened in America until the Europeans arrived; that American southwestern residents anxiously awaited the Anglo[2] invaders so that they could whip things into shape. Reading the histories of the Southwest in Texas schoolbooks makes me sick—Tejanos[3] breathlessly awaiting the arrival of the skilled Anglo Generals to lead them against the incompetent Mexican Generals—the brilliant Anglo leadership and stupid Tejano followers beating the hell out of those Mexican bastards. Who do the Anglos think taught those "foreign" Anglo Generals how to fight Mexicans—other Anglos?

Did those authors ever stop to think that for every official Anglo liberation hero like Jim Bowie, Sam Houston, and the others, probably a hundred nameless Tejanos died valiantly alongside them? And where is there even a foot-note reference to them? Can anyone really believe that Jim Bowie and his special knife held off hundreds of armed Mexicans? The truth is that people lived on this land before the Anglos invaded and took their land away from them. They fought for their freedom, loved their chil-dren, cared for their families and old people, and practiced religions which produced more brotherhood and less hypocrisy than what I see among the Anglos today. You know, my ancestors worked, sweated, loved, and died with-out knowing how damned inferior they were to Anglos. Me? I'm lucky that I was told, or I surely wouldn't have guessed it.

Historians and educators have permitted gross misrepresen-tations to creep into standard history texts concerning the conquest era of the Southwest and the cultural and political contributions of Mexican Americans in that area. This has led to an Anglicized version of historical events that selectively overrates Anglo contributions and relegates those of the Mexi-can American to an inferior historical and cultural position. For this minority group such an artificially contrived inferior-ity creates an ethnic image of defeat, humiliation, and failure.

For example, of the many military heroes who helped to bring about Texan independence, honor has been bestowed almost exclusively on Anglos. The names Stephen Austin, Sam Hous-ton, James Collingworth, James Bowie, and James W. Fannin bring to mind images of gallantry and pride in the battles at the Alamo and San Jacinto, whereas the names of General Cos and Santa Anna are equated with cowardice, incompe-tency, and infamy.

Reconstructing the period preceding the battle of the Alamo, historians describe a condition of continuing political insur-rection in Mexico that pitted those who desired a representative type of government against the faction desiring a centralized system. Troop defection throughout Mexico was common, as one faction lured men away from the other with promises of better conditions (Cumberland, 1968:179–183). In American history books, these sudden declines in troop strength have been attributed to a lack of courage and a fear of the superior Anglo heroes. Yet the story of the Alamo written from the diaries of Mexican officers and writers of that era, especially the memoirs of Lieutenant Colonel Navarro, describes the Anglo leaders of the Alamo quite differently than do present Anglo histories. Navarro wrote in his diary, "Travis, commander of the Alamo, died like a hero. Bowie, the braggard son-in-law of Veramendi, like a coward." While Travis, Bowie, and other Alamo heroes are praised in song and story, a deaf ear has been turned on the Mexican American heroes. Gregorio Esparza, the only Alamo defender whose body was allowed by General Santa Anna to be buried rather than burned, fought against his own brother, who was on call to Santa Anna during the storming of the Alamo. Eight other Mexican Texans— Abamillo, Badillo, Espallar, Fuentes, Gregorio, Losoya, Nava, and Rodriguez—are among those not mentioned who *also* died defending the Alamo (I.T.C. 1971:15).

Plácido Benavides led Mexican ranchers in Texas against Mexican troops during the 1836 Texas revolt. Captain Jesús Cuellar defected and joined General Fannin's troops during this struggle for freedom from Mexican rule. Juan Seguín, whose father had financially supported the move toward Texas independence, led thirty Tejanos in the cavalry charge at the deciding battle of San Jacinto in 1836. Lorenzo de Zavala, José Antonio Navarro, and José Francisco Ruiz attended the Texas convention that convened to sign the Declaration of Independence. These outstanding leaders served in various political and administrative positions in the new republic. Ramón Musquiz and Erasmo Seguín, friends of Texas colonists, and Martín de Leon and José Antonio Saucedo, Texas ranchers and founders of educational facilities, are rarely mentioned in histories of Texas (I.T.C., 1971:12–17). The positive role of Mexicans in the cultural, political, military, and economic development of the Southwest has been unjustly overlooked.

Occasions of justified retaliation are often distorted into incidents of banditry and lawlessness, as is the case with Juan Cortina, the prominent Tamaulipas governor who in 1859 sent armed forces into Texas to correct injustices against Mexican citizens residing in the United States. Hollywood versions of Pancho Villa's raids in Sonora and west Texas, of Joaquín Murrietta's activities in California, and of Juan Flores Salinas' exploits in Texas are seldom cast as angry recriminations for past indignities and injustices; rather, they are simply characterized as the criminal acts of "outlaws" (Cuellar, 1970). This continuous portrayal of Mexican Americans as the "bad guys" of American history creates an ethnocentric pride among Anglos at the expense of historical accuracy and indirectly contributes to the stereotype of the Mexican American as a border outlaw.

The present relations between Anglos and Mexican Americans cannot be understood without a review and scholarly clarification of the historical setting from which they emerged. Otherwise, our story would be biased by the many underlying falsehoods concerning this minority that have been perpetuated by both popular and "scientific" writers (Vaca, 1970a; 1970b). To expose these ludicrous inconsistencies necessitates a large dosage of "reality therapy," not unlike that demanded of the Anglo majority by black Americans (Rose, 1969:288–289). Thus the student who demands that we "tell it like it is" is requiring the more difficult prerequisite of uncovering and refuting the traditionally accepted misconceptions concerning the past and present characteristics of American citizens of Mexican descent.

Notes

[1] The February 20, 1970, issue of *Current Population Reports* estimates that the Spanish American population of Mexican descent is 4,073,000, plus 1,582,000 other Spanish Americans.

[2] The term *Anglo* (short version of Anglo American) is generally used throughout the Southwest for all Caucasian-type peoples.

[3] During the era of Texas independence, a loyal supporter of the Lone Star republic who was of Mexican descent.

Chapter 2 ◉ From Whence and to Where?

Specific migration patterns of Mexican Americans have resulted in their concentrations in certain areas of the United States. The oldest segment, the Spanish American population, predates Anglos in the Southwest by nearly two centuries. Later immigrants, Mexican Americans, make up the bulk of the present Mexican American population in America. By analyzing the historical development of the Southwest and the various patterns of immigration and internal migration, we see the dramatic effects of these movements on the development and population concentrations of this minority. These traditional settlement and migration patterns, especially within the United States–Mexico borderland region, have had a large impact on Mexican American identity, minority stereotypes, and the processes associated with language maintenance and cultural ties with Mexico itself.

SPANISH AMERICANS: CITIZENS BY CONQUEST AND ANNEXATION

Throughout the Southwest it is common to hear Anglo Americans say of persons with Spanish surnames, "Why don't they go back where they came from if they won't learn our language?" The facts are that many persons now residing in northern New Mexico have forbears who lived in the area since early in the seventeenth century, almost 150 years prior to annexation of New Mexico in 1848, after the war with Mexico. Prior to acquisition of the region by the United States, its indigenous populations had been dominated alternately by the Spanish crown, by France, and by Mexico. For them, Anglo Americans were but the most recent of a long list of conquerors, none of whom took much interest in the people of the area but rather sought to own the land and to exploit its natural resources.

The earliest historical accounts of Hispanos in the Southwest territory are of Spanish expeditions in search of precious metals. Prompted by stories of the legendary Seven Cities of Gold to the north, Francisco de Coronado, with a sizable expedition, penetrated far into the Southwest territory during the mid-sixteenth century, and further exploration was undertaken by Chamuscado, Rodriguez, and Espejo. The first serious colonization by Spaniards was directed by Don Juan de Oñate in 1598, who, with eighty-three wagons, hundreds of men, and thousands of cattle, journeyed up the Rio Grande almost to the Chama river valley, where he founded the communities of San Juan de los Caballeros and Villa de San Gabriel. A decade later, the main colony was strategically relocated southward at La Villa Real de la Santa Fe de San Francisco (Santa Fe). Spanish military forces subdued the Pueblo villages, exacting tribute and forcing natives into servitude, while Catholic missionaries zealously proselytized them. Hatred among the Pueblos for the Spanish oppressors smoldered for many years and eventually erupted to open rebellion during the Pueblo Revolt. The Spaniards and the Christianized Indians retreated southward, village by village, and at last proceeded to El Paso to await reinforcement. Once arrived, Spanish military forces began the long fight to recapture the 300-mile area lost, which took a dozen years (Moquin, 1971:43–58).

Throughout the following century, fighting between the Hispanos and their Indian subjects was frequent. The Pueblos now possessed only half the land they had owned a century before, and their population of 50,000 had been reduced to 8,000, primarily through war and disease. Although the rural villages of the Pueblos in the river valleys had been subjugated, marauding Indian parties halted further expansion of Hispanic colonists into adjoining areas in Colorado, Utah, Arizona, and Texas.

In 1800 these [Spanish dominated] areas all seemed to be islands of civilization in the midst of vast tides of savagery which pounded upon every shore; Apaches on the south and west, Utes on the north, Comanches on the north and east. It is clear that these nomadic Indians were a much more dangerous foe in the last years of Spanish rule than in the first, for they were now in some cases mounted on horses and armed with guns . . . and were everywhere deeply embittered by a long history of harsh punitive Spanish retaliations [Meinig, 1971:14–15].

By 1821, when Spanish rule in the Southwest territory came to an end, the northern New Mexico villages were so far from the central seat of power that hardly a ripple occurred there. Sanchez (1967:9–13) described this as the first step in a rapid succession of "protective governments," which were all ineffectual in politically integrating this isolated area into their governmental policies or threatening the dominant Hispanic cultural traditions. The newly formed Mexican regime, knowing little of the northern lands or its inhabitants, gave land grants encompassing vast acreages east of the Rio Grande to select individuals. At this same time, Chihuahua City merchants were eager to build up their trade to the Santa Fe region, which had previously consisted of a single caravan every two or three years carrying military and civilian supplies and bringing back sheep, wool, hides, and sometimes nomadic Indian slaves. Since Santa Fe was the southernmost point of the Santa Fe trail (extending from Kansas City along the Arkansas river to the upper Rio Grande region), the midwestern trading centers were all anxious to compete for this same market. By 1840, Anglo companies from the East and Midwest had resident agents in every principal trading point from Kansas City through New Mexico and Arizona and on into California. The stage was set for the 1880s, when the railroad lines would follow these old trade routes and trails.

In 1846 the War with Mexico brought military forces westward. Forts were established to preserve the peace, and these became a main outlet for Anglo traders stocking food and supplies for military outposts. The western migration prompted by the Gold Rush of 1849 created a further volume of trade and enhanced the economic position of the established Anglo merchants.

Further Anglo domination in the Southwest occurred in 1850, when New Mexico, Utah, and California were designated as territories by the United States. The Anglo system of property ownership was replacing the Indian and Hispano systems of possession or use. Spanish American heirs to ancestral land grants were unable to compete with Anglo lawyers, who could sometimes hold up their titles in technical court proceedings for as long as two decades, during which time taxes had to be paid by the owner and the land could not be sold to pay the tax liens imposed. Morever, Anglo functionaries appointed for the new territories were the validating officers for land claims and sometimes themselves shared in the acquisition of enormous acreages at a cost of little or nothing to them personally.

Anglo cattlemen from Texas and Oklahoma expanded westward, pushing the Spanish American ranchers back into their river valleys. Decades of hostilities between the two factions culminated in the decisive Lincoln County Wars, fought from 1868 to 1881. Meanwhile, on the western border of the Hispano settlements, Anglo cattlemen from California and Arizona were encroaching upon traditional Hispano grasslands. To the north, the creation of the Colorado territory in 1861 had cut off the San Luis region (including the Rio Grande headwaters) from Santa Fe control, and the Mormon colonists coming south from the Utah territory made further Hispano expansion in that direction impossible. In 1892 the last and final blow to the Hispano economy was dealt when grazing privileges in United States forest lands were extended to persons other than Hispanos from whom the land had been taken. Depriving Spanish Americans of their traditional economic base—the land—was the critical factor that changed the Hispano-dominated system into an Anglo-dominated system in which Spanish Americans were solely occupants of the lower strata of society when once they had penetrated every level. Since a full understanding of Hispanos attitudes toward dominant Anglo institutions as a result of these land grabs is necessary to comprehend their current bitterness over dependency, a more detailed explanation of the land-grant systems and Hispano treatment under Anglo law follows.

In the Treaty of Guadalupe Hidalgo, signed at the close of the war with Mexico in 1848, ancient Spanish and Mexican land grants in northern New Mexico were validated as a legal basis for land ownership. These consisted of two basic types. The "common" or group ownership of land (constituting by far the greatest total acreage) did not coincide with the Anglo legal pattern of individual land ownership. From 1854 to 1880 the policy of the office of United States surveyor general was to reject this group form of land ownership. Thus acreages owned under common land grants were declared public property and officially surveyed as government land. The vast majority of this newly acquired federal land was set aside as national forests and park lands during the early years of the twentieth century.

Rightful land-grant heirs, trying to legitimize their claims, found the established governmental processes highly involved and cumbersome. Often, vague policies and lack of standardized legal procedures led to "legal" piracy. For example, there are numerous recorded accounts of lands having been confiscated for delinquent taxes or nonpayment of water fees. The legal separation of water rights and land ownership under Anglo laws, a maneuver not understood by those familiar with Spanish legal traditions, allowed easy acquisition of land once full control of water rights was obtained. The practice of purchasing property impounded for delinquent taxes or water liens, without making reasonable attempts to advise owners or accepting partial collections, was a calculated use of Anglo legal institutions to overcome land use rights. Further, since the practice of demanding ownership transfers in writing was not common among illiterate peoples, many land titles were legally defective and thus prey to false claims. In some extreme cases even legitimate deeds were destroyed when archives were looted and burned by Anglo officials (Knowlton, 1970:1064–1065). Extended court battles with complicated proceedings were little protection to the illiterate, poverty-stricken landholder who had to refute illegal claims made by others. During the last half of the nineteenth and early part of the twentieth centuries, unscrupulous lawyers had reaped huge fortunes from court cases in which the claimants received nothing. Swadesh notes the instance of a lawyer who represented the heirs to the Canyón de San Diego in 1904. After he had successfully established their claims to 80 percent of their original 110,000 acres, he promptly claimed one-half of the land as his legal fee. Alfonso Sanchez, shortly before he became district attorney in the First Judicial District of New Mexico, administered a legal suit on behalf of some Tierra Amarilla heirs. (Chapter 7 discusses in detail Sanchez's involvement in another famous incident in the history of the Chicano movement, the Tierra Amarilla Courthouse Raid.) The heirs got nothing, but Sanchez came into ownership of some of the Tierra Amarilla acreage (Swadesh, 1968:167). But the most notorious theft of land-grant acreage in New Mexico[1] was executed during the last half of the nineteenth century by the "Santa Fe ring," a collection of Anglo lawyers and Spanish American collaborators. Their abuses were so flagrant that they invoked the wrath of President Grover Cleveland, who rebuked them and attempted to break up their operation. Knowlton lists some of the real estate that "passed" into the estate of only one "Santa Fe ring" member, Thomas G. Catron, prior to 1893: 50,000 acres of the Mora grant; 80,000 acres of the Beck grant; two-thirds of the 78,000 acres of the Espiritu Santo grant; one-half of the 21,500 acres of the Tecolote grant; 7,600 acres of the Juana Lopez grant; 24,000 acres of the Piedra Lumbre grant; 11,000 acres of the Gabaldon grant; 15,000 acres of the Baoa grant; a portion of the Tierra Amarilla grant; 8,000 acres in patented homesteads (1967b:6; 1970:1067–1068).

It is quite clear that current economic problems among the Spanish Americans of northern New Mexico have arisen as a natural consequence of the economic, social, and legal losses associated with land grants and land use. They have never been able to recover from these losses, and the resentment accompanying the questionable methods whereby these lands were obtained still burns deeply within their offspring.

The contemporary myth of "pure Spanish ancestry" among

the socially prominent Spanish American families of northern New Mexico and southern Colorado is culturally rather than genetically based. Although the Spanish Society of Castes was in operation in the Santa Fe region as it had been in central Mexico, more than three centuries of history had led to genetic dilution. Soldier settlements alongside the villages resulted in many mixed-bloods, as did the forced Indian labor in towns and in Spanish homes. Captured Indians from the nomadic plains tribes were sold as slaves and their offspring added to the rapidly rising Mestizo population. Meinig (1971:14) claims that from 1600 to 1800, only rarely was the claim of pure ancestry valid. He writes:

> Of the estimated 20,000 "Spanish" in 1800, only a few hundred were wholly that in ancestry. . . . The rest were an indigenous mixture, Mexican or New Mexican, now more numerous than descendants of either of their progenitors, and the solid nucleus of that steadily enlarging people which in later years became known as the "Spanish Americans" or "Hispanos."

Though twentieth-century Spanish Americans, accentuating their light skin shade, claim to be an endogamous elite of pure Spanish ancestry, most authorities reject such a facile explanation, pointing instead to their Indian ancestry (Edmonson, 1957:16). Some authorities feel that compared with other "white-skinned" peoples, the Spanish American's complexion is swarthy. This is, of course, a result of previous racial mixtures with darker-skinned peoples (Mörner, 1967). During the latter half of the nineteenth century, when, because of redistribution of wealth and land, elite Hispano families were rapidly being deposed and others were taking their place, many Hispanos with Indian ancestry who conspired with Anglo lawyers to obtain disputed land-grant acreages were elevated to elite status. Thus, many Manitos, who claim Spanish purity, were really Mestizos in the days prior to the Pueblo revolt.

The label "Spanish American" did not come into social usage in New Mexico until the period of mass exodus from Mexico following the Revolution in 1909 (Gonzalez, 1969: Chap. 8). During the early decades of this century, Anglo immigrants to northern New Mexico who were cattlemen, those connected with mining or the railroad, and mercantile or trading-company representatives, became a dominant economic and political force in the Santa Fe region. These Anglos regarded both Hispanos and Mexican Americans simply as "Mexicans." As the refugees from Mexico became more numerous, Hispanos, who did not wish to associate themselves with the impoverished Mexican immigrants, experienced an identity crisis. They went to great lengths to refuse Mexicans assistance in order to avoid the onus of identification with them (Servín, 1965:148). It was at this point that the term "Spanish American" became reserved for the traditional Hispanos, whose ancestors were native to the area, and all others were labeled "Mexicans" or "Mexican Americans."

The attempt to maintain the myth of pure Spanish ancestry has caused Spanish American families of all social levels to avoid intermarriage with Indians. Kluckhohn and Strodtbeck (1961) found this practice to be very strong in the rural New Mexico villages. Evidence of this anti-Indian attitude came forth during the early 1960s, when Reies Tijerina and his militant Alianza de las Mercedes group fought to reclaim lands illegally taken from them in the nineteenth century. When Tijerina openly supported a move to restore lands to the Taos Pueblos, he lost a huge portion of his local Spanish American support (Swadesh, 1968:167).

Today, historical differences are evident between the Spanish Americans of northern New Mexico and the more recent Mexican immigrants, but the racial differences claimed by the Spanish Americans are socially based and genetically unfounded.

Mexican Americans are a composite of Spaniards and Mexicans who were either absorbed under Southwest expansionist policies or who immigrated voluntarily to the United States following the cessation. Unlike the sudden leap forward into the isolated Indian villages of the Santa Fe region of Spanish America, there was only a gradual extension of the Spanish empire or Mexican nation into the Southwest, followed by a colonial relationship between Spaniards and the dominant Anglos. Moore (1970b) characterizes the Spanish American

system in New Mexico as "traditional colonialism"—the transfer, intact, of an entire social system from central Mexico, complete with both Spanish-surname elites and Spanish-surname
lower classes—during the latter part of the sixteenth century.
The California experience is termed "economic colonialism,"
wherein Mexican Americans were subjugated through the economic power of the Anglos. In Texas, "conquest colonialism"
characterizes the social position of the "vanquished people"—
the "Meskins" within Texas borders. These early differences in
attitudes toward Mexican Americans are borne out later in the
treatment of Mexican Americans in these different states.

Prior to 1769, only Baja California had been exploited by
Spain, but no serious attempt had been made to colonize California. When a representative of the crown, José de Galvez,
commissioned Captain Gaspar de Portola and Fray Junípero
Serra to open up the new San Diego colony, it was principally
out of fear of possible encroachment by the Russians south of
Alaska (Moquin, 1971:98–102). During the next half century
the Franciscan order established twenty-one missions, each
about thirty miles from the next, extending north from San
Diego along the Pacific slopes. The priests were in charge,
while the officials, soldiers, and civilians gave their support.
Thus, nearly all of the best, most fertile land in California had
come under church control by 1800. Local Indians, under the
direction of the priests, worked the land. "Each mission forms
an indivisible society, of which the fathers are the kings and
pontiffs," commented a ship's captain in 1808 (Moquin,
1971:119). In spite of this, however, the Franciscan fathers
supported the Spanish crown against the Mexican colony as
the gap between the two grew wider. Thus, after 1821 there
was increased pressure from the *presidios* to secularize the
missions and place them under government direction. Local
governors and military leaders were not altogether altruistic in
their suggestions, inasmuch as they hoped to avail themselves
of some of the rich lands that would be "liberated" from mission control. Finally, in 1834, the missions were secularized.
The current government and military officials availed themselves of the huge landholdings freed from church control, as
did some aristocratic families recently arrived from Spain or

Spanish dominions. The family names of Pico, Carillo, Ortego, Alvarado, Bandini, Vallejo, Pacheco, and others were now numbered among the elite Californios who dominated the region for the next century. Dana, the author of *Two Years Before the Mast*, comments as follows on the gradual decay of this landed aristocracy elite by describing a Bandini descendant:

> I could not but feel a pity for him, especially when I saw him by the side of his fellow passenger and townsman, a fat, coarse, vulgar, pretending fellow of a Yankee trader, who had made money in San Diego, and who was eating out the very vitals of the Bandinis, fattening upon their extravagance, grinding them in their poverty; having mortgages on their lands, forestalling their cattle, and already making an inroad upon their jewels, which were their last hope [Moquin, 1971:170–71].

Following the Treaty of Guadalupe Hidalgo in 1848, the question of Spanish and Mexican land grants, an issue central to the problems of the Spanish Americans of northern New Mexico, was also undertaken in California. Just prior to the admission of California as a federal territory in 1850, two reports were made on land grants in California that proved to be somewhat contradictory. The investigation by the Department of Interior generally concluded that the existing land grants were legitimate, but the report from officials of the territory of California took the view that the existing grants were highly questionable, many of them vague and unmanageable due to their enormous size. The federal government then appointed a land commission in 1851 to decide on the validity of each grant, and it decreed, in addition, that each grant holder would be required to file suit against the United States government at his own expense to prove why the land should not become part of the public domain. Between the years 1852 and 1855, a total of 812 suits were filed (Moquin, 1971:202). But while the legality of these claims was being decided, the payment of property taxes by the owners was still required, even though the land could not be sold until a clear title was obtained.

Squatters took over the lands, in some instances going so

far as to build fences between landholders' houses and farms
and threatening death to trespassers. The Gold Rush brought
together in "Sonora Towns," which sprang up throughout the
Southwest along the routes to California, the Mexican ne'er-
do-wells and the less than puritanical gringos. In the eastern
United States, rumors of the rich opportunities in the West,
especially California, brought "hordes of solid, but perhaps
sanctimonious and prosaic, middle westerners" into the West
and Southwest (Servín, 1965:145). California's "first families"
were numerically overwhelmed by the Anglo immigration
(Pitt, 1970:83, 251–254) and by 1891 it was reported that
only thirty of the elite Spanish families (the Californios) still
retained any wealth or influence (Moquin, 1971:235). Although a few Mexican Americans still worked as ranch hands,
the "Foreign Miners Law" of 1851 restricted them from being
employed in the mines. Reduced to mere economic production
units in the California agricultural market, the Mexican Americans would never again emerge with the power they com-
manded during the golden age of the Californios.

In Arizona Mexican American influence was minimal.
Although the Jesuit missionaries worked among the Pima (or
Papago) Indians in the late 1600s, missions, ranches, and
presidios were established along the Santa Cruz river only as
far north as present-day Tucson. Because of the roving Apache
tribes that raided the cattle and razed homesteads of rural
families, little expansion beyond the central "urban" settlements had occurred up to the early 1800s. As army outposts
reduced the Indian menace, Texans and other Anglos drove
their cattle herds into the broad basin between the Rio Grande
and the Santa Cruz. In the early 1870s, droughts in California
brought Anglo cattlemen and sheepmen to the lower Gila River
country. The Mormon settlers from Utah established irrigation
agriculture colonies in the "Little Colorado" area of northern
Arizona. Collectively, these Anglo expansions not only encircled
the Spanish American domain of New Mexico, but created a
thin occupation of the best Arizona range land (Meinig,
1971:35).

Because Arizona was sparsely populated, it was dominated
by its urban centers and railroad junctions. Although Arizona

and New Mexico considered entering the Union as joint territories, the idea of Anglo-dominated Arizona combined with
Hispano-dominated New Mexico made each area aware of its
own self-interests. Thus, in 1863 Arizona and New Mexico
became separate federal territories. The Arizona Hispanos, as
an ineffectual minority, are characterized by Meinig as follows:

> Arizona itself did not have really serious internal prob-
> lems. The Anglos were completely dominant and although
> there were differences in background among those of the
> north (mostly Midwestern), center (many Californians),
> and south (Texans and Southerners), they tended to work
> well together in order to block the two political minorities,
> the Mormons and Hispanos (the Indians did not have the
> vote), from exerting any influence. . . . The fact that the
> Mormons were in all three areas was a special spur to
> cooperation, while the fact that the Hispanos were very
> largely in the Southwest somewhat undercut the power of
> population numbers in those counties [1971:62].

The overpowering influence of the California Anglos in Arizona
was evidenced by the fact that in 1887, over one-third of the
territorial legislators were either natives of, or had come from,
California. This provided sharp contrast to the weak Hispano–
New Mexican influence in the state.

In the early 1900s, following the development of an effective, low-grade ore-processing system, Arizona became an
important source of copper. Mining districts had a distinctive
community pattern. Typically, there was an old town, the
archaic remains of a former mining camp; a new town, the
small formal section for Anglo officials, engineers, and fore-
men; and a sprawling slum where workers lived. If Mexican
Americans resided in this type of community, they were to be
found in the slum.

The dry farming and new federal irrigation programs developed during the early decades of the 1900s created the need
for farm labor and hand labor at harvest time, and Mexican
immigrants were able to obtain employment in these low-
paying industries. But Mexican Americans never became part
of Arizona's political, economic, or social elite classes, as they

had previously in New Mexico and California, nor did they form a great percentage of the state's sparse population.

Texas was on the northernmost border of the Spanish empire in the New World. Although there was some fear of French encroachment in Texas, the cession of Louisiana by France to Spain in 1762 reduced this threat. Spain gradually lost interest in this distant part of its empire, and, in 1773, the Spaniards abandoned the whole east Texas mission area as an economy measure. Prior to 1800, only San Antonio and two smaller Texas communities (La Bahía and Nacogdoches) contained a sizable concentration of Spanish administrators and residents. Scattered missions, mostly along the Rio Bravo, were the remaining evidence of Spanish penetration into this uncolonized area. Plains Indians and buffalo herds roamed freely throughout the region.

When Texas came under the control of Mexico in 1821, a land grant from Antonio Martinez, governor of the province, to Moses Austin was only the first attempt among many to attract settlers to Texas. A generous colonization policy encouraged migration from the United States and from European countries to the extent that these new settlers swelled the Texas population of 4,000 to four times that number in a single decade. Most of the new immigrants were Anglos. The lack of Mexican control of their individual colonies caused some misgivings on the part of the Mexican officials. Believing that it was losing control over its territory, the provincial government issued a decree on April 6, 1830, forbidding further immigration from the United States into the province of Texas. The Texas Anglos, wishing to preserve their land and their self-determination, gained the support of Spanish and Mexican families of influence, who also wished to be separate from the strong "dictatorial" government recently formed by Santa Anna, and together they organized to declare their independence from Mexico. The Mexican general, Martin Perfecto de Cos, was defeated in San Antonio on December 10, 1835. On March 1, 1836, Texas declared its independence, but suffered the total annihilation of a garrison in the battle of the Alamo some five days later. In April the Texas forces, which combined the Texan Anglos with the Tejano Mexican Americans and Mexicans, defeated Santa Anna's army and thus assured Texas her independence.

The Treaty of Guadalupe Hidalgo that followed the War with Mexico in 1846 raised the question of Spanish and Mexican land grants in New Mexico and California. Texas, however, a republic with its own constitutional authority, decided the issue in favor of local power blocs, without utilizing federal guidelines. The Anglo Founding Fathers of the Texas Republic had cooperated with aristocratic Spanish families—the mayors, state senators, and wealthy sponsors of the Texas push for independence. After one or two generations, however, these prominent Tejano families—De Leons, Seguíns, and Carbajals —were relegated to a subordinate social and political position (I.T.C., 1971:15, 20). Clearly, the Anglos had assumed control in Texas. With the termination of the Civil War and the clearing out of the buffalo herds and the Comanche Indians from the west Texas plains, the cattle industry drew even more Anglos into the territory, just as the railroad lines had done during the 1880s. Mexican Americans in Texas were treated socially, politically, and economically as a "conquered people" in a structure referred to by Moore (1970b) as a "conquest colonization" social system. This complete domination of Mexican Americans by Anglos, which extended throughout the early twentieth century, was challenged only after World War II by the emergence of the G. I. Forum and later by the Chicano movement in the 1960s. (see Chapter 7 for a discussion of contemporary ethnic organizational development.)

MEXICAN AMERICANS: CITIZENS BY IMMIGRATION

Except for the population of the early Spanish American colony in northern New Mexico, only 200,000 persons born in Mexico were living in the southwestern territories of the United States by 1909 (the year of the Mexican Revolution). Prior to that time, immigrants from Mexico had come in a slow trickle. However, the Díaz benevolent dictatorship in Mexico was drawing to a close, and the stable social system of the hacienda patron and his peons was about to be shaken. Within the next two decades in the United States, a torrential stream of Mexican immigrants would come northward to seek refuge in the southwestern states.

In 1910 the wildly cyclical power plunges and counter-revolutionary thrusts of the Mexican Revolution spurred the first substantial movement of large numbers of Mexican citizens into the United States (Cline, 1963:24–30). Most of these refugees retained their Mexican loyalties, fully expecting to return to their homeland when the internal political and military conflicts there had subsided. Although the land-reform speeches or patriotic appeals of the revolutionary leadership of the period may have attracted a limited number of Mexicans back from the United States, the tide of peasants released from peonage on the larger haciendas and those fleeing from the hostilities of the Revolution itself produced the largest influx of Mexicans to the United States of any decade in its history.

Because the U.S. Reclamation Act of 1902 had forced many large sheep and cattle ranchers on the United States borderland to make way for crop farmers, the subsequent decade showed an accelerated need for farm laborers. Likewise, there was a shortage of field workers in the lush agricultural regions of southern California. United States officials, having viewed with alarm the growing Oriental population in the United States, had halted the importing of Oriental labor through the so-called Gentleman's Agreement of 1907. Military demands during World War I further diminished the local farm-labor supply, and Mexican immigrants were actively sought to fill the labor void, even though prior to this period Mexican immigrants had arbitrarily been refused entry into the United States because it was thought they would become public charges. Although Western hemisphere countries were excluded from immigrant-quota laws, Mexicans generally had not been welcome in the United States until farm-labor supplies became short. Therefore, special regulations were issued by the government in 1917 to admit "temporary farm workers" from Mexico without the economic tests previously used as restraints. Many

Mexicans entered the United States as temporary laborers, but, seeing a bright future for themselves and their families, continued to reside in the Southwest until they were forced to leave during the California purges of the 1930s or the "Operation Roundup" repatriation of the mid-1950s.

Prior to 1920 the immigration pattern of the Mexican was to locate in farm areas or small towns very near the Mexican border, specifically, in the agricultural regions of southern California and the lower valley of Texas. There were smaller movements toward the West Coast, and some migration north to the Rocky Mountain region, but these were usually seasonal, in pursuit of work connected with sugar beets and fruit. (While these first-generation communities of borderland Mexicans remained somewhat permanent, second-generation Mexicans were to become part of the larger West Coast migration that followed the close of World War II.)

For several years during the 1920s another pattern of immigration became visible: Mexicans were lured to the United States by the expanding northern industrial manufacturing centers in Chicago, Detroit, and Milwaukee. There, as untrained factory employees, they had a chance at steady employment and an income that was generous compared with farm wages. Coming from Mexico and not from border towns in the United States, they were thrown directly into contact with Anglo society, and some became rapidly acculturated. However, most continued to occupy the bottom rungs of the economic ladder. Their settlements became urban "seeding areas" for subsequent dropouts from the migrant agricultural stream. Although this group never did comprise more than 10 percent of the entire Spanish-surname population within the United States, its distinct migration pattern and comparatively better economic situation did point up more poignantly the economic exploitation suffered by Mexicans who had chosen to locate in the agricultural regions of the United States–Mexican borderland.

During the 1920s immigration from Mexico reached its peak, with a half-million Mexican immigrants entering the United States on visas. The attractive labor opportunities during that period coupled with the aftermath of Mexico's civil strife had both a push and a pull effect on this mass relocation of people. By the beginning of the 1930s there were nearly 1.5 million persons of Mexican extraction in the United States, according to the U.S. Census. Then, abruptly, the economic impact of the Depression enveloped the United States. Industry slowed and then halted; farming became more of a family operation than before. Compounding this reduction of farm-labor employment was an accelerated rate of mechanization in crop farming. Farm laborers in general, and Mexicans in particular, found little demand for their services throughout the entire Southwest.

In Texas Mexican immigrants were not legally eligible for welfare assistance, and although no overt means were employed to deport Mexican immigrants, it became increasingly difficult for those who were unemployed to remain in Texas.

California, with its liberal relief policies, had attracted vast numbers of unemployed Anglos from urban centers, as well as Dust Bowl migrants, to fill the decreasing number of farm-labor jobs. McWilliams (1939:305) notes that during this period, half of California's farm-labor force was Anglo. Most relief agencies that had established bread lines or federal works projects now restricted their services to United States citizens. But the relief policies had already taken their toll of tax dollars by this time. For instance, in 1925 Riverside, California spent 90 percent of its welfare budget on Mexican cases, and in 1927 Los Angeles spent 27 percent of its welfare funds on the Mexican population, which at that time comprised only 7 percent of the city's population (McWilliams, 1939:127). When mounting unemployment signaled financial disaster for local welfare and relief agencies, communities took action against their noncitizen residents.

Thousands of Mexicans had departed for their homeland of their own volition. Of those who had not, many were deported, as revealed in the following account of an incident that occurred in Los Angeles:

It was discovered that in wholesale lots, the Mexicans could be shipped to Mexico City for $14.70 per capita. The sum represented less than the cost of a week's board and lodging. And so, about February, 1931, the first trainload was dispatched, and shipments at the rate of about one a month have continued ever since. A shipment consisting of three special trains left Los Angeles on December 8. The loading commenced about six o'clock in the morning and continued for several hours. More than twenty-five such special trains had left the Southern Pacific Station before last April [McWilliams, 1933:26].

A mere 27,000 persons came into the United States from Mexico during the 1930s, and by the end of the Great Depression not only had immigration from Mexico dropped sharply, but a mass exodus from the United States back to Mexico had taken place. Eventually, the return to Mexico slowed, and by 1940 it had all but halted.

The decade from 1940 to 1950, beginning with the industrial production brought on by America's involvement in World War II, brought an economic boom. High wages in urban factories created another agricultural labor shortage in the United States, as rural Anglos and some native-born Mexican Americans migrated to industrial centers. However, unlike the situation some twenty-five years earlier during World War I, there was during World War II a corresponding prosperity in Mexico due to the unlimited markets abroad for its entire agricultural production. Moreover, coming to the United States as a permanent legal resident during that time presented some risk of having to serve in the United States Armed Forces. When because of these and other related factors Mexican immigration was insufficient to supply the labor force for United States agriculture, the *bracero* program was born (see Galarza, 1964).

The bracero project was devised to recruit and redistribute labor from drought and poverty areas of Mexico to American farms. Commencing during the years of World War II, it continued in force until the end of 1964, with some modification during the period from 1948 to 1951. Under joint United States–Mexican governmental sponsorship and regulation of transportation, housing, and wage contracts, fees were collected at governmental recruitment centers for the processing of workers. Contingent costs were collected from applicants shipped to the United States, who were hired out under contract for specific time periods to do agricultural work. United States government representatives collected fees from prospective employers to cover the cost of coordinating the program.

While the bracero program was an economic boon to participating Mexicans, it proved an anathema to Mexican Americans who had followed the agricultural migrant stream. They were working alongside the legally protected braceros, but without similar governmental protection from exploitation, intolerable housing, and dangerous transportation facilities. This degrading comparison germinated intense bitterness against the American system, which allowed loyal citizens to suffer humiliation at the expense of protecting "foreign" Mexican braceros. This bitterness was especially strong among the generation of children that grew up in the harvest fields, at the mercy of capricious growers and of their own crew chiefs. By the middle of the 1960s, the Mexican American migrant laborers who followed the sun, harvesting the food and fiber for other, privileged Americans, were ready for organized action against exploitation and inequality. The recent collective action in the citrus groves of southern Texas and the grape arbors of Delano, California, might well be the harvest of seeds of bitterness planted in the postwar years, ripened during the affluent fifties, and seasoned during the sixties, along with other militant movements of that period. Indirect consequences of the bracero program are also evident. It stimulated unlawful migration into the United States, no doubt by advertising the need for Mexican labor in the United States. Moreover, the returning braceros encouraged their own children to seek a higher status within the local community or to migrate to the United States–Mexican borderland in hopes of obtaining a better existence than their parents enjoyed.

A postwar economic boom followed the decade from 1940 to 1950, and a sharp rise in immigration began. In Mexico the wartime economy no longer dominated the scene, and without a fully operating industrial complex to absorb workers and production materials, the lack of agricultural prosperity was again felt by many Mexicans in semirural areas. An increasing number of *wetbacks*[3] (slang for a Mexican who enters the United States illegally by swimming across the Rio Grande.

In the process of fording the river, he becomes wet—hence the term "wetback.") entering the United States during this economic-boom period resulted in a concentrated effort by United States immigration and border-control authorities to capture all illegal aliens and return them to Mexico. The 1952 legislation against harboring wetbacks or abetting their entry was a prelude to a Special Force Operation program that was fully inaugurated by 1954. This procedural cordon designed to trap the wetback also exposed many earlier immigrants who had entered without proper credentials. Unfortunately, these immigrants, though only technically "aliens," were processed and deported along with the wetbacks. This generated displeasure on the part of Mexican officials, making the formal relations between the United States and Mexico understandably tense. Liaison personnel from both countries were under constant pressure from those demanding a more thorough search and seizure operation as well as from those resenting the deportation of older residents for minor breaches of bureaucratic procedure.

At the beginning of the crackdown, in 1953, four aliens were apprehended by the U.S. Border Patrol for every one agricultural laborer admitted legally. Of the 187,000 persons "arrested" during that fiscal year, 30,000 had industrial and trade rather than agricultural jobs. The bulk of the 3.8 million persons affected by the Special Force Operation were caught and returned to Mexico during the year 1954. In that single year, over 1 million persons were repatriated, and by 1956 another 90,000 had been returned. The flood of illegal immigration had been reduced to a trickle. Of the total, however, only 63,000 persons can be classified as deported, the rest returning "voluntarily" in lieu of deportation procedures. Except in northern New Mexico (including southern Colorado) and in borderland hamlets that were annexed during the past century, this roundup of illegal immigrants has left a Mexican American population in the United States consisting largely of families that remained here during the Depression years.

Within the Republic of Mexico three major demographic patterns have been evident all this time that not only affected past immigration trends but that may well affect potential immigrations into the United States, barring quota restrictions. These three patterns are: (1) a high increase of births over deaths; (2) an overall movement from rural to urban areas within the nation; and (3) a large migration northward to the states adjacent to the United States, especially to the urban *municipios* located on the Mexican–United States border.

In regard to the population increases, it is generally agreed that the continental area of Latin America has the highest birth rate in the world. In 1960, with a population growth rate of nearly 3.5 percent annually, Mexico was ahead of most other nations in Latin America, and at that rate, Mexico's population will have doubled within two decades. Thus, urban planning programs designed for presently needed economic, educational, occupational, and community services are even now inadequate.

The second aspect of Mexico's population change, the shift from rural areas to urban centers, has deposited 80 percent of those moving from their state of birth into the urban municipios. With the exceptions of the Distrito Federal (Mexico City) and the contiguous state of Morelos, the municipios showing the greatest growth rate of all in Mexico are those located along the entire length of the Mexican–United States border.

Average figures for the nine largest Mexican border cities indicate that they have doubled their population over a period of twelve years. (Four of the nine Mexican border municipalities cited more than doubled their population just from 1950 to 1960: Ciudad Juárez, 136 percent; Mexicali, 123 percent; Tijuana, 115 percent; and Ensenada, 113 percent.) But the pull of the borderland areas affects much more than just the nine major border municipios. The Mexican states fronting on the United States had an average population increase of 5.0 percent in the decade from 1950 to 1960, with an increase of 5.7 percent projected for the next ten years. The Mexican state of greatest population growth, Baja California, is situated just below southern California. During the period from 1940 to 1950 the population nearly doubled (to 98,000). This was followed by a similarly fantastic growth rate of 129 percent for the 1950–1960 period and only a slightly lower rate of 112 percent growth from 1960 to 1970. That reservoir of uprooted, young, uneducated, and economically underprivileged Mexicans at the border looking toward the "promised land" is possibly future citizenry. The overall pattern of population characteristics within the United States mirror those found in Old Mexico. Thus there is a notable shift in population density from rural regions to urban centers, an increase of births over deaths resulting in a rapidly expanding population, and a migration westward. Similarly, except for some Spanish American enclaves in northern New Mexico, the same trends are demonstrable among Mexican Americans as among Anglos, but although their regional migration is similar to that of the Anglo component, their residential patterns are more defined and limited within the larger urban metropolitan areas.

Before 1930, fifty percent of all Mexican Americans in the United States lived in rural areas. They were mainly located in the borderland counties from Texas to California, while Spanish Americans were found in northern New Mexico (including southern Colorado). By 1950 the ratio of Mexican Americans in rural areas had decreased to 30 percent of the total population, and in 1960 it dropped below 20 percent, as shown in Table 2–1.[2] Until 1960 more of this minority group lived in Texas than in any other state. But after that time continuous migration to the West Coast shifted the population balance, and California became the state with the greatest number of

Table 2–1   Distribution of Spanish-surname Persons in the Five Southwestern States: 1960.

	Total	Urban Residents (%)	Rural Nonfarm Residents (%)	Rural Farm Residents (%)
Arizona	194,356	74.5	19.0	6.1
California	1,426,538	85.4	10.8	3.8
Colorado	157,173	68.7	25.2	6.1
New Mexico	269,122	57.7	36.7	5.7
Texas	1,417,810	78.6	15.0	6.5

SOURCE: U.S. Census, 1960, *Persons of Spanish Surname*, Table 2.

Mexican Americans. Colorado, which had a spectacular increase in Spanish-surname residents during the decade from 1950 to 1960, still has a small Mexican American population in comparison with California. Yet because California has the largest population of all fifty states, it still has a smaller percentage of Mexican Americans than any of the remaining four southwestern states.

In the 1950 census Mexican Americans are classified as foreign-born (comprising 17.2 percent) or native-born (of which one-third are second generation and the remainder third generation or later). New Mexico and Colorado have a predominance of Spanish American residents of native-born parents. California and Arizona, which both attract large, mobile Anglo populations, have had the largest increase in foreign-born Mexican Americans, and Texas occupies an intermediate position on the scale (Browning and McLemore, 1964:54). There was a time when most foreign-born Mexican Americans came across into Texas and settled there permanently, but now the immigrant either goes from Baja California into southern California or crosses into Texas and then migrates westward, principally into the metropolitan centers of San Francisco or Los Angeles, or northward to San Antonio. Thus, the old pattern of large Mexican immigrations into rural borderland areas has been broken.

During the early 1960s there was a brief upsurge in permanent immigration to the United States. This was followed by a sharp decline in 1964, when administrative restrictions were established to curb unlimited immigration from Mexico. A ceiling of 120,000 immigrants from countries in the Western Hemisphere was established by congressional action, to go into effect in 1967. As a result, immigrant labor would become scarce, placing additional stress on the "commuter labor" immigrants to participate in the economic life of the United States. Families from the interior of Mexico who were unable to obtain permanent immigration visas to the United States pushed toward the border municipios, causing economic and population pressures throughout the area. The obvious poverty and overcrowded living conditions of Mexican families along the international boundary perpetuate negative stereotypes commonly applied to all Mexican Americans. Also, because they are so close to Mexico and Mexican culture, border residents have a lower assimilation rate into American culture, thus reinforcing the "Mexican" stereotype.

MEXICAN AMERICAN BORDER CULTURE

Of special importance to Mexican American identity within the United States is the borderland area lying along the United States–Mexican frontier. Although Steiner (1970:141) maintains that Los Angeles is the capital of La Raza, its "umbilical cord" is the Mexican borderland region. The blending of American and Mexican ways in this area has resulted in a culture traditionally associated with the southwestern United States. The architecture, art, literature, and music of this region rely heavily upon this cultural fusion, and the bilingual and bicultural institutions that developed there have been a training ground for Mexican American authors, educators, and social and political leaders. Unfortunately, this border region has also been a source for the perpetuation of ethnic stereotypes, especially negative ones. With the constant immigration and constant international interplay, the basic social, cultural, and legal differences between Mexican nationals and Mexican Americans often become blurred, especially since elements of prejudice toward Mexican Americans are already firmly established in the social structures and traditions of the region.

The official boundary line between Mexico and the United States is 2,500 miles long and runs along the Rio Grande and through the desert. It contains thirty-one legal ports of entry. At the conclusion of the war for Texas independence in 1836, the Rio Grande became the dividing line between the Lone Star Republic and the Republic of Mexico. When Texas joined the Union in 1845, this river became the border between Mexico and the United States. For nearly one hundred years after, the meandering course of the Rio Grande created bitterness between Mexico and the United States, and various international conferences were held to resolve disputes over surrounding land. These hostilities were not finally resolved until the

Chamizal Convention of 1963. Subsequently, a treaty was signed in November 1970, establishing the El Paso–Gulf of Mexico segment as the main channel of the Rio Grande, regardless of future changes in the channel caused by river erosion.

The line dividing the United States and Mexico in the desert was initially set forth in 1848 at the Treaty of Guadalupe Hidalgo, following the war with Mexico, in which the southwest territory was claimed by the United States. A minor change in that border occurred in 1853, when a large desert tract of land belonging to Mexico was acquired under the Gadsden Purchase. This acquisition allowed the construction of a direct railroad route to California as well as the transferral to the United States of land that contained high-grade copper ore (Moore, 1970a: 37–38).

The division of the desert was difficult to establish and is even more difficult to maintain. Hostility has arisen among Baja California farmers because of the high saline content in the waters resulting from Americans polluting the streams feeding that Mexican area. The call for relief by President Echeverria in his June 1972 visit points this up as a source of future antagonisms between California and Baja California agricultural interests. There are pressures constantly working to equalize cultural, social, and economic differences across this political barricade. There is a tendency among Americans to view the poor, uprooted Mexicans living in the *colonias* (squatter suburbs) adjacent to the United States as typical of Mexican American citizens in the United States.

Across the Rio Grande from El Paso are the squatter suburbs of Ciudad Juárez spreading rapidly across the hills. These suburbs are largely without schools or parks, and only a few colonias have electricity or water. The Mexicans living in shelters made of brush or adobe look across the river at the opulence of American life, and visitors from the United States touring these Mexican border cities deplore the economic and social conditions that they find there. However, the truth of the matter is that in these urban slums the per capita income is two or three times higher than the average in other regions of Mexico. What these invidious comparisons of life across the border with life in the United States bring to consciousness is that conditions throughout Mexico are intolerable and in dire need of change.

The Mexican living next door to the United States who is exposed to the American way of life becomes anxious to participate in it. Sometimes his dreams are realized through legal means, but illegal procedures are also common. Legally he can live in Mexico and work in the United States as a "green card" commuter. A resident of Mexico who has not fulfilled all of the requirements of United States citizenship but who declares his intentions to do so in the future is issued a green card from the Immigration and Naturalization Service that allows him (or her) to commute daily into the United States for work and still reside in Mexico. Most of these commuters are hired as manual laborers or domestics. Because of lower rent and food costs in Mexico and because wages paid to even skilled labor are low by United States standards, a green card commuter can live as well as a skilled urban worker in Mexico, despite the low wages the former receives in the United States; and it is because of these low wages that he is in demand by United States employers and patrons in the United States.

A 1968 Senate hearing on Western Hemisphere immigration, which convened in El Paso, verified that more than 12,000 green card holders crossed daily from Ciudad Juárez to El Paso. It is also reported that of the 50,202 Mexican commuters located along the Mexican border more than one-fourth commute directly to El Paso. From 1968 to 1970, 10,996 more Mexicans became green card commuters, with 2,469 new commuters concentrated in the El Paso area alone. Daily, 7,450 green card commuters pass into San Ysidro, 200 into Tecate, and 7,849 into Calexico-Mexicali. The economic impact of green card commuters can be seen in Valencia's study (1969: 35,37), which reports that in 1960, 36 percent of the total wages earned by Ciudad Juárez residents working in the United States was paid to green card commuters and 85 percent of the million dollars in wages earned in the United States was in turn spent in El Paso.

In addition to green card entry, some illegal means are also used by Mexican citizens attempting to work in the United States. They can obtain a seventy-two hour visiting pass ("local passport") and, once over the border, remain for a week or longer to work as farm laborers, gardeners, or maids. In the El Paso region alone, more than 300 female Mexicans working as domestics are picked up and returned to Mexico each month, according to border immigration officials.

Wetbacks also enter the United States for agricultural jobs. Since Mexicans are now included in the Western Hemisphere immigration quotas, legal entry into the United States will be harder to obtain, and illegal entry will become a more critical problem. Immigration statistics by region in 1968 show only 200 Mexican aliens illegally entered in the Northeast, 832 in the Southeast, 6,700 in the Northwest, and 143,948 in the Southwest. The number of illegal Mexican aliens has continuously increased—from 39,124 in 1963 to 201,636 in 1969—according to official immigration figures. In 1970, thirty-five million dollars was required just to return the more than 350,000 illegal aliens apprehended in this country. During the first three-quarters of 1971 this rate of illegal entry rose by 27 percent. In El Paso alone, 6.7 percent of all juveniles in the county home have been detained for violating immigration laws, and the public is now asking whether the expense of detention for this cause is warranted. In San Antonio and various West Coast metropolitan areas, the presence of the wetback is often "overlooked," because of a lack of funds for his detention and transportation back across the border.

These immigration statistics present only a limited picture of the problem, however, and do not include the many Mexicans picked up close to border entry points who voluntarily return to avoid deportation proceedings. Of the 150,000 or more illegal Mexican aliens apprehended in 1968, one-fifth were caught as they entered and another fifth within seventy-two hours. Relatively few are apprehended after one year in the United States except in special campaigns such as those conducted in the mid-1950s and the recent ones being conducted in Los Angeles and San Antonio.

Although El Paso, a major port of entry, apprehends a high percentage of Mexican aliens (in 1970, 53,173 illegal aliens were apprehended in the El Paso area, of which 2,873 were actually smuggled into this country by trucks, vans, and other means), with current quota restrictions there has been a sharp increase in illegal entry since 1969, and this rate should increase even more dramatically during the next five to ten years. Officials state that only 30 percent of all illegal Mexican aliens are apprehended. When applied to an average yearly figure, this would indicate that mcre than 180,000 immigrants cross the border into the United States illegally through El Paso alone.

Mexican farmers feel the drain on available Mexican labor as the wetback crosses to work at more lucrative jobs in the United States. President Echeverria, in his official visit to the United States in June 1972, startled the United States Congress by his pointed criticisms of American employers who entice wetback labor across the border in violation of both Mexican and American statutes. Moreover, Mexican farmers have demanded that government troops be employed along heavy-crossing areas to keep Mexicans in Mexico and available for employment in Mexican agriculture. However, the alien working illegally in agriculture is taking a big chance because ruthless American farmers may work him for weeks and then let him be "discovered" at the end of the season, just before payday. His questionable status leaves him without legal recourse to collect his wages. Such exploitation lends further credence to the stereotypes of the "dumb" Mexican and the "shrewd" Anglo employer.

Official regulations governing entry across the border are implemented by local formal and informal procedures that are elastic enough to be workable yet legal. But in spite of local interpretations and modifications of international border regulations, the resentments that have smoldered for many generations are fanned into active antagonisms from time to time. The most recent instance of this was Operation Intercept in 1961, an ill-fated attempt to restrict narcotics smuggling. The actual effect was to put economic pressures on border business interests in Mexico to become active in the destruction of marijuana fields in the interior. Likewise, the relay points within Mexico for hard drugs from Europe and the Orient were to come under local surveillance and measures would be taken to reduce the drug flow across the border (Price, 1971:33–41). This economic boycott produced a counter measure in Mexico called Operación Dignidad (Operation Dignity). Ciudad Juárez residents were exhorted not to go into the United States to buy goods and services. This directly affected many major businesses in the cities that cater to the Mexican customer.

A recent study of the Economic Development Administration shows that the borderland region adjacent to Mexico is economically underdeveloped and needs outside investments and other assistance to raise average wage rates and standards of living. Organizations such as the United States–Mexico Border Cities Association are actively engaged in promoting the growth of twin plant arrangements, in which inexpensive assembling and hand labor in Mexico can be combined with highly technical operations in a sister plant in the United States. Unfortunately, the present high rate of population growth in border areas neutralizes the rate of industrial development and trade.

Within this depressed economic area, ethnic minorities are caught at the bottom of the economic strata. At hearings before the Select Commission of Western Hemisphere Immigration in El Paso in 1968, findings of a special commuter survey were presented. It was found that firms which employ Mexican commuters pay lower wages for the same work than firms employing only United States residents, because United States residents say they are not willing to accept the lower wage paid to the commuter. Moreover, green card commuters may be hired to replace striking workers during labor disputes for that period between the time of the strike and a later date when the strike is certified as legitimate by the secretary of labor. Border city trade unions, consisting predominantly of Mexican American members, vote overwhelmingly to restrict the competition of other foreign labor, while at the same time proclaiming their cultural identity with Mexico. It is this situation that discourages effective union organization and trade bargaining. All this makes the border milieu a pressure pot where romantic dreams of wealth and happiness are constantly being shattered by the sordid realities of hunger, disease, overpopulation, and underemployment.

Notes

[1] Though far less publicized, Texas land grants were also legally ravished. Between 1840 and 1859, for example, all but one Mexican-owned grant in Nueces county, Texas, passed into the hands of Anglos. Pitt (1970: 83–103, 278) describes in great detail the four ways used to dispossess the lands of "the twenty-five families" of the Californios—by squatter, legal chicanery, joint ownership, and money lending devices.

[2] The main census data in tables throughout this volume are from the 1960 census. The 1970 census materials for Spanish-surname peoples are soon to be released. However, since different methods have been used to arrive at the current figures, the reader is warned against faulty inferences. Ethnic sampling quotas have been reduced to 5 and 15 percent of total households (from 20 to 25 percent in 1960), and the new Spanish-surname and Spanish-language composite category is based on household rather than family units. For example, if a grandfather whose mother tongue is Spanish is listed as the head of household, then all members of that household will be included in the Spanish-surname and Spanish-language category, even if none of these others speak Spanish or carry a Spanish surname. According to Leo Estrada, some 4,667,975 persons of Spanish surname are listed in the 1960 census for the five southwestern states, but figures for 1970 increase this total by one-third to 6,188,362—an additional 1,520,397 individuals. The reader is therefore advised to be cautious in comparing past demographic figures with current ones.

[3] "Wetback" is a misleading label since illegal immigrants can cross to El Paso through a dry Rio Grande riverbed during about ten months of the year.

Chapter 3 ◉ A Search
for Identity

A person's self-image—who he is and what he thinks he is worth—arises from acceptance of him and socialization by him within the group with which he most readily identifies. Thus individual identity is determined to a great extent by group identity. The graphic impressions associated with racial, religious, ethnic, and nationality groupings are a vital key for each individual in his understanding of himself and the world about him.

In the past, negative status has been bestowed upon Mexican Americans by the dominant Anglo Americans. Anglo reasoning begins with the ethnocentric ideas that Caucasian Americans are superior to non-Caucasian Americans and that foreigners are not equal to Americans. According to such reasoning, Mexicans, as foreigners, are inferior, and, since Mexican Americans are simply displaced Mexicans, they are equally inferior. To rid himself of his inferior status, a Mexican American must either reject his ethnic ancestry or reject the dominant society —repudiate its right to determine his identity. In recent years the latter alternative has become increasingly popular among the more radical ethnic movements.

A Mexican American who identifies with his ethnic group loses the social and economic rewards reserved for "Anglo-type" individuals. On the other hand, a minority person who identifies with the larger Anglo society and succeeds within that structure is attacked and rejected by his own ethnic group. He is accused of "selling out" his cultural heritage. Identifying with either societal segment will tend to alienate the person from membership in the other. Wiley (1967:151–154) compares upward mobility to climbing a tree with many branches.

The decision to climb out on a limb of ethnic separatism initially provides a degree of upward mobility, but also draws the person further and further from the central trunk. Such action may become a "mobility trap," inasmuch as the means for moving up within an ethnic system are contrary to those for moving up within the central system, or the larger society. Nevertheless, in the central system obstacles often prevent further ascension, thus making the limb a welcome alternative. Wiley continues:

> Mobility comes not only from persistent and dedicated climbing. More important is knowing how to distinguish the limbs from the trunk, and even in knowing when to climb out on a strong safe limb to avoid falling from a slippery trunk [1967:149].

Identity is defined differently when it is self-designated than when it is bestowed upon one by someone outside the group. Thus, we can expect vast differences between a Mexican American's self-image and the view of him held by external observers. In addition, the way in which Mexican Americans project their image to other groups reveals elements of their own view of themselves. Using these three basic distinctions for identity—(1) externally bestowed, (2) projected, and (3) self-designated—we can review professional and popular literature for different usages and acceptance of disparate categorical names and titles, as well as for the emotional connotations of each and the contexts in which they are deemed appropriate or inappropriate.

AN OUTSIDER'S VIEW OF MEXICAN AMERICAN IDENTITY

American writers have created and perpetuated popular stereotypes of the quaint, romantic life among the docile Mexican American. Simmen (1971) traces some of these trends throughout the century and finds that only during the past decade has there been a long-awaited shift toward authentic self-portraiture by writers of the "awakening minority." Even respected historians and social scientists have perpetuated in their writings the stereotype of this ethnic minority as having had no heroes, having made no cultural contributions in the Southwest, and having needed Anglo domination for lack of internal leadership (Romano-V., 1967). A 1970 report to the Texas State Education Commissioner found an "inexcusable bias" in textbooks used in lower grades within the state, and publishers were warned that future textbook adoptions would be made only when all ethnic groups were accurately portrayed. Sometimes, rather than being stereotyped, this minority was simply not represented in novels and textbooks read in school. Even more devastating was the fact that students were basically unaware that such omissions had occurred.

Social scientists, because of their claims to accuracy, have been far more damaging than had they made no pretense to having scientific knowledge of Mexican American culture. Five approaches used by social science in analyzing the relationship of Mexican Americans to the larger society will be examined here: (1) the development of the "folk-culture" model; (2) the "value-orientation" model; (3) the sequential stages of superordinate-subordinate interethnic relationships; (4) the demographic and attitude comparisons between Mexican nationals and Mexican Americans; and (5) the rebuttal of previous "scientific" contributions by social scientists of Mexican descent.

The initial development of a folk-culture model for Mexico probably began with Redfield's work (1930;1941), which was critically reformulated later by Lewis (1951). These anthropological accounts of isolated Mexican villages were mistakenly thought to be accurate reflections of rural Mexico in general and therefore applicable to Mexican immigrants in the United States who had come from rural areas. This simplistic notion of Mexican homogeneity is clearly repudiated by current, respected historians and writers. For example, Simpson's *Many Mexicos* (1964) emphasizes the historical differences in the various areas and among the people of Mexico. Cline (1963) stresses the differences between rural and urban Mexicans and between value orientations of Indian and non-Indian groups, as well as other regional variations that prevail. Hayner (1966) discusses in detail the varied life styles of the social classes, the various ecological and residential patterns in town and metropolis, and the recent changes in Mexican culture resulting from increasing professionalism, decreasing militarism, and marked shifts in population concentrations. The writings of Simpson, Cline, and Hayner show a far greater range of life styles in Mexico than do the earlier studies of semi-isolated folk cultures in Mexican villages.

Mounting criticism of the folk culture of Mexico model as a valid approach to understanding contemporary Mexican American society in the United States has been voiced by sociologists, anthropologists, and Mexican American spokesmen. As Peñalosa (1967:408) notes, present-day urban Mexican Americans can be understood little by studying rural Mexicans. Foster declares that physical displacement of isolated folk peoples to urban areas functionally changes the institutional influences upon them and eventually dissipates their folk beliefs.

The urban classes which are characterized by an essentially folk culture do not constitute a distinct society, since the lives of individuals of these classes are geared to the organic functioning of a society which includes and is dominated by non-folk [1953:170].

Leeds points out that in considering Mexican Americans as a folk culture other anthropologists display the most blatant methodological bias, implicitly ascribing to Mexican Americans a homogeneity of behavior and beliefs that their urban and regional heterogeneity does not reflect. He writes:

Anthropologists have tended to perpetuate traditional concerns—kinship, the community, child training, study of associations, etc.—transferring these, first, forty to fifty years ago, to the quite different societal context of rural communities and then, more recently, to the drastically different context of the city in large-scale society. Some of the methodological problems regarding tribal societies were never resolved. . . . In this transference of traditional concerns from tribal experience to city studies, these problems were perpetuated and intensified [1968:32].

If this folk model of Mexican Americans ever did fit a substantial number of Mexican Americans (which is presently being questioned by an increasing number of scholars), it has not been an accurate picture of the majority of Mexican Americans for some decades. Even attempts at converting the folk culture model to a simplistic Mexican American culture model is not valid because of the stereotypes that are still perpetuated. As Peñalosa summarizes this point:

> Existentially there is no Mexican-American community as such, nor is there such a "thing" as Mexican American culture. This group is fragmentized socially, culturally, ideologically, and organizationally. It is characterized by extremely important social class, regional and rural-urban differences [1967:405–406].

Again, the category of Mexican American, with all its rich variety, has been simplistically labeled as "homogeneous" to fit stereotyped notions. This label has been further reified by scholars who have attempted to build modal value orientations for the complex Anglo and Mexican American cultures. Because these orientations have impeded an accurate view of Mexican Americans in contemporary United States society, they will be discussed now in some detail.

THE VALUE-ORIENTATION MODEL From concepts originated by Florence Kluckhohn at Radcliffe College in 1937, the idea of separate value orientations for Mexican American and Anglo American cultures emerged. Using this idea as a basis for further investigation, Saunders (1954) did a comprehensive health study of Mexican Americans. Mead (1955) similarly described the Spanish Americans of New Mexico, emphasizing their lack of formal organizations, their village and familial loyalties, and their special norms concerning time and work, which were not like those in Anglo societies.

Edmonson (1957) ascribed to Los Manitos of northern New Mexico six basic value orientations, which are: traditionalism, familism, paternalism, personalism, dramatism, and fatalism. Kluckhohn and Strodtbeck (1961) further specified that the value orientations toward rationality, toward man's relationship to nature, toward the inherent goodness in man, and toward perceptions of time and space were different for Mexican Americans than they were for Anglos.

From this and other data on Mexican Americans as a single, homogeneous group, Vaca (1970b:45) compiled, and rejected the validity of, the following list of specific values itemized under the Mexican American and Anglo American headings:

Table 3.1   Ascribed or Inferred Value-orientation Differences between Anglo American and Mexican American Cultures

Mexican American	Anglo American
Subjugation to nature	Mastery over nature
Present oriented	Future oriented
Immediate gratification	Deferred gratification
Complacent	Aggressive
Non-intellectual	Intellectual
Fatalistic	Non-fatalistic
Non-goal oriented	Goal oriented
Non-success oriented	Success oriented
Emotional	Rational
Dependent	Individualistic
Machismo	Effeminacy
Superstitious	Non-superstitious
Traditional	Progressive

SOURCE: El Grito (Fall 1970), p. 45.

Madsen (1964:15–16) described the Latinos of lower Texas within this general orientation. His account is saturated with symbolism of La Raza—the fierce nationalistic pride of Mestizo Mexican citizens, their hope for an ultimately glorious destiny brought about through cosmic intervention (Vasconcelos, 1926). Likewise, Rubel (1966) tacitly accepts the legitimacy of this bicultural model in his analysis.

Such a dogma as represented by the value-orientation approach, which infers that all members of a given ethnic group have similar values regardless of social class, age, wealth, and education (to name only a few social variables), finds itself precariously close to supporting racist doctrines of genetic or cultural determinism. Vaca correctly indicates (1970b) that any social scientist, whether of Anglo or Mexican American extraction, who begins with the premise that these value orientations correctly reflect either of the specific groups indicated, reinforces the erroneous stereotype that even Anglos have a homogeneous culture and that any pattern which varies from it is wrong. More and more criticisms are being leveled against the universal application of value-orientation interpretations. For example, Swadesh (1972), in her extensive research in northern New Mexico villages, found that the Spanish Americans are indeed goal directed, future-time oriented, progressive, and capable of rational thought *when these values are interpreted* in terms of *their own* rather than Anglo *culture.* Moreover, when lower-class norms predominate among ethnic respondents, these attitudes toward physical or mental aggressiveness are interpreted as valid ethnic differences and are stigmatized as inferior to the values of both middle-class researchers and the larger Anglo society. A recent study of urban Mexican Americans (Chandler and Ewing, 1971) reported their value orientations to be not significantly different from either rural or urban Anglo value orientations. This lack of difference between Mexican Americans and Anglo Americans was ascribed to full acculturation within the urban milieu. Whether former differences were due to normative criteria used for evaluation or were indeed accurate, subsequent research would indicate the necessity of applying these value models to categories smaller than entire cultures.

THE ACCULTURATION MODEL   Some social scientists, attempting to find an alternative to the folk-culture and value-orientation models for examining Mexican American culture, have employed a differential acculturation typology, emphasizing value differences among various generations of immigrants arriving in the United States during different eras. A statement by Broom and Shevky exemplifies this approach:

> The twentieth century Mexican immigrants found already established in the United States an indigenous Spanish-speaking population of long standing. This group, localized in the Southwest, was a legacy of the land accession

of the nineteenth century. The Mexican-American population is differentiated on the basis of this fact [1952:151].

Saunders (1954:44–64), studying cultural differences in medical care, breaks down Spanish-speaking Americans into three
subcategories: (1) the *Spanish Americans*, early residents of
the Southwest, with mixed Hispano-Indian ancestry. Isolated
in northern New Mexican villages, they still exist today as a
residue of the precolonization era. At various times in their
history, Indian, Spanish, and Anglo nations all battled over
them and their lands; (2) the *Mexican Americans*, genetically
similar but perhaps more Indian than the inbred Spanish
Americans. Mexican Americans are distinguished by their residence in, and loyalties toward Mexico, coupled with their recent
arrival from that country; and (3) the *Mexican*, a still more
recent arrival than the Mexican American, with a very close
attachment to Mexico. He fully expects to return there someday.
Saunders' distinctions on the basis of national loyalty are
modified by Burma (1954:35–36), who distinguished between
Mexican American and Mexican on the basis of legal citizenship. Others have followed this trend with only minor modifications, for example, D'Antonio and Samora (1962:18–19);
Madsen (1964); Heller (1966:10–11); and Sanchez (1967),
to name a few.

Other scientific writers, using these three arbitrary subcategories, have noted some similarities and differences between
history and self-identity among Spanish-speaking peoples.
Whereas the Spanish Americans can be distinguished by both
geographical isolation and historical differences, the separation
of Mexican Americans (the largest segment of Spanish-speaking Americans) into distinct types on the basis of acculturation
is beset with methodological controversy. The first difficulty is
to decide whether the basic Mexican background or the subsequent Anglo acculturation will be the standardized unit against
which current behavioral patterns are compared.

If we accept the concept of Mexican-American culture
. . . as a variant of the United States working class subculture, but influenced to a lesser or stronger degree by
traditional Mexican folk culture, it follows that these peo-

ple should be regarded as partially Mexicanized-Americans rather than as partially Americanized-Mexicans [Peñalosa, 1967:410].

The traditional approach (which has assumed that Mexican Americans are merely transplanted Mexicans, saturated with Mexican values, but subject to Anglo influences) would consider Anglo and Mexican values as opposite poles on a continuum. Mexican American values would lie somewhere between these polar types. Yet, two social scientists reject this model, proclaiming instead that Mexican American values do not merely mix Mexican and Anglo values, but comprise indeed a distinct culture. Nall (1962:37) in comparing Mexican, Mexican American, and Anglo students found that Mexican Americans expressed values with a distinct cultural dimension, often representing a more extreme position along the continuum than those of either the Mexican or the Anglo samples. Another comparison of university students in Mexico City and Austin with Mexican Americans from the borderland zone resulted in similar findings. The American attitude toward respect, for example, was one of detached, self-assured equalitarianism, whereas Mexican students displayed a close-knit, highly emotionalized, reciprocal dependence and dutifulness within a firm, authoritarian framework. Mexican Americans, rather than combining the two attitudes, were further removed from the core-culture pattern of the other two than they were from each other's.

The model of acculturation stages is not yet a useful analytical tool for differentiating between former and latter generations of Mexico immigrants, although the factor of generation-in-the-United-States combined with "allegiance" group has enabled researchers to more accurately portray the distinct frustrations in social adjustments and group identification encountered by the novice, hard-core, transitional, and mainstream types of Mexican immigrants.

Spanish-surnamed persons in the southwestern United States are far below the national average in income. It is this situation, a result of low educational achievement and past discriminatory practices, that allows members of the larger society to consider Mexican Americans of many years residence and recent Mexican immigrants as identical.

In the beginning third of the twentieth century, some social scientists mistakenly concluded that because Mexican Americans with Spanish as their mother tongue scored below normal on I.Q. tests written in English, this was due to genetic deficiencies. The conclusions of many writers of this era who reflect a similar persuasion were examined in some detail by Vaca (1970a), and their instruments and data were found to be lacking in validity. Yet, stereotypes concerning the physical appearance and the mentality of the Mexican American still flourish. Some qualities that are said to differentiate Mexican Americans from Anglo Americans are skin hue, hair color, body odor, intelligence, brain size, body weight and/or form, and even accident proneness. With the current, sophisticated methodological procedures and research designs of most social scientists revealing the spurious relationships between constitutional factors and mental ability, perpetuation of these Lombrosian-type explanations of human behavior is linked more to the maintenance of traditional social and power structures than to valid scientific explanations of the mental potential of minority peoples. Casavantes (1969) claims that the Spanish language, family names, music, food, festivals, celebrations, and literary traditions (both oral and written) constitute the most objective criteria for differentiating Mexican Americans from other ethnic groups. Since language and surnames will be discussed in detail later in the book, it is sufficient to say here only that these are extremely important criteria for Mexican American identity.

Ethnic backlash from advertising, caricatures, and social science reports that intensify stereotypes of genetic and cultural inferiority has been varied. Since the middle 1960s there have been ever-increasing shouts of discontent from the barrio. Mexican American medical doctors, educators, and other professionals have used their occupational status to counter the insidious disparagement of Mexican Americans as a people, and of Spanish, their mother tongue. There are also a growing number of Spanish-surnamed social scientists and scholars who repudiate the fallacies and misconceptions concerning

Mexican American character perpetuated by other social scientists.[1]

More recent protests against the biases of history and social science scholars have been raised by Mexican American writers such as Casavantes, Arciniega, Guzman, Romano-V., and Vaca. Casavantes (1969) declared that the notions of dependency, fatalism, and paternalism—values of the folk-culture model— were indeed "false attributes" of the Mexican American. Instead, he maintained the true characteristics which signify his national origin are language, food, music, and literature. Arciniega has pointed out that erroneous interpretations by "outsiders" of the behavior of recent Mexican immigrants has been supportive of the stereotype of Mexicans as lazy, indifferent, and irresponsible.

> The time that the individual allots to the allegiance group is sometimes mistakenly judged by "outsiders" to be wasted time, or proof that these "types" lack ambition because they devote so much time to recreation and family even when almost starving to death. *Outsiders miss the point entirely!* The allegiance group performs the function of educating the individual for existence. There is no [other] school for these "types" [1971a:9].

In strongly emotional rhetoric, Guzman (1967:247) points out the lack of objectivity currently presented in "scientific" works and the role of these works in perpetuating erroneous stereotypes. Romano-V. (1967; 1968), in a lengthy counterthrust at current distortions in the writings of social scientists and historians, offers historical evidence of Mexican American accomplishments—organizational skill, union organizations, strikes and marches—to show the falsehood of this image of the dependent, traditionalistic, and fatalistic Mexican American. He levels charges of distortion at such authors as Tuck, Saunders, Edmonson, Kluckhohn and Strodtbeck, Madsen, and Heller, and even at Samora and Lamanna. Randomly selected comments from his charges follow.

> According to Madsen, Mexican-American culture represents a retreat, whereas acculturation represents creativity and change. . . . [1968:14]

. . . As Ruth Tuck before him, Lyle Saunders distorted history, essentially rewrote history and perpetuated the concept of an ahistoric people, the Mexican lazily asleep under the cactus, in the popular and ignorant mind. . . . [1968:16]

. . . Edmonson goes on to say Hispanos do not cry at funerals; they just give a "characteristic shrug." Hispanos have no "individual responsibility" in sexual relations, are fatalistic about the "natural order of things" due to their religion, are willing "to live with failure," live in "mañana land," are politically apathetic, and finally, ". . . where Hispano culture is fatalistic, American culture is markedly activist." Like Tuck and Saunders before him, Edmonson cleanly wipes out history and simultaneously classifies these people of New Mexico as basically Un-American. This is a theme that is incessantly recurrent in all of the social science literature on Mexican-Americans. . . . [1968:17]

. . . Contemporary social science views of Mexican-Americans are precisely those held by people during the days of the American frontier. . . . Contemporary social scientists [are] busily perpetuating the very same opinions of Mexican culture that were current during the Mexican-American War [1968:24].

Vaca (1970a; 1970b), in a lengthy review of social science literature, offers a critical analysis of writers from 1912 to the present. He maintains that the earliest tendency among scholarly writers was to ascribe to genetic inferiority the inability of Mexican Americans to compete in American schools. Subsequently, their lack of success was attributed to cultural inferiority, a viewpoint Vaca calls "cultural determinism." Describing the "folk culture" and "value-orientation" models as simplistic explanations for the present problems of the Mexican people, Vaca suggests that cultural determinism has been eagerly embraced by educators and other representatives of the larger society since it infers that present minority problems are in the minority culture itself, not in the present institutional structures of the dominant society. Whether couched in the emotional language of a Chicano barrio newspaper or in the carefully worded style of the professional article, these charges that social science *has* been, though sometimes unwittingly, a party to the perpetuation of negative ethnic stereotypes have been substantiated.

The dangers of anti-Mexican American stereotypes are that they not only produce a negative self-image among members of the minority which suppresses motivation, but that they legitimate discriminatory behavior toward this minority from the larger society. For instance, during a recent Arizona OEO project to produce barrio housing and health reforms, stereotypes of Mexican American "passivity and non-goal-directed values" (from the value-orientations model previously discussed) were so fully accepted by Anglo functionaries that, when a study was made showing a high rate of activism toward specific reforms by the barrio residents, the program sponsors insisted on attributing the results to "outside agitators" and "behind-the-scene-manipulators." Local probation officers in that Arizona community were convinced that the "barrio culture" was the causal factor in high juvenile delinquency rates, and local educators and religious leaders so wanted to believe that Mexican Americans were a "childlike people" that they would not change their opinions even when presented with evidence to the contrary (Spicer, 1970:16).

THE SEARCH FOR CORRECT ETHNIC LABELS

So far in our discussion, the economic, political, and social problems of the Mexican American have been approached as either deficiencies within the minority group itself or deficiencies within the institutional structures of the larger society. An alternate approach, popular with educators and journalists, is to view interethnic clashes as resulting from a "lack of communication." In other words, this approach views existing interethnic problems as a function of the interrelationships between the groups themselves and considers that the solutions are to be found in the dynamic processes concerned. Communication depends upon symbols, and if incorrect symbols are used, hostility rather than cooperation is engendered. How-

ever, interethnic animosities are not incurred through the mis-
use of terms. Rather, these terms are merely symbolic of
feelings of hostility and mistrust underlying outward gestures
of goodwill. Some attempts at "lexicography" reveal the etio-
logical nightmare involved in creating acceptable ethnic nomenclature. Sanchez discreetly refers to the total citizenry of
New Mexico as "New Mexicans," differentiating the Spanish-
speaking minority by the phrase "citizens of Spanish descent
in New Mexico [1967:28]." Not only is this phrase excessively
long, but the exclusion of people of Indian ancestry and the
unique regional setting mentioned prohibits the widespread
adoption of this term to include all Mexican Americans. "Hispanos," an all-inclusive term used by many scholars, refers to
"pureblood" immigrants from the Iberian peninsula rather
than to the Mexican American Mestizo population. Some two
decades ago, the Bureau of the Census searched for a non-
controversial but appropriate title for the Mexican American
minority. A functional approach was to describe this minority
in terms that could be applied to census materials, and "persons
of Spanish surname" became the basis for demographic reports
in the five southwestern states. When the Inter-Agency Committee on Mexican American Affairs was created in 1967, its
initial chairman, Vicente R. Ximenes, insisted that the term
"Spanish Surnamed Americans" (without the hyphens) become
Washington officialese throughout administrative areas of government.[2]

With large numbers of Spanish-surnamed peoples from
Puerto Rico and Cuba relocating in the United States, the
demand for change in the Mexican American title—coinciden-
tal with the demise of the Inter-Agency Committee on Mexican
American Affairs—led to the establishment of the permanent
Cabinet Committee on Opportunities for the Spanish Speaking
(CCOSS), which has shifted the basic ethnic criterion from
Spanish surname to those identified as Spanish speaking. This
places a new emphasis upon language as the identity key for
this minority.

Lest observers be lulled into a false sense of complacency,
it must be emphasized that whatever term comes into use, it
soon absorbs emotional meanings already existing between the

person using the term and the person to which it is being applied.

A PROJECTIVE VIEW OF
MEXICAN AMERICAN IDENTITY

Within an action frame of reference, an individual uses selected means to gain priority goals. His voluntary choice of means and ends reveals his values, which in turn are an accurate indicator of his social origin. Just as the path of a bullet following a trajectory can be retraced to discover the point of origin, so too can a "value trajectory" be constructed to locate the societal position of a person or group espousing a given attitude. Ethnic groups reveal their class origin and self-identity by the criteria they use to evaluate other groups and the manner in which they react to the behavior of others.

For example, in Old Mexico, the upper class perceive the Anglo as a "Babbitt" type (Humphrey, 1954:116–125). He may be shown courtesy by a member of the upper class because the Mexican elite pride themselves on being hospitable and gracious at all times. In addition, the wealthy and powerful Anglo receives social amenities from this Mexican in spite of, not because of, his cultural ethnocentrism. Whereas Anglo arrogance might be resented by lower-class Mexicans or Mexican Americans, its acceptance by the more secure upper class is considered necessary in dealing with what they consider to be an immature but financially more powerful group. In social situations where upper-class Mexicans and upper-class Mexican Americans interact, such as a country club, for example, there is a common bond overriding citizenship considerations. Indeed, when these elite are asked to indicate the criteria by which their "ethnicity" is measured, they are hard pressed to respond. Since their elevated social position has always been taken for granted, they have never had to identify themselves in any manner other than as members of the social elite. The upper- and middle-class families of Mexico enjoy a privileged position within their specific social structure. United States citizens of similar status who wish to enter Mexican politics, to inherit real estate in the Republic, or to own a commercial enterprise there, change their citizenship to Mexican. There appears to be little social adjustment in shifting from one elite to another, however, the change being one of expediency rather than of ethnic identity.

Middle-class Spanish-speaking immigrants to the United States whose characteristics more nearly correspond to those of Anglo middle-class types seem to have fewer adjustment problems than poverty-class immigrants because they are able to maintain a positive self-identity throughout the adjustment period. A study by Portes (1969) of Cuban exiles from the Castro regime illustrates this quite well. During the early revolutionary period in Cuba, the more economically powerful and well-educated citizens of Cuba's Establishment were forced to flee to the United States. Unlike subsequent waves of lower-class refugees, they possessed educational and professional skills that were immediately salable, and these "golden exiles" felt no resentment or hostility toward the dominant Anglo society. The projection of hostility and envy so often evidenced by Mexican Americans in less advantageous social positions was absent.

Lower-class persons project their awareness of subordination through resentment toward their superiors. Still, in terms of the reality of their powerlessness, persons of a subordinate status must define their roles with reference to the power of the dominant group and should anticipate possible punitive reaction or embarrassment from the dominant group for actions that show disrespect toward these "social superiors."

> When inferiors extend their most lavish reception for visiting superiors, the selfish desire to win favor may not be the chief motive; the inferior may be tactfully attempting to put the superior at ease by simulating the kind of world the superior is thought to take for granted [Goffman, 1959:19].

This accommodating attitude is a planned charade and is functional only so long as the subordinate group feels its present station in life is appointed by destiny or that it has no way of changing the status quo. Nowhere does the self-image relate

more to projected status based on relative deprivation than in
the case of the Mexican immigrant. The lower classes of Mexico
are destitute and are the classes desiring most to come
to the United States, since they have literally nothing to lose
and believe they have great possibilities for bettering their
situation through such a change. Newly arrived Mexican immigrants measure present opportunities against conditions in
Mexico. They are satisfied with the Anglo society and the promises of future attainment within it (Dworkin, 1965:215). They
do not have to rationalize about their present low status in the
United States because, compared with their life in the destitute
suburbs of Mexican municipios, even slum living here is a
substantial socioeconomic jump. Thus, although the new migrant has the least status, lowest income, and poorest food,
shelter, and basic services, he is still most appreciative of his
present conditions and less likely to become violently opposed
to his situation.

In some areas slum-dwelling Mexican Americans turn their
frustration toward the newly arrived Mexican, calling him a
"cholo" (an equivalent of the word "nigger" for black Americans) and savoring whatever prestige accrues from being able
to look down upon someone lower in status than themselves.
This resentment might reflect the lack of upward mobility
experienced by the lower-class Mexican American slum dweller
who is a second- or third-generation American and still finds
himself near the lowest rung of the social ladder. Subsequent
generations, conditioned to expect even more regarding education and ability, become increasingly aware of the disparity
between American ideals of equality and the existing inequality
of opportunity for minority-group members. And because there
are so many lower-class Mexican immigrants, all Americans
of Mexican descent are blanketed with the poverty stereotype
—regardless of their present class level or the number of generations their fathers have been citizens. This is especially evident along the southern border, where the perpetual stream
of new immigrants from Mexico keeps alive the low-class
image. Not only do the incoming immigrants reinforce traditional Mexican customs, language, and style of life, but their
very presence keeps alive the misconception that all Mexican

Americans are poor. Their obvious presence in substandard housing in ghetto areas focuses attention on them. However, the underlying fact that, while some are moving into the barrio from Mexico, others are leaving the barrio to better themselves financially and socially is obscured by the "apparent" fact that the characteristics of people in the ghetto continue unchanged over long periods of time.

Two opposing reasons given for the Mexican American's acceptance of an inferior socioeconomic position are that he internalizes a sense of ethnic inferiority in contact with Anglo institutions or that his outward acceptance is a superficial, role-playing device for eliciting majority-group approval. Guzman maintains that the negative images projected by Mexican Americans in their relations with others were internalized along with the rest of the content within the formal education institution.

Tragically, these external social judgments have been internalized by many Mexican Americans. Recent surveys in San Antonio and Los Angeles show a tendency for Mexican Americans to agree with the negative judgments that the larger society has passed upon them [1967:246].

In contrast to the "internalized-inferiority" hypothesis, Carter (1968:218) postulates that minority school children studied in a California community were aware of the stereotypes used against them. Solely to reduce friction with school authorities, they adopted behavior patterns consistent with Anglo expectations. Such poses as "hanging one's head and playing dumb," which were often interpreted by teachers as manifesting a "negative self-view," were but purposeful tricks developed by the subordinate group members to avoid Anglo antagonism directed toward their ethnic group. In describing themselves, group members were quite positive in the images they used. Their repetitive school failures, according to Carter, reflect the irrelevance of the Anglo skills being taught to these minority students rather than any internalized sense of inferiority they might have. These two different interpretations of sociopsychological research raise the questions of whether these minority-student attitudes are merely what the students perceive as majority-group expectations for their ethnic group or whether the students reveal their deepest personal feelings, uninhibited by fear of retaliation from figures in authority. It should be quite obvious that further examinations of minority-student motivational levels are futile until this methodological problem of reliability has been resolved.

The claim has been made that in any and all social systems inequality must exist between social positions constituting the various social strata to ensure that all societal functions are carried out properly. Yet, these strata need not be determined by ethnicity, race, creed, or color but may be differentiated on the basis of training or performance skills. Even within the utopian democratic model—that of the ancient Greek forum —only the *citizens*, comprising less than half of the total population, had power to decide the destiny of the nation. Slaves carried out the menial functions, which the citizens, debating in the forum, did not have time to do. Slaves were taught from birth that they were only an appendage to the person of their master. Their own identity was inextricably connected to the maintenance of the master's welfare, and satisfactions were gained only by obedience to, and protection of him. Slaves were not conscious of discrimination against them because the acceptance of their identity as slaves denied them any other option.

In a similar manner, subordinate groups and individuals must meet certain prerequisites in order to perceive and react against the inequalities of their present social standing. Such persons must have the freedom to recognize the unequal treatment dispensed by institutions within the system and have some awareness of alternative status positions open to them within the larger society. They must also be partially aware of the channels and processes involved in achieving upward mobility within that system. Then and only then can their personal or ethnic identity become a dominant factor in directing their mastery of their own destiny. These goals are probably the ones being met most adequately in present ethnic studies programs. It is ironic that this sensitivity to inequality and a need for a positive self-image occurs among lower-class Mexican Americans only after exposure to the workings of the larger society (usually through formal schooling) accompanied by "partial Anglicization." By this means barrio residents are introduced to the processes within the larger society that can lead to greater privileges and expanded personal opportunities. Knowledge of these processes provides the basis for personal and group motivation, ethnic autonomy, and the creation of a more positive self-identity, while a continued acceptance of subordinate status promotes a defeatist attitude among the minority members and ultimately results in failure. The process leading to failure, known as the *self-fulfilling prophecy process*, occurs when a *false* assumption evokes the type of behavior that makes the originally false conception come true. For example, in an experimental situation, a few California teachers were told that some of their students were rapid learners or "spurters." Although these students were chosen randomly, the teachers, in anticipating their rapid learning, elicited behavior that resulted in the students actually becoming rapid learners (Rosenthal and Jacobson, 1968).

The self-image a member of a minority group has is in large part a result of the labels that are used to identify his minority group and his acceptance of these labels. Derogatory names that are used to identify a group as undesirable are called *ethnophaulisms* (Palmore, 1962). Social psychologists claim there is a close association between the amount of prejudice directed toward a given minority group and the number of ethnophaulisms coined to describe it. In the United States, such ethnophaulisms as *kike*, *polack*, *wop*, *nigger*, *meskin*, and *greaser* are used to label people of "foreign" extraction, thereby subtly conferring on them an image of inferiority. A study of ethnophaulisms directed toward minority groups in America showed that the greatest number were directed toward Negroes, the next greatest toward Orientals, and the fewest toward Mexican Americans. Ethnophaulisms are used by minority- and majority-group members against others of their own group as well as against members of other groups. Some examples of ethnophaulisms used by Mexican Americans against Anglo Americans are *gringo*, *bolillo*, *gabacho*, and *extranjero*. In recent years, Chicanos, following the Black Power model of using derisive terms openly during confrontations, have often used these terms and others to irritate functionaries representing the Anglo (or WASP) middle class.

A given minority group can use negative labeling of other minority groups to raise its own social status. By projecting an even less desirable image upon others, one appears to enhance one's own position. This occurs among Mexican American groups as it does among all minorities, as is evident in the lower Rio Grande Valley in Texas. Inasmuch as the Anglos of that region have reserved for themselves the exclusive rights to the title of "white," all other groups are arbitrarily placed in the "nonwhite" category. In the lower valley there is a strong resentment on the part of the Mexican Americans at being thought of as black. Of course, this suggests that the Mexican American is as guilty of prejudice against Negroes as is the Anglo. But an alternate explanation is the existence of a rivalry between the two subordinate minorities, vying for *relative acceptance* by the dominant majority at a higher status level. An aversion to interracial mixing on a large scale might be more of an attempt by Mexican Americans to preserve their position of *relative acceptance* than a manifestation of racial bias. Similarly, Anglo prejudice toward Mexican Americans seeking complete social equality might reveal insecurity among Anglos, who, without the existence of an "inferior group," would be required to demonstrate their superiority rather than maintaining it by ascription.

When the dominant society fails to allow minority groups equal access to social betterment, minority members must defy the present structure, and therefore they see it as an obstacle to their ethnic goals. Urban Mexican Americans in California view Anglo society as a barrier between them and the fulfillment of their aspirations (Peñalosa, 1967:414). This rejection of the larger society has been linked by the Mexican American Study Project to the degree of self-hatred extant among members of a minority group. Mexican Americans in Los Angeles and San Antonio who were highest in anti-Anglo sentiment showed a higher level of hatred toward their own group and toward themselves.

SELF-DESIGNATED
MEXICAN AMERICAN IDENTITY

A single term by which Mexican Americans in the Southwest could distinguish themselves from all other peoples is conspicuously absent. In addition, there is little consensus as to which specific term they would prefer others to use in referring to them. The most preferred name changes according to where in the Southwest it is used and also by which social class and in what historical era. Some names are appropriate to English (i.e., Spanish-surname Americans), while others are more meaningful in Spanish (i.e., La Raza, La Causa, La Gente). Some ethnic labels are polite terms suitable for formal settings, while others are more suitable to the argot of the barrio. Knowing the wide diversity and heterogeneity of the Mexican American people, one expects that no simplistic, single label will capture these variations, nor is one single term functionally desirable (beyond the mere fact of having an overall category for Mexican Americans).

> If the day should ever come when all of these people are willingly subsumed under one laber or banner, when they align themselves only under one philosophy, on that day, finally, they will have become totally and irrevocably Americanized [Romano-V., 1969:45].

Interesting enough, the author just quoted recoils from the use of a single label for all Mexican Americans and yet is willing to assume that all persons who become "Americanized" may be conveniently regarded as homogeneous.

There are two approaches used to explain the origin of descriptive terms used by various segments of the Mexican American population. One suggests that their self-images originated in their homeland and were brought with them at the time of their immigration as part of their cultural heritage. The other claims that prior to arrival in the United States, the adjustments in acculturating to the dominant Anglo middle-class value system produced identity strains. Both of these explanations have some merit and will be discussed separately.

To become familiar with the Mexican self-image, it is necessary to turn to some of the leading writers and poets of the
Republic. In general, Mexican authors delight in analyzing
their own identity and the motivational factors that cause
them to feel the way they do. A major theme is the fight
between pride and emasculation, partially reflecting a feeling
of uncertainty as to identity. Alba, the Mexican poet, describes
a Mexican as a "person in whom the Indian and Spaniard are
still at war within himself [1967:248]." The question is whether
to identify with one's victorious Spanish or conquered Indian
ancestors. Paz, a Mexican philosopher, describes the Mexican's
need to prevent the outside world from intruding on his privacy and to show manliness by "not backing down [1961:29–
30]." An extensive survey of Mexican authors writing of the
causes for this deep-seated sense of inferiority among Mexicans
reveals a multiplicity of factors considered. Some are significant historical events, a revolt against patriarchal tyranny, a
reawakened *indigenismo* (nativism), the Mexican cinema,
changing life expectancy ratios, and even nutrition. It is not
these specific attributes that focus our attention on these
writers but rather the central theme: the deep sense of inferiority and uncertain identity that is discussed by Mexican
writers as an "ethnic attribute." If their perceptions of the
"Mexican character" are correct, feelings of inferiority among
Mexican immigrants should be ascribed to Mexican culture
and not attributed to acculturation or the cultural adjustments
required for living in the United States. As Luis Miguel Valdez,
poet-creator of the California farm workers' theater group *El
Teatro Campesino*, cogently states: "It is not enough to say we
suffer an identity crisis, because that crisis has been our way
of life for the last five centuries [Steiner, 1970:327]."

Forbes (1968:56), a noted scholar of the peoples of the
Southwest, declares that the Mexican learned to cherish his
Spanish lineage and deny his Indian background. The Mexican
social structure was saturated with the racial beliefs that Europeans were superior to Indians culturally and genetically and
the Mestizo offspring took pride only in his Hispano blood. The
Anglos' preferential treatment of light-skinned Mexicans further reinforced a resentment against the Indian ancestry

among those persons trying to gain acceptance in the larger Anglo institutions. A careful historical analysis by Mörner (1967:45–55) documents the existence of a "pigmentocracy" of status levels determined by skin color throughout the conquest and colonization of Mexico, as suggested earlier by Forbes. At the top of the Spanish American Society of Castes—which imposed the hierarchical estate society of medieval Castile on a multiracial colonial situation, although without the total inflexibility of, say, India's caste system—were those of light skin color. The repudiation of one's Indian ancestry was necessary to survive and prosper in Mexico prior to the twentieth century. The "conquest philosophy" that demanded that Indians give up their native languages and culture and become Mexican educated and fluent in the Spanish language was the official policy of the Mexican government until just three short decades ago. Even the famous Benito Juárez, a Zapotec Indian who became a president of the Republic, was noted far more for his separation of church and state affairs in Mexico than for any programs for preserving the culture of Mexico's indigenous peoples. Only recently, in 1940, the Inter-American Indigenist Congress, held at Pátzcuaro, Mexico, declared that Indians had a moral right to maintain their ancient languages and culture (Aguirre Beltrán, 1953: 33, 48). The Instituto Nacional Indigenista was subsequently organized, and a visible turn toward the glorification of Indian culture and heritage became evident in Mexico. In 1949, Cuauhtémoc, the last Aztec ruler, became officially accepted as the symbol of the Mexican nation. Although Romano-V. (1969:37) claims that the nativistic movement to increase pride in Indian ancestry has been supported by Mexican immigrants to United States barrios since 1910, it is obvious that this acceptance of Indian ancestry is of more recent vintage even than that in Mexico.

In the United States, prior to the rise of militant ethnic movements during the 1950s and 1960s, Mexican Americans were reluctant to openly proclaim their Indian heritage. Many writers reported that Mexican Americans who aspired to upward social mobility claimed to be Spanish to remove from themselves the stigma generated by the terms "Mexican" or "Indian." But during the years following World War II, a self-declared liberation from Anglo evaluations of non-Anglo ethnic groups emerged. Peñalosa and McDonagh (1966:504) observed a trend in southern California away from the Spanish emphasis and toward a growing pride in the designation of "Mexican." During this same period a number of organizations dedicated to extolling the Indian's contributions to Mexican culture were spawned, and popular histories of southwestern United States had to be revised for a more accurate portrayal of the role of Indian culture in that area. One of the first formal steps taken to glorify Indian Mexican rather than Spanish Mexican heritage was found in the Mexica Movement (pronounced "Mexchica," in the Aztec fashion) in southern California. The same Indian pride, combined with cultural identity and the philosophical focus of Chicano student organizations, formed the basis for the Movimiento Estudiantil Chicano Hijos de Aztlán (MECHA), emphasizing their historic linkage with the Aztec race and discounting their reliance on black or white assistance in their continuing struggle for recognition. In April 1971 the following appeared in *Machete*, a Chicano press outlet:

Our land is here and it is today. Black or White Nationalism implies that we are to accept their leadership and merely replace one system with another. If Blacks and Whites are to relate to us, it must be on the basis of absolute equality and mutual respect. . . . We are not Americans. We are Chicanos. THEY are the Americans. . . . If you are a White or Black Revolutionary, we don't need you to tell us how to run a War of Liberation. We have been doing it for a lot longer than you have. . . . [Signed] MOVIMIENTO ESTUDIANTIL CHICANOS HIJOS DE AZTLAN, occupied California.

It has become fashionable in recent years to claim an Indian background. During the 1970 fall registration at Texas A & I University, 175 students who had formerly registered as Mexican American now claimed to be "American Indians." For college students especially, minority status has become a vehicle for involvement in a cause, qualifying them for special programs, and demonstrating to others their liberal social and political views. It is no longer necessary to be ashamed of a non-Anglo cultural background.

Variations have also been found in the self-images of foreign-born and native-born persons of Mexican descent living in the United States. Dworkin (1965:220–221) reported that the foreign-born Mexican American field workers he studied saw themselves as proud, religious, gregarious, and happy; they were tolerant, short, fat, dark, practical, and well-adjusted. Of these attributes cited, ten were considered positive by the immigrant respondents. In contrast, the native-born Mexican Americans studied characterized themselves as emotional, unscientific, authoritarian, materialistic, old-fashioned, poor, and of a lower social class. They felt they were uneducated or poorly educated, short, fat, dark, caring little for education, mistrustful, proud and lazy, indifferent, and unambitious. Of these twelve attributes cited, only one is considered to be positive by the respondents. The shift from a positive self-image to a predominantly negative one in just one generation can be ascribed to a shift in evaluation criteria. It could also have resulted from a new interpretation of the criteria themselves. Dworkin's (1971) comparisons of stereotypes held by Mexican Americans about themselves over the period from 1963 to 1968 showed that the adjectives used for description did not change appreciably but their meaning changed drastically. Whereas Mexican Americans were still classified as "emotional," the meaning of this attribute had changed from lack of self-restraint to "soul"— the positive ability to enjoy life fully. There was a similar trend in Anglo stereotypes held by Mexican Americans. The Anglo characteristic of "materialism," which had formerly been considered an indication of progress, success, and other middle-class virtues, was now felt to imply an attachment to the Establishment, which subjugated ethnic and racial minorities. Chicanos who were college educated manifested a significantly greater positive self-image than did those who were not. Moreover, Anglo college students expressed an increasingly positive attitude toward Chicanos, while other Anglos manifested little change in their attitudes for this same period.

When Mexican Americans of the second and third generation reside in areas where there are concentrations of foreign-born Mexican immigrants, use of the term "Mexican" is often restricted to designating those who are foreign-born. One further variation of this was reported in a California village in which Mexican Americans who had become citizens called themselves "Mexicans" to distinguish themselves from both the "Nationals" (recent immigrants) and the *braceros* (temporary laborers). There were attempts by the native-born Mexican Americans to limit their social intercourse so as not to become linked with Nationals in the eyes of the dominant Anglo group (Parsons, 1965:63).

The most comprehensive study to date on the Mexican American's identity problem is the one done in Los Angeles and San Antonio by the Mexican-American Study Project. From it we gain some general picture of trends in labeling among Mexican Americans:

> These three names—Mexican, Spanish-American, and Latin American—are the three designations about which there has been the greatest status battle. "Mexican-American" and "Mexican American" (with and without a hyphen) are increasingly used, at least in California and Arizona, as acceptable and honorable names. An increasing number of bold U. S.–born individuals risk the "negative implications" of calling themselves "Mexican." In recent years, *chicano* (diminutive of *mexicano*) has come into increasing use as a self-referent, notably among the young and especially among the militant. . . . Some Mexican Americans altogether reject the "Mexican" designation, refusing to be known other than as "American" [Grebler et al., 1970:386–387].

In this same study Mexican Americans were asked to select the titles by which they preferred to be called, both in English and Spanish. In Los Angeles, the preferred English name was "Mexican" whereas "Latin American" ranked first in San Antonio. In Los Angeles "Mexicano" ranked highest among English and Spanish labels popularly used in the Southwest. In San Antonio, medium-income residents preferred "Latino," whereas low-income respondents preferred "Mexicano" (Grebler et al., 1970: Table 16-2). In another study, done in Albuquerque, most Mexican Americans wished to be called "Spanish-American." These data demonstrate the regional and class variations accompanying the different titles deemed acceptable within various segments of Mexican American society.

The perennial topic of discussion in Mexican or Mexican American organizations in the United States is, "What shall we call ourselves?" In 1958 the Mexican American Political Association (MAPA) was organized on the West Coast and the Political Association of Spanish-speaking Organizations (PASO) was organized in Texas. When attempts were made to consolidate these two into one powerful political arm of the Mexican American minority in the Southwest, the ethnic leaders from Texas rejected the "Mexican American" nomenclature and the California group would not assume the euphemistic and compromising ethnic label of "Spanish-speaking" (Cuellar, 1970: 148). These names reflected distinct images even to their own regional councils. In Los Angeles, a similar situation occurred in a new political action organization being formed by Mexican Americans. The younger participants demanded the word "Mexican" outright in the organization name, whereas the older generation sought to have the word "American" as its focal point (Martinez, 1966:54–55). Another study, done in 1962 among influential Mexican American males in Los Angeles, reflected age and status differences in labeling preferences. Nearly 40 percent of those studied wanted to be called "Mexican American" by their own ethnic group, whereas less than 20 percent selected "Mexican." "Mexicano" and "American" were selected by barely 18 percent. But when those men studied were asked what they wished to be called by people *not* of Mexican descent, the "Mexican" or "Mexicano" category dropped to 10 percent, "Mexican American" sagged slightly to 33 percent, and "American" vaulted to a strong 30 percent (Sheldon, 1966:150–151).

During the 1960s the term "Chicano" developed popular momentum, especially among young, militant Mexican Americans in the barrios. "Chicano" was a term of derision when applied to Mexican Americans by members of the dominant society. Thus it was selected as a rebuff to the larger society's power over Mexican Americans and became the militants' favorite designation, symbolizing their drive for autonomy and pride. Initially, it was difficult for sympathetic Mexican American adults, especially those in the professions or in business, to embrace these "lower-class" methods of dealing with ethnic issues. However, in time, and in light of the achievements that resulted from the zeal of these youthful Chicanos, the more conservative Mexican Americans proclaimed openly their support for La Causa and were less reticent about being subsumed under the Chicano label. But nevertheless, the gains of youthful activists have discomforted many older, traditional ethnic leaders.

> The Chicano movement poses a very difficult dilemma for most older Mexican Americans. They sympathize with the goals of *chicanismo*, yet they fear that the radical means used to pursue these ends will under-mine their own hard-earned social and economic gains . . . but for the older leaders to oppose the Chicano protest might be a slow form of personal political suicide as well as acting to exacerbate divisiveness in the Mexican American community [Cuellar, 1970:154].

As with many other beginning social movements, there was at first little differentiation evident among Chicanos other than their claim to Mexican descent. However, as the movement grew larger and proclaimed its cultural, racial, and political goals, self-identity became a major concern for the movement leadership. For example, the speaking of Spanish was itself enough to legitimate one as a potential Chicano leader. One would then be required to master barrio dialects in order to assume local command. More stringent rules were applied in some localities, such as excluding Mexican Americans who had one Anglo parent, who were married to an Anglo, who had a non-Spanish surname, or who were of a religious faith other than Catholic. Those born outside the state, community, or barrio and those who had achieved middle-class life styles were declared "Uncle Toms" (*"Tío Tomás"*) or given similar labels denoting ethnic disloyalty.

During the 1970s a reverse trend in membership requirements has become evident. More than language fluency, Spanish surname, barrio residence, and so forth, dedication to the cause of Mexican American cultural pride now seems to identify one as a "true" Chicano (Estrada, 1972).

There is some evidence that many of the "Mexican attributes" to which militant Chicanos point with pride are actually combinations of lower-class Anglo-Mexican values, solidified within the barrio, rather than truly ethnic characteristics. Casavantes complains that with the resurgence of ethnic pride noted during the last five or six years, Mexican American youth are not absolutely sure what aspects of their ethnic heritage they should take pride in. He asks,

> How can we ask our children to be proud of being terribly poor? . . . *a false stereotype of the Mexican American is represented by a description of the Mexican American as possessing only those attributes accurately associated with the lower-lower socioeconomic class.* . . .

Unless Mexican Americans *themselves* come to distinguish clearly between ethnicity and social class, a Mexican American youngster might well be ostracized by some peers when he tries to live the life of a middle-class Mexican. As matters stand now, far too often the feeling is that any Mexican American individual who tries to be middle class in his style of life is "not a true Chicano" [1969:7–8].

Professional observers agree that this confusion of ethnic and class identity is the "Achilles heel" of ethnic socioeconomic liberation, and whereas a drive for autonomy and for identity indicates the maturity of the movement, there must be some way for Chicanos to accept middle-class Mexican Americans instead of branding this style of life as *malinchismo*, or "selling out."[3]

The question arises, What are those attributes that designate *ethnic* rather than *class* differences in the Mexican American? Casavantes maintains that "to speak Spanish well, to enjoy Mexican music and Mexican food, to periodically recall the customs and ways of life of Spain and of Mexico—these are truly Chicano." Mexican American literature, movies, and even band music, added to the traditional folklore of the past, are, according to Garza (1969), Chicano. But whatever the criteria used here, Mexican Americans themselves must eventually determine what constitutes their cultural heritage and then work to preserve it. With present differences in class, education, age, and background, agreement is not immediately forthcoming.

Verbal declarations of unity between Mexican Americans and the peoples of Mexico are numerous. In reality, however, cultural and class cleavages are apparent. During a forced relocation of Mexican American families from the Chamizal area (prior to settling an international border dispute between Mexico and the United States), there were serious neighborhood misunderstandings between families of third- and fourth-generation Mexican Americans and recent immigrants. While those who had been citizens longer were more supportive of local institutions (i.e., schools, churches, voluntary organizations, etc.), the recent immigrants ridiculed them and praised the Mexican ways (Stoddard, 1970b:17–18). Also, during labor union disputes Mexican Americans competed with commuting Mexican green card workers, thus making Mexican American union membership the vanguard issue of those condemning both the "foreign worker" and the system that allowed them to take away jobs from "loyal" Americans.

As was suggested earlier, names used by members of the ethnic minority for themselves are not those that they would have nonethnics use in referring to them. Anglo Americans who come into constant contact with Mexican Americans have experienced the negative reactions engendered by the indiscriminate use of certain ethnic names or labels. The effort to find "neutral" labels that will expedite communication between functionaries in the larger society and Mexican Americans, has created the mistaken impression that "correct" or "open sesame" words will dissipate existing animosities. Yet the etiology of the titles or labels has very little to do with the hostile reactions they engender. Rather, the social distance between the minority group and the dominant society is the basis for reaction to names or labels.[4] Within an ingroup, various names or titles can be used and accepted as positive communication from one's fellows, but if those same names are used by an outgroup member (i.e., an Anglo) it may be viewed as an attempt to humiliate. Heller notes:

> People of Mexican descent . . . call themselves *Chicanos.*
> . . . They also refer to themselves as "Mexicans" or "Mexi-
> canos," but tend to resent these terms when applied to
> them by the majority population because of the deroga-
> tory connotations attached [1966:7].

This pattern was documented in a field study of Mexican American youths from El Paso, Texas. When queried as to what Anglos currently called them, two-thirds of the youths answered "Mexican." When asked to indicate what they would *prefer* Anglos to call them, however,. 40 percent answered "Mexican American" or "Spanish speaking" and 43 percent chose "American" or "U.S. citizen." This selectivity of name usage was prevalent in spite of the fact that the Mexican Americans believed that Anglos used basically the same criteria for identifying their ethnic group as they themselves did, as evidenced by table 3.2 on the following page. When asked what their immediate friends called them, 64 percent replied "Chicano" and 24 percent, "Mexican." These data support the existence of differences between ingroup slang and formal titles in communication with outgroups.

In summary, self-identity provides the motivations for fulfilling subservient roles or for seeking channels of upward social mobility. Traditional labels that have been applied to the Mexican American minority by nonethnics describe a simple homogeneous culture similar to the folk cultures of Mexico, whose value orientations are less desirable than those of Anglo Americans. These labels project an erroneous, distorted picture. The most significant change in ethnic identity has been the push toward ethnic autonomy—the creation and bestowal of labels *by* Mexican Americans *for* Mexican Americans. Though no single label is accepted generally within their ethnic group, those names chosen by Mexican Americans themselves carry with them a more positive self-image and a connotation of ethnic pride than the names formerly ascribed to Mexican Americans by the larger Anglo society.

The new label, "Chicano," which emerged during the past

Table 3.2 Self-Identity Criteria Used by Self and Attributed to Anglo Use by Mexican Male Youths*

IDENTIFICATION CRITERIA	USED BY SELF			ATTRIBUTED TO ANGLO USE		
	Modal Rank	Number of Respondents	Percent	Modal Rank	Number of Respondents	Percent
Family name	1	21	57	3	19	51
Language	2	20	54	1	25	68
Skin color	3	17	45	2	22	59
Nationality	4	12	32	4	7	19
Religion	5	3	8	4	7	19
Place of residence	5	3	8	7	1	3
Income	7	2	5	6	5	14

* Total sample = 37.
SOURCE: Stoddard, 1970a: Table III.

decade, may be so closely associated with lower-class norms of the barrio that it will prove unacceptable as a term applicable also to middle-class Mexican Americans. There has been a tendency for middle-class values to be considered "deviant" from the lower-class barrio style of life and thus deviant from the "true" Mexican heritage. Until the Mexican Americans stop confusing Mexican heritage with lower-class norms, frustration will accompany the efforts of Mexican Americans attempting to participate more fully in the "good life" of America. However, it is assumed that if educational opportunities for the younger generations of Mexican Americans improve and if Mexican Americans with training and skills become more evenly distributed in society, the future guardians of Mexican heritage might well be middle-class Mexican American families rather than the militant barrio groups.

The remaining chapters of this book will deal with the various social institutions operating within the Mexican American ethnic system and their relation to the social institutions of the larger system. Whether they are an aid or an obstacle in obtaining ethnic goals depends upon how these goals are defined and the priorities given to occupational mobility, family dependencies, ethnic isolation, and ethnic stereotypes.

Notes

[1] Social scientists of Mexican descent are marginal men. When individuals serve both as success models for *Chicanismo* and as qualified professionals, some role conflicts are inevitable. In their eagerness to attack the traditional ethnic biases among historians and social scientists, some Mexican social scientists have inadvertently supported a quasi-racist dogma that genetic makeup and Spanish surname are the criteria for expertise in Mexican American affairs.

[2] Some Mexican American leaders have suggested that the hyphenated term "Mexican-American" is an Anglo technique to relegate ethnic members of the group to the level of pseudocitizen. Actually, similar resentments have been expressed throughout history by minority groups such as "German-Americans," "Italian-Americans," and the like. Theodore Roosevelt successfully waged

a campaign against the hyphenation of minority titles, and when Wilson declared war in 1914, minorities became "100% American [Higham, 1970:195, 204]."

3 Malinche was the Aztec mistress of Cortéz. Hence, any Mexican American who sells out to the larger society instead of promoting the goals of his own ethnic group is called a "malinche," a cultural traitor or ethnic prostitute.

4 Words focus existing sentiments but do not create the sentiments or beliefs themselves. Thus, negative sentiment toward *Pachucos* during the Zoot-suit era had really existed prior to the wearing of distinctive clothing and needed only a symbol to bring forth latent hostilities (Turner and Surace, 1956).

Chapter 4 ◉ Clashes of Values:
Race, Religion, and Family

The dominant values of a society are transmitted to its members through the process of socialization. This process involves religious training, family relationships, and education, all of which condition the individual to internalize as his own attitudes the existent values of his society. Among the many values that become internalized are those dealing with ethnic classifications—recognizing "them" and "us." Not only are ethnic groups perceived as separate entities, but salient characteristics that distinguish them from other groups are noted. Once a person has learned his own culture's stereotypes regarding other groups, it becomes increasingly difficult for him to replace these with new, reliable data. And interestingly enough, a person *learns* the prejudices of his own group toward others by contact with prejudiced persons within his group rather than by actual contact with the "less desirable" groups in question. Subsequent contact only gives him the opportunity to reinforce stereotypes already learned and accepted from members of his society.

In the United States there have been extremely rapid changes in urbanization and technology, especially since the end of World War II. As a result, unusual strains have been placed on the social institutions of the dominant Anglo society as well as those of minority societies in the United States. For the Mexican American in the Southwest, this has been principally in the area of adapting his life style from rural or semirural to urban, requiring a rearrangement of nearly all of the major priorities in his traditional value system. Within this milieu of dynamic social flux, the problems of racial tensions, religious challenges, and family disintegration figure predominantly. In the sections that follow, the effect of modernization on the basic structure of the family, religion, and race relations will be examined.

RACE AND SKIN COLOR

Physical differences (i.e., skin color, facial structure, hair, etc.) are determined genetically. However, *attitudes* toward these physical features are *learned* and therefore *changeable*. Present sentiments toward Mexican Americans are inextricably tied to the history of conquest and colonization in the Western Hemisphere. Therefore, a brief chronology of racial practices and policies leading up to the formation of contemporary society in the Southwest will place present racial attitudes in a clearer historical perspective.

Stratified societies have existed since before 2000 B.C. Thus, these are not a unique creation of Spanish or American colonialists. However, racial superiority *based on skin color* is a relatively recent idea. For centuries, racist theories in Western Europe were based on a people's technological superiority. Then, such models were used to justify the conquest and plunder of nonwhite peoples around the world. Prior to the Spanish conquests in the New World, the dogma of "white superiority" had already pervaded Europe (the Iberians having been in intimate contact with the Moors as a conquered people for four centuries). As early as one hundred years before Cortéz conquered the Aztecs, the Iberians had already adopted the practice of buying and selling slaves. Moreover, the many peoples from non-Western cultures living under the Spanish feudal system who were proselytized into the Catholic faith, were allowed only subordinate positions within the social hierarchy of the Spanish Empire. The same system was used in the New World by white Spanish conquerors to subordinate Indians.

Arriving in New Granada, Cortéz discovered the dominant, Nahua-speaking Aztecs dictating racial and religious ideologies throughout their sprawling empire. Had he arrived some two centuries earlier, he would have found the Aztecs a nomadic band seeking refuge from humiliating defeats suffered at the hands of their stronger neighbors. In the relatively short period of 100 years, the Aztec leaders had made alliances with other Nahua-speaking groups and had formed a well-administered empire that represented vestiges of the former tribal democracies of the region. Supported by religious practices that involved human sacrifices, a small but effective military force, and a highly centralized economic system, the Aztecs kept a much larger population in total subjugation. By the time Cortéz arrived, the Aztecs had become undisputed masters of the region —but the role of conqueror was soon to be reversed for them.

The arrival of Cortéz and his men produced overwhelming changes in Aztec racial policies. The Indian leadership was destroyed (Cumberland, 1968:53–54) and all indigenous peoples, regardless of their positions in Indian society, were subordinate to the Catholic church and its leaders, appointed by the crown. In a few rare instances, dedicated missionary orders attempted to educate the Indian aristocracy, but the Spanish government forbade this practice by legislative decree, lest the natives be provided with the tools to resist their fair-skinned conquerors. Indian communities were allowed to keep some of their administrative functions, serving principally as relay stations between the Spaniards and Indians.

During the colonization era racial purity became a prominent concern of Spanish nobles. It, for example, was a prime requisite in selecting colonists to America. A colonist's genealogy could show no Moorish ancestry for at least three generations back, and this had to be certified by the church. However, present evidence suggests that the criterion for "purity" was measured more by religious fervor than by evidence of non-Moorish ancestry.[1] There are accounts of peninsular (Spanish and Portuguese) women painting their faces white and red to hide a swarthy appearance, which was considered a sign of ugliness in that era. Hoetink (1967:171–176) comments further that the darker peoples of the New World received better treatment from the swarthy Iberian aristocracy than they did from the lighter northern and western Europeans because of the Iberian's similar skin hue. Though in reality the Spaniard's own background was mixed, he espoused the dogma of racial purity as the basis for the Society of Castes in the New World. So adamant were the Spanish in maintaining purity among the colonists, that even the direct offspring of "pure" peninsulars born in the New World were placed in a secondary position to those born on the Iberian peninsula. Further down in the social hierarchy were the nonwhites—the Mestizo, the darker "pure" Indians, and the Negro slaves, who constituted the lowest stratum of colonial society.

Table 4.1   Ranked Racial Categories Denoting Ancestry in New Spain during the Eighteenth Century

| PARENTS | | OFFSPRING |
Male	*Female*	
1. Spaniard	Indian	Mestizo
2. Mestizo	Spanish	Castizo
3. Spaniard	Castizo	Spaniard
4. Negro	Spanish	Mulatto
5. Spaniard	Mulatto	Morisco
6. Spaniard	Morisco	Albino
7. Spaniard	Albino	Torna atrás
8. Indian	Torna atrás	Lobo
9. Lobo	Indian	Zambaigo
10. Zambaigo	Indian	Cambujo
11. Cambujo	Mulatto	Albarazado
12. Albarazado	Mulatto	Barcino
13. Barcino	Mulatto	Coyote
14. Indian	Coyote	Chamiso
15. Mestizo	Chamiso	Coyote Mestizo
16. Coyote Mestizo	Mulatto	Ahi te estás

SOURCE: *Race Mixture in the History of Latin America*, Magnus Mörner, p. 58. Copyright © 1967 by Little, Brown (Inc.). Reprinted by permission.

During conquest and colonization, the keeping of concubines and illicit sexual unions between Spaniards and Indians or Negroes produced a large group of racially mixed progeny. Mörner writes that the darker skin color of Negro slaves and freemen was diffused throughout nearly all social strata except the most select Spanish and Creole castes. Interracial unions were common; but because they were often casual affairs, the name "Mestizo" applied to the offspring of such unions, became a synonym for "illegitimate." The darker Mulatto and Mestizo peoples settled into the lower social strata, and the increasingly stable social structure, based on the Society of Castes, effectively deterred any sizable redistributing of dark-skinned persons into a higher social strata.

The Spanish came to the New World looking for gold and other precious metals. When they found these riches, the exploitation of the dark-skinned natives to mine it and prepare it for shipment to Spain became a matter of course. Not only was the native population exploited, but the Spanish conquerors and colonizers justified it on racial grounds.

> The early assumptions that the native would not work for personal profit, that he was childlike and could not learn the skills necessary in a complex economic system, and that he could never achieve an intellectual sophistication equivalent to the European gave birth to the *encomienda* [forced labor], the *repartimiento* [forced labor with guaranteed wages], and to debt peonage. Even the great reforms of 1609, ostensibly eliminating the most vicious and exploitative aspects of the *repartimiento*, clearly sprang from the same assumptions [Cumberland, 1968: 83].

During the sixteenth century, the Indian population of central Mexico dropped sharply from an estimated 25 million to 1 million (Borah, 1951). The large number of native deaths as a result of military conquest and forced labor was increased further by the spread of European diseases to which Indians had little resistance—syphilis, malaria, and especially smallpox, which decimated entire native village populations.[2]

Through economic exploitation and disease, the native Indian population on Hispañola (Haiti and the Dominican Republic) had been annihilated, thus forcing the Spaniards to import slave labor from Africa. Now similarly, in New Granada, the rapidly declining Indian labor force called for the introduction of new institutions that would be more efficient than the wasteful institutions of *encomienda* and *repartimiento* that had been in effect. As free labor (Mulatto and Mestizo) became available to replace the inefficient Indian slave in the urban areas and mining communities, wages and production rates soared. The majority of remaining Indians were relocated to central Mexico to be used as agricultural labor. Sexual exploitation accompanied this economic servitude, and offspring from illicit liaisons between Spanish and non-Spanish were downgraded to the social level of the non-Spanish partner—usually the mother. Not until the church promoted legal marriages between members of different social classes did racially mixed offspring have the legal rights to claim their social inheritance from either parent, thus causing some redistribution of mixed breeds throughout the society. However, this came much too late to lift the stigma of inferiority from the dark-skinned peoples and to change the practices that held them in economic and social subjugation.

By the middle of the eighteenth century, the Society of Castes, with its legal, religious, and economic support system, had begun to crumble. In addition to skin color and lineage, other criteria were now used to determine social standing. Among these were village of origin, past military or governmental service, style of clothing, correctness of etiquette, and even the mastery of hygienic practices. Wealth or prestige also "lightened" one's complexion, but even among the well-to-do elite, dark skin color was looked upon with suspicion regardless of lineage. This is reflected in written comments of that period such as the following: "Manuel Hilario Lopez, Spaniard as he says but of very suspect color . . . Juan Antonio Mendoza, Castizo of obscure skin [Mörner, 1967:697]."

According to Othón de Mendizabal (1968) the combined number of peninsular whites (born in Spain) and Creoles (Spanish of pure-blood parents but born in America) at the beginning of the nineteenth century approximated one-third the combined Mestizo and Indian population (see also Borah, 1951:181). The Creoles, chafing at the inferior position they were forced to maintain with respect to the *gachupines* (a derisive term used for peninsulars), encouraged the Mestizo and Indian populations to revolt. But circumstances in Europe soon brought peninsulars and Creoles back together. A new consti-

Table 4.2   Estimated Population (by Race) in New World: 1800

Spanish born in Spain (peninsular)	70,000
Spanish born in America (Creole)	1,245,000
Indian	3,100,000
Negro	10,000
Castes (mixed)	1,412,000

SOURCE: (Othón de Mendizabal, 1968)

tutional government offered to the citizens of Spain by Ferdinand VII in the early 1800s weakened the traditional social structure, which was based upon the principle of white superiority. Spain, threatened by internal dissension, became preoccupied with its domestic problems, and the colonies saw their chance to break free. Peninsulars and Creoles in the New World were united in a common cause to gain national independence from their mother country. But the desire for freedom spawned earlier by the Creoles among the Indian and Mestizo masses had already swept the countryside. Rallying behind religious leaders such as Father Miguel Hidalgo and Father José María Morelos, and supported by Guadalupe Victoria (Miguel Fernandez) and Vicente Guerrero, the Mestizo-Indian population declared itself to be part of the Mexican nation and culture, not of the European Hispanos.

During the Popular Revolt of 1810, native bands roamed through the country killing Peninsulars and Creoles, both of whom were considered gachupines and foreigners. Among those killed were many mine owners and operators, and with their deaths the technical and managerial skills necessary to the mining industry were lost, thus causing the mines to close and destroying the economic base of the country. Even under these conditions, the traditional power structure still remained intact until 1850. The debilitating war with France in 1838, the loss of two-fifths of Mexico's territory during the Texas succession, and the reign of Emperor Maximilian during the 1860s were followed by the stability and masked despotism of the Díaz regime just prior to the Revolution of 1910.

At the beginning of the twentieth century the age-old racial dogmas still prevailed. Mestizos, and more so Indians had been denied social equality principally upon the basis of skin color. And except for brief economic or political upheavals, which allowed some Indian and Mestizo peoples to gain entry into the elite, the social position of the Mexican peasant was an inheritance from an earlier caste system, which dictated class and cultural differences as well.

The Mexican government did little to support cultural pluralism for racial and ethnic minorities until after 1930. Programs initiated by government to speed up acculturation among Indians geographically and racially isolated from other Mexicans became, surprisingly, the means for preserving Indian culture. The "conquest philosophy," complete acculturation by the indigenous peoples, was replaced by a philosophy that accepted cultural pluralism. In 1940 the first Inter-American Indian Congress in Mexico officially sanctioned the practice of teaching Indian languages (along with Spanish) to Indian children, and some efforts were also made to record, and thus preserve, these Indian tongues. With staunch governmental support, the Indigenista movement flourished. However, in the United States as well as in Mexico, traditional feelings of inferiority associated with being dark skinned had to be challenged and changed. Manuel Gamio, the Mexican anthropologist, lamented racial discrimination in the southwestern United States during the early decades of this century, but he mistakenly suggested that such discrimination was not operative prior to the Anglo invasion in the nineteenth century (1930:50–52). Noguiera (1959:167–172) stresses that prejudice concerning skin color is dictated by *origin* (i.e., genealogy) in the United States, whereas in New Spain it was dictated by *mark* (i.e., physical appearance), and this difference may have been what Gamio reacted to in describing Mexican American–Anglo relations in the Southwest.

In the first quarter of the twentieth century, "scientific" I. Q. tests, which were really culturally biased, substantiated an erroneous notion about the relationship between lower mentality and dark skin color. Gradually, anthropologists and sociologists have proved that these tests measure *social-class skills*. The impact of these proofs on Supreme Court decisions since

1915 covering housing, voting, intermarriage, employment, and transportation are well documented. The 1954 Supreme Court decision involving segregation in schools, for example, was based upon social science evidence discounting skin color as a measure of intellectual capacity.

Many studies have shown that Mexican Americans are highly sensitive about skin color and avoid identification with darker-skinned races. Samples collected from Mexicans, Mexican Americans, Spanish Americans, and Anglo respondents during recent decades have shown a high rejection rate toward Negroes in all groups, and this is essentially true among Mexicans or Mexican Americans residing in rural areas, as shown in Table 4.3 on the following page. As expected, intermarriage evoked the highest resistance. Attitude studies of Mexican Americans in Bakersfield, Los Angeles, and San Antonio (Grebler et. al., 1970: Table 16-6) further confirm these findings, with all groups overwhelmingly opposing intermarriage with blacks. Even the radical coalitions of Chicanos and blacks during the past five or six years have been relatively unstable and unproductive. This is summarized by a Mexican American writer:

> The Black and Mexican-American rank and file consider the arrangement [joining of Brown Power and Black Power organizations] a tactical necessity. . . . The fact of the matter is that Blacks and Mexican Americans barely know each other [Lara-Braud, 1970:13].

Whether this interminority prejudice will diminish as the idea that "brown is beautiful" becomes accepted among Mexican Americans and Anglos alike remains to be seen.

There are marked differences between older Mexican Americans and the youth in preoccupation with skin color and its relevance to ethnic identity. The earlier generations who fought for their citizenship did not give the priority to skin color that their children and their children's children do. Until two decades ago it was common for Mexican Americans to trace their genealogical lines only through their Hispano ancestors (Burma, 1954:96). This desperate desire to belong to the "superior" white group has caused some to ascribe "whiteness" to the

Table 4.3   Rejection Rates of Negroes at Various Levels of Social Encounter

	White (N=1357)*	Spanish-speaking (N=105)*	Urban Mexican (N=1126)*	Rural Mexican (N=288)*
Relatives by marriage	89.4	62.8	59.0	78.4
As Neighbors	50.7	45.4	43.2	71.5
As Co-workers	21.1	8.0	39.2	70.0
To become Citizens by Naturalization	5.1	4.3	41.5	74.9

* N = number sampled.
SOURCE: Loomis, 1970: 148–149.

Aztec nation (Forbes, 1968). Once a dark-skinned person has internalized the idea that light skin is more desirable, he begins to develop a negative attitude toward himself, an intense self-hatred that produces feelings of inadequacy and inferiority. Sometimes he attempts to whiten his skin by use of cosmetics, skin bleaches, and similar measures. This acceptance of dark skin as a sign of inferiority (with its corollary, a preference for lighter skin shades) begins earlier than grade school. Experiments show that ascribing badness to dark colors and goodness to white, seeing dark objects as smaller than they really are and seeing white objects as larger, and other positive-negative color evaluations begin in early childhood. Because of a darker skin color, self-debasement results, with accompanying adverse effects on the individual's personal motivation. When social and economic opportunities are consistently offered to the lighter-skinned person in the larger society, there develops despair and hopelessness among darker-skinned minority members. This is witnessed by youth in Castroville, California:

> The teen age boys said "there wasn't much use of finishing High School if you are dark . . . you couldn't get a good job anyway." Mexican girls who recently graduated from High School reported that they had many difficulties in finding secretarial or clerical jobs in the Castroville and Salinas area. They said that girls who looked "almost white" got jobs first but that some of the Mexican-looking girls never did find the kind of employment they sought and finally had to go to work in the "sheds" [of the local packing company; Parsons, 1965:150].

Skin-shade consciousness within the minority group produces segmentation and marital barriers: parents wonder whether children of "mixed" marriages will be rejected with the dark-skinned parent or be accepted with the light-skinned parent. Some Mexican American girls admitted to Parsons that they spurned Anglo suitors for fear they would have to choose between identifying with a dark-skinned offspring and maintaining acceptance with their light-skinned spouse.

The acceptance or nonacceptance of a person because of skin shade occurs at two levels: in groups or individually.

When a sizable percentage of a community's population is comprised of a single minority group, individuals from that group are identified more on the basis of the traditional group stereotypes than are minority group members who comprise an insignificant percentage of the community population. In the latter case, powerful figures in the larger society are less resistant to minority achievements because there is little danger that vast numbers of the minority group will suddenly become active and destroy the current power balance. In other words, when the minority group is numerically small, acceptance does not pose a threat. Single persons with light skin are accepted readily, and assimilation is relatively easy. Even when marked differences in skin color are evident, minority members are accepted, but only until their numbers appear to threaten the power of the larger society. This ratio can be a factor in the availability of economic, or occupational opportunities for minority peoples. However, with the beginnings of militancy and the introduction of organized leadership in minority groups, these observations regarding population ratios may no longer apply. The impact of ethnic organization will be discussed in a later chapter.

A departure from the prevailing attitude of shame over brown skin color was noticeable some years prior to 1950 during the period of militant separatism. Pride in being called Mexican and in *being* Mexican was beginning to take hold, although it was still clear that, as one descended the occupational ladder, the prevailing skin color became darker. The final turn from resignation to pride was obvious above all during the early 1960s, when, on the heels of the "Black Is Beautiful" movement, Chicanos repudiated entirely the white-supremacy models that formed the basis for the established social structure. As they become more vocal in proclaiming their non-Spanish heritage, Mexican Americans also claimed the right to decide their own destiny according to their own criteria. It was a critical turning point in the development of self-pride among Mexican Americans in the Southwest.

Yinger (1963) cites examples of court decisions and legislative actions designed to curtail color discrimination during the period from World War II to the 1960s, and although much more has occurred since then, there is much still left to do. Even a change in the legal code is not implemented immediately within the informal patterns of society. The Urban Coalition, a nonprofit organization devoted to the protection of minority rights, seeks immediate behavior changes to conform to legal statutes, regardless of the attitudes held by the persons involved. Even a forced, superficial acceptance of darker-skinned peoples tends to undermine the psychological mechanisms that maintain racial prejudice and allows the minority group the chance to develop a positive self-identity.

In summary, discrimination on the basis of skin color had its genesis in Western Europe and later was carried by European settlers to Mexico and the southwestern United States. Prejudice against dark skin color is deeply a part of the historical heritage of Mexicans, Mexican Americans, and Anglos. It is not so much that Anglo colonists in the United States were the originators of anti-Mexican attitudes (regarding dark skin), but rather that they did nothing to change those attitudes. The feeling persists among many dark-skinned Chicanos that they need to ensure their "equality" by forcing the larger society to give preferential treatment—a form of reverse racism—to darker-skinned peoples; this is an expected transitional development during a period of rapid identity change. However, the major hurdle for future generations of Mexican Americans has been cleared if this generation has learned to have a positive self-image, without feeling shame over their Indian ancestry and racial heritage.

RELIGION AND CHURCH

The popular stereotype of the Mexican American is that he is always Catholic and always religious, and it is rare that this notion is not perpetuated by social scientists. A typical example is found in the work of Broom and Shevky (1952:157), who maintain that the church is the principal agency of cultural conservatism for Mexicans in the United States and that it reinforces the separateness of the group. Madsen (1964:Chap. 3) uses the religious background of rural Latins in Texas and the spiritual overtones of La Raza in almost every description or explanation of the Latino culture. Others have described Catholicism as a powerful instrument for the conservation of the ethnic tradition, but less powerful than the forces of organized discrimination against the dark-skinned peoples (D'Antonio and Samora, 1962:18). Yet, in spite of these assessments of the importance of the church and of religion in the lives of Mexican Americans, there is historical as well as recent evidence to question their dependency on Catholicism.

At the time of Cortéz's invasion in 1519, Spanish monarchs, in reward for their expulsion of the heathen Moors from Spanish soil, enjoyed a more intimate relationship with church officials than any other European royalty. As a result of this intertwining of church and state, persons could transfer from church office to secular position and back again with a great deal of ease. This same system of politico-religious government was introduced by Spaniards into settlements in the New World. Church vows could be administered or enforced through civil authorities, and church titles were handled by secular officers. To ensure doctrinal purity among ranking leaders of church and state, the Office of Inquisition was brought into Mexico City in 1571. As an institution, the church supported the existing social structure, which was the Society of Castes; this structure, as was explained earlier, preserved the privileges of the upper strata, which were, as might be expected, heavily represented by church officials.

At this time, however, there were differences developing in the church structure in America. The stability sought through liaisons between church and government officials was upset by the proselytizing efforts of various religious orders whose efforts to Christianize and educate the Indian leadership posed a potential threat for the unquestioned supremacy of the Spanish monarchy. Moreover, the social, economic, and geographical distances between the reigning church "princes" and the rank-and-file local priests or "padres on horseback" indicates anything but a consensus on the role of the church in the Christianizing of the Indian. Intraorder struggles to determine "who owned the Indian" were but a reflection of differing procedures adopted by the various religious orders.

The squabbling, quarreling, and backbiting, notorious in
the first generations, did not occur over the creation of
new experimental institutions; they concerned the selec-
tion of old institutions and the exercise of power—economic, political, social. Even among those whose very
creeds and oaths bound them to gentility and brotherhood
—the clerics—the din of quarrel resounded. . . . Franciscan suspected Dominican, both feared Jesuit; and all
three engendered jealousy among secular clergy. But all
the clergy agreed on one thing; catastrophe lurked in a
grant of power to lay authority [Cumberland, 1968:43].

The Spanish crown agreed that the education of the indigenous
masses would threaten the stability of the New World colonies
(and therefore their source of mineral wealth), and by the
seventeenth century it had issued legislative decrees forbidding
clergy to educate the Indian. Schisms between the various religious orders and the central church authority became more and
more disturbing to the social stability of colonial power; and the
expulsion in 1767 of the troublesome Jesuits from all Spanish
dominions was a final move to curtail internal dissension.

The Popular Revolt of 1810 and the circumstances leading
up to it demonstrated the cleavage between the church structure and the Mexican people. During the eighteenth and nineteenth centuries a substantial gap had become evident between
everyday actions of church leaders and the religious precepts
that they proclaimed (Vallier, 1970:26). Moreover, the indigenous peoples were ill-equipped to understand the sophisticated
theological reasonings of the erudite church princes.

The Mexican understood his religion poorly if at all. . . .
The Church . . . had made the average Mexican merely a
surface practitioner of a religious rote, deeply imbued
with a form of religiosity but not necessarily loyal to the
Church as the hierarchy defined both loyalty and Church
[Cumberland, 1968:179].

Church representatives and priests trained on the Iberian
peninsula did not relate well to the indigenous peoples and
their culture, nor did they attempt to understand any of the

problems outside their spiritual realm. No attempts were made by the hierarchy to integrate the layman into religious activities or to provide him with religious responsibilities (Vallier, 1970:59). The church was foreign, guided by foreigners, and inaccessible to the mass of Indians and Mestizos, although Mestizos of higher-caste parentage were allowed to enter the priesthood. Soon the meaning of church and religion for the average Mexican was limited to that of personal contact with his priest or with the padre on horseback who served his needs. A further dimension of internal dissent existed between the white peninsulars (Spaniards born in Spain) and the Creoles (their offspring born in America). The church had traditionally aligned itself with the white peninsulars and with the Spanish monarchy. As the pressures arose for independence from Spanish rule, the Creoles promoted enmity toward the peninsulars among the Mestizo and Indian castes. As the church continued to oppose a policy of separation from Spain, increased hostility was directed toward it by the disenfranchised Castas (Mestizos), and this contributed to the Popular Revolt of 1810, which was led by local priests against the higher church authorities. The Popular Revolt revolved around the personalities of the church padres and their zeal for reform. One such padre, Father Hidalgo, accumulated more than 80,000 followers in just a few months, but these inexperienced and poorly trained volunteers were a problem to control and discipline. They soon became a mob, out for vengeance against the foreign whites, and, once the revolt was crushed, Father Hidalgo and his insurrectionist followers were killed—with the full approbation of the reigning church authorities. In such circumstances, the Mexican church member was hardly capable of deciding whether the local church fathers or the distant church hierarchy was the true representative of the church and of God.

At the beginning of the nineteenth century, the Catholic church was one of the largest landholders in Mexico. In exchange for church support most government leaders refrained from public criticism of the church, but few of them were happy about the vast church-owned acreages that stood largely unused at a time when starving citizens were demanding land of their own. Initially, territory belonging to the Inquisition and to the outlawed Jesuits was seized. The Lerdo laws of 1856 provided the legal means to acquire all the rest, and land claims led to the War of the Reform (1858–1861), in which a coalition representing conservatives and the church was the target of liberal-supported, disenfranchised Mestizos and Indians. Under the leadership of Benito Juárez, the liberals were victorious. During the period from 1867 to 1876, many anticlerical laws were passed, including ones that limited church-owned property and activities of the clergy. During the latter part of the nineteenth century the Catholic church recouped some of its power, and it had a brief period of autonomy during the Díaz regime. During the Revolution of 1910, however, the church was one of the targets of the revolutionaries.

The social and economic disorganization coming in the wake of the Mexican Revolution saw the ravishing of church properties by marauding bands that were living off the land. The revolutionary leaders fought among themselves; for years both the army led by Pancho Villa in the north and the forces of Emiliano Zapata in the south continued to engage in military operations of various sorts. Agricultural production was dramatically lowered. Starvation as well as military conflicts caused deaths and, coupled with the large emigration to the United States, resulted in a sharp population drop.

In 1926, the clergy refused to perform church functions, protesting government actions restricting their religious operations, but they soon found to their dismay that the people were content to practice their religion without formal services (Cumberland, 1968:270). The 4,493 "registered" priests in Mexico prior to the Revolution dropped to a mere 230 by 1935. Some returned to Spain while others emigrated to the United States and elsewhere. Those who settled in the Southwest were faced with the hopeless task of ministering to the needs of the immigrant poor with a minimum of personnel and with inadequate economic support.

An already understaffed and underfinanced regional church in Mexico was also faced with the task of ministering to an economically deprived population. Priests who remained in

Mexico were mostly concentrated in urban areas, and tended to rural Catholics only occasionally. The majority of the rural Catholics had little opportunity for religious instruction and a minimum of direct contact with the priest. As summarized by McNamara: "The emerging profile of the Catholic Mexican immigrant, then, is hardly that of the practicing Mass-and-Sacraments Catholic normative of northern European, Irish, and therefore, of American Catholism [nd:9]."

The impoverished immigrant who had come to the United States during the years of the Mexican Revolution had no skills by which to become economically independent. Thus he was a poor candidate for the middle class, from which has come the mainstay of financial support for Catholic programs. Moreover, it was not his custom to contribute regularly to church and to the clergy. The numerous Mexican immigrants in the United States had a strong love for religious ceremony and especially those major sacraments centered about the family such as baptism and marriage, but they felt little loyalty to the Catholic church as a formal institution and received little support from it.

In describing the four distinct types of Catholicism practiced in Mexico, Spitzer (1960) employs the following typology: *formal* Catholicism, *nominal* Catholicism, *cultural* Catholicism, and *folk* Catholicism. Each of these produced a distinct religious heritage among Mexican American Catholics in the United States.

Formal Catholicism requires an adequate knowledge of church dogma, rituals, and proscriptions. Few families qualify under this classification, but there are Catholics who follow church doctrines rigorously, are totally committed to parochial schooling, and attend religious services regularly. Clerics and church educators from all of the various socioeconomic strata constitute this limited group. Because of their religiously oriented life style, they are not as widely accepted outside their own group as are Catholics in the other classifications.

Nominal Catholicism requires an identification with, and an allegiance to the Catholic church but only perfunctorily. The nominal Catholic's practice of independently interpreting Catholic doctrine means that birth control and extramarital sexual relations, for example, are not problems for people in this very large category. The wife and children are usually the regular attenders of church services, occasionally escorted by the father. It would appear that this type of Catholicism is the most common among Mexican Americans in the United States today, and especially characteristic of barrio residents.

Cultural Catholicism is a nonspiritual affiliation with the church. Cultural Catholics consider the church as just another vehicle to be used in obtaining social, economic, and political goals. Members in this category are generally quite prosperous and may publicly display their generosity to the church for social considerations, but they are rarely church attenders. They feel that their lives are little influenced by spiritual affairs or doctrinal pursuits.

Folk Catholicism is practiced outside the formal scope of the Catholic church. Native rites are performed in the home or within the neighborhood. Elements of pagan worship and folk ritual are present in the festivities. These practices are somewhat independent of formal church attendance. Characteristic of Mexican Catholics in small, rural areas or of uneducated Mexican Americans in isolated areas of the urban Southwest, folk Catholicism is often portrayed by popular writers as the *most* common form of Catholic worship. Recent evidence, however, indicates that it is probably one of the *least* common of the four types of religious practices.

In the United States today, most Mexican Americans are nominal Catholics, and they reflect an extremely wide variety of attitudes toward the church as an institution and toward specific church dogmas. Overall attendance at Catholic mass for Mexican Americans is from 10 to 20 percent lower than it is for American Catholics as a whole. Moreover, in this ethnic group there is especially low attendance among the young. Among lower-class Mexican Americans, the most faithful church attenders are women with small children. Data from the recent Mexican-American Study Projects shows that attendance at mass decreases for both males and females as income rises. Among adult Mexican American males in Los Angeles, attendance at mass for grade school–educated respondents was 50 percent, for high school–educated, 25 to 30 percent, and up slightly to 38 percent for college-educated males. There are noticeable variations from one geographical region to another; male attendance at church in San Antonio was nearly double that of Los Angeles. In Los Angeles, during the 1966–1967 school year, only 16 percent of the Spanish-surname students of grammar school age were in parochial schools. Perhaps this has had some impact on low attendance at Catholic mass. In any case, residents in both cities were substantially under the national average for attendance at mass by Catholics. Incidentally, the figure for church-performed marriages, on the wane for many years, is now below 50 percent among Mexican American Catholics (Grebler et al., 1970:473–477; Mittlebach et al., 1966).

In Los Angeles and San Antonio, Mexican American Catholics were far less supportive of church policies on birth control than other Catholics throughout the nation. About 33 percent of the Mexican Americans surveyed agreed with church policy, whereas 44 to 68 percent of the Catholics surveyed nationally responded favorably, their attitudes varying according to the amount of religious schooling they had completed (Grebler et al., 1970:474). Even of the respondents who attended mass every Sunday or oftener 50 percent disagreed with the church teachings on birth control. Inasmuch as church attendance is a fairly strong indicator of overall religiosity, this weak tie between church participation and positive attitudes toward specific religious dogma is strong evidence of a lack of dependency on the church among urban Mexican Americans. Though they are highly religious, with long-standing family traditions of Catholicism, the formal church does not appear to be an important part of their lives.

Other contemporary studies also discount the supposedly strong attachment of Mexican Americans to the formal church structure and its religious doctrines. A study by Ulibarrí of Mexican American migrant laborers concluded that the church was not a strong factor in their lives, nor was religion a strong influence in determining their attitudes and behavior (1966: 362–363). Clark's study in San Jose, California, reports that among those studied the religious complex is not the all pervading influence that it is said to have been in Jalisco,

Michoacán, and Guanajuato, Mexico—their areas of origin (1959:96–97). One study of 2,000 boys in twenty urban Catholic high schools revealed the preponderance of the home and neighborhood in influencing basic attitudes, with much less influence coming from church and school. Nearly one-half of the boys indicated that their schools did not influence their vocational choices, and only 12 percent named the priest as their primary source of counsel on personal matters. Those things of greatest value to them were, in order of importance, money, material possessions that would provide them with pleasure, and religious salvation (Fishman, 1961:184).

During this century, the processes of urbanization and secularization have changed the roles of all religions, non-Catholic and Catholic alike. Formal Catholicism and folk Catholicism in isolated communities (in which the local priest or traditional religious practices dominate the style of life) are especially vulnerable, because the central role of the church is diminished when the family relocates to an urban milieu. Nominal Catholicism and even cultural Catholicism become more common as nonreligious institutions and agencies perform the functions traditionally performed by the church alone. Thus the church hierarchy, which has been traditionally identified as the dominant institution in the community, is unable to spring itself loose from the power liaison of community leaders and is forced to abdicate the role of catalyst for social change in urban society.

Just as the Catholic church in Mexico has generally been against reform or civil rights in the past (Cumberland, 1968: 181–186), so the contemporary Catholic church in the United States (and especially in those dioceses having the more conservative prelates) is also reactionary. The traditional church role of providing education and sacraments for its people is discounted by the masses, who demand church support for social action programs. Reactions by church authorities to these pressures vary considerably from region to region.

For example, during the Delano grape strike, when the National Farm Organization requested local priests to provide religious services for the farm laborers out on strike, its request was refused by the conservative Cardinal McIntyre, of Los Angeles, who also forbade any local clergy to bless the marches.

However, another prelate, Bishop Hugh Donohoe of Fresno, agreed to supply strikers with "priests at large" (independent and therefore not subject to local authority) to minister to their needs. Priests from San Antonio, carrying forth the liberal social action program of Archbishop Robert E. Lucey, were in the forefront of the 1966–1967 demonstrations by field workers petitioning for a minimum wage of $1.25. In events such as these the lay church members are bound to evaluate the clergy and the church as an institution by whether they support the status quo or change. The presence of priests at demonstrations indicates some interest on the part of the church, whether or not the action to improve existing conditions is successful. The feeling that prevails among many lay church members of being isolated from those who determine church policies is a reaction to the insensitive attitude of many clergymen in the upper echelons of the church hierarchy. One result is that in the Chicano press the church has become synonymous with the Establishment.

The great majority of lower-class Mexican Americans—and especially militant Chicanos—claim that the Catholic church has been hypocritical on the matter of racial discrimination. The Roman Catholic Bishops of America, in their November 1967 National Conference in Washington, condemned institutional racism:

> We must recognize the fact that racist attitudes and consequent discrimination exist; not only in the hearts of men, but in the fabric of their institutions. We must also commit our full energies to the task of eradicating the effects of such racism on American society. . . . Catholics, like the rest of the American society, must recognize their responsibility for allowing these conditions of racism to persist [Barragan, 1969:49].

Yet, barrio priests declare that "institutional racism" abounds within the church structure, as indicated by the paucity of Chicanos in the higher ecclesiastic offices and the low number of Chicano pastors in Spanish-speaking barrios. One group of social action priests, PADRES (Priests Associated for Religious, Education and Social Rights), has urged immediate church action to increase the number of Chicanos appointed to positions in church government. PADRES has stressed the need for the church to provide more financial assistance for social action projects, more adequate education in barrio parochial schools, and more church-sponsored community development programs in the Mexican American barrios (Barragan, 1969: 50, 54–57). As secular-sponsored programs for social action increase, the church structure seems more and more like an obstacle to the amelioration of social and economic inequities among Mexican Americans than their champion. Grebler et al. note (1970:477) that the church cannot assume, as in former eras, that the Mexican American will turn to it for comfort and support. Rather, it must reach out to him if it is to perform its spiritual role and be identified as a friend by this ethnic minority.

At present, liberal movements and social action related to the Catholic church are fomented by individual priests or by persons not integrated into the formal church hierarchy. Grebler et al. point out that "individuals and groups most prone to the liberal position are those divorced from the structure of the institution [1970:447]." Such a group was the Spanish Mission Band, a group of six or seven priests who lived with the alien migrants during the Bracero program a decade or so ago. Independent of direct orders from local parishes and from ecclesiastical authority, these priests could initiate programs of immediate relevance to the needs of the migrants. Similarly, in Delano, California, during the grape pickers' strike, and in south Texas, the priests bearing placards and marching in the picket lines were not the local parish-based priests, who were more often than not restrained from overt participation by local authorities. These were the "outside agitators," who came, sometimes against the wishes of their superiors, to convert Christian doctrine into visible actions for humanity—claiming as their authority the "higher law of charitable service to mankind." But such unauthorized commitments make the participants vulnerable to reprisals by both secular and ecclesiastical authorities.

For most Mexican Americans, the local parish priest is the spokesman for the church, and therein lies the problem for the liberal priest. He is restrained by church policies set up by his immediate superiors. It is not unusual for local agencies or their regional and national offices to ask a local clergyman to assist in the distribution of welfare commodities or in public assistance programs. As his involvement increases, there comes a time for this local clergyman to decide whether he must place formal church procedures or governmental and social action policies first. To be effective in promoting social and economic change, leadership roles often demand the circumvention of official church channels. The clergyman is thereby forced into a role conflict (McNamara, 1968:177–185). This is more extreme among the older priests than the younger, more liberal-minded ones. A recent national poll showed a distinct difference between Catholic priests under forty and over forty years of age regarding acceptance of birth control and celibacy rulings by the Catholic church. Younger priests, by a two to one margin, disapproved of the church's ban on artificial birth control measures, and most of them said they prescribe such measures to their congregation when asked. Priests over forty years of age seldom recommended artificial methods of birth control and by a two to one margin accepted the church's stand. Seventy-seven percent of the younger priests approved of marriage for priests, while only 36 percent of the older priests approved. Clearly, the age of a priest is a salient factor in his attitude toward church doctrine and social action.

Foreign clergy (including Spanish-speaking clerics from Spain), Anglo-Irish Catholics, and "Nordic" types, currently have difficulty being accepted in the barrio area, not on religious grounds but because of their ethnic identity and language limitations. However, all is not easy for the dark-skinned Mexican American priest either. For example, if, because of his middle-class training, the priest supports programs with long-range goals when lower-class barrio residents want instant action (not realizing it might be less effective), he is caught in a class conflict, sometimes drawing the ire of his fellows, who proclaim him to be a "Tío Tomás," or a "coconut" (brown on the outside, but really white within). Among Anglos, the myth still persists that the local Catholic priest always has the unquestioned loyalty of the Mexican Americans in his area, and he is considered their spokesman. But whether he fully agrees with their objectives or not, the priest's physical presence in the barrio many times provides the needed legitimation for a given project of reform.

No one will deny that despite an overall lack of social action, the Church's symbolic role is far from dead. Labor organizers and Vista volunteers know well the value of a Roman collar at a barrio protest meeting or marching in the front ranks of a demonstration . . . a legitimating endorsement of the cause in question [McNamara, nd:14].

THE CATHOLIC CHURCH AND PROTESTANTISM

Today, Catholic leaders are aware of the possible loss of members to the Protestant religion. However, they were not always so concerned. During the earliest period of immigration northward, the church was strongly committed to the Spanish-speaking aristocracy in the Southwest. It needed their financial support as well as their sanction of church monopoly on religious activities. In subsequent areas, especially during the early twentieth century, Mexican immigrants found little sympathy for their plight among Spanish-speaking elite. They were ignored and despised by the resident, Spanish-speaking aristocracy, and likewise they received little or no help from the impoverished Catholic church.

The Roman Catholic Church, aside from building churches and stationing refugee Mexican priests in Spanish-speaking parishes, did little to aid materially or socially. It is, therefore, not strange that bitterness toward the Spanish-speaking aristocracy and some antipathy toward the Church . . . resulted in the conversion of many Mexicans to Protestantism [Servín, 1965:148].

And the Catholic church, concentrating still on its central duty as guardian of the Christian faith, remained apparently unconcerned about the temporal welfare of its people. More pressing than the revitalization of the religion among nominal Catholic and folk Catholic immigrants was the perpetuation of sacra-mental purity and traditional dogmas.

For many Mexican Americans, conversion to Protestantism signifies social acceptance as much as does the embracing of Protestant theology. Many values associated with the "Prot-estant Ethic" are subscribed to, and practiced by the upper social strata of Catholics in the United States. This would minimize the differential in aspirations and achievement im-puted to Protestant conversion (Lazerwitz, 1961:574).

Many Mexican immigrants have been attracted by Protestant programs of economic aid and compassionate help to the down and out rather than by its religious credo. For some, their new religious outlook has been an answer to a spiritual and social void in their lives. For others, it provided an escape from the constrictions of Catholic traditions, which were infused into all their societal institutions. When Protestant-sponsored welfare during the Depression caused the religious loyalties of many needy Mexican American families to shift, local Catholic lead-ers retaliated by establishing church-sponsored relief and wel-fare projects. A more liberal clergy became concerned with the physical needs—food, clothing, shelter, and medical assistance —of its flock. With some financial support from government, these church-sponsored agencies became the vehicles for artic-ulating emergent programs for the needy. In the larger urban centers, Catholic agencies and administrators have been in the vanguard of the "social gospel." But this social awareness has not been so evident in the impoverished and economically over-committed parishes and dioceses of the southwestern United States. During the last decade, the Catholic church has shared the fate of other major religions: spokesmen for the radical Left have labeled them all "Establishment." Chicano leaders have felt particular hostility toward the church because its proce-dures and policies have often seemed to be obstacles rather than aids to the cause of Mexican Americans—a traditionally loyal Catholic ethnic group. These leaders have been given more open support from non-Catholic religious groups and clergy than from the Catholic church in most cases. However, strong disaffection toward Catholic officials and the church per se should not be interpreted as a shift away from Catholicism and toward other religious orientations. The original bond of Mexican Americans to Catholicism was not a rational acceptance of sophisticated theology. Official church stance on birth control, celibacy, and social action that precipitated the recent revolt by some members of the clergy may now be more apparent among rank-and-file church members. It is entirely possible that this reduction in church loyalty is in the nature of an awareness of the *ecclesia* rather than a bolt from Catholicism to Protestantism. In 1970 not only Catholic officials but leaders of all religions were shaken to find that *all major churches* in the United States had suffered a loss in membership.

Since Max Weber's classic study of the "Protestant Ethic," the hypothesis has been advanced that Mexican Americans who embrace a Protestant faith and internalize its theology will thereby increase their motivation to "get ahead." However, one study of political participation—a "get ahead" indicator—revealed more attitudinal and behavioral differences among the various ethnic segments of the Catholic sample than when Catholics were compared with Protestants (Greeley 1972). In one study, Protestant converts were people already aspiring to move upward economically and hence were selectively recruited for conversion because of their life style. In Chicago, Mexican Americans from lower socioeconomic levels who had been converted showed little upward mobility following the change, while the upwardly striving middle-class Catholic was found to be strongly integrated into his church, according to Samora and Lamanna (1967:42–44, 135–136). Peñalosa and McDonagh (1966:503), from their research in southern California, concluded that upwardly mobile Mexican Americans changed their *class* values but retained their designation as Catholics. In that region, conversion to Protestantism was a substitute rather than a vehicle for achieving upward mobility.

A functional alternative to the "Protestant Ethic" thesis became apparent in many private conversations I have had with Protestant professionals of Spanish American or Mexican American origin. They claimed that the reading skills garnered through Bible study and the profuse use of doctrinal tracts and religious literature were extremely valuable in preparing them for formal schooling and further professional advancement. Therefore, the study skills emphasized by the evangelistic workers rather than the act of embracing the Protestant credo appeared to be the major factor in producing their upward mobility.

Perhaps the Chicano movement will be the most serious competition for both Catholic and Protestant religions, inasmuch as the problems of ethnic purity and Mexican American identity are the basic causes of the Chicano movement. Unless the Catholic church takes a more realistic view of its role in social action, the Mexican American minority may be forced to consider the church as its enemy, just as it did in Mexico in 1857 when the church elite openly supported the established order in declaring that civil liberties were an obstruction to religion and religious ideals.

FAMILY LIFE

Current Mexican American society is too complex and heterogeneous to select a single family model to represent the entire ethnic minority. As succinctly stated by Romano-V.:

> Traditionally, in the United States, the Mexican family has been dealt with as if it were monolithic, authoritarian, and uni-dimensional. . . . The truth of the matter is that virtually every Mexican-American family takes several forms and includes many types . . . from assimilationist to Chicano, to cultural nationalist. . . . In short, the same complexity that is found in the general Mexican-American population is also found in the family of virtually every Mexican-American [1969:45].

Heterogeneity in the family structure is somewhat of a recent phenomenon and has been heavily influenced by the increasing urbanization and mobility of the Mexican American population. Nevertheless, the Mexican American family is still depicted in current social science literature as an extension of the traditional Mexican family. For example, an account of the Latino in south Texas states:

> The most important role of the individual is his familial role and the family is the most valued institution in Mexican-American society. . . . The worst sin a Latino can conceive of is to violate his obligations to his parents and siblings. . . . The oldest male is head of the household and rules it. The old command the young and the males command the females. Latin society rests firmly on a foundation of family solidarity and the concept of male superiority [Madsen, 1964:17].

Rubel's (1966:55–70) account of Mexican American families in Weslaco, Texas, and the description by S. Ramirez (1967: 185) of a typical Mexican American family both echo Madsen's view and perpetuate the model of an age- and sex-graded, multigenerational, authoritarian, patriarchal family and similar pictures of the Spanish American families of rural New Mexico are given by other sociologists. Such descriptions may have been partially true some generations back, when the majority of the early Mexican immigrants with peasant backgrounds settled in rural areas or small towns in the United States. At that time, their family structure reflected their Mexican heritage more closely then than it does today, when more than 80 percent of the families of this ethnic minority are highly mobile and urbanized. Today, nuclear families are predominant, and female heads of households are prevalent in the barrios.

Two approaches have been used in describing the dynamics of Mexican and Mexican American families. The historical approach centers on racial mingling and the identity problems that have resulted from the sexual exploitation of the Indian female by the Spanish male, whose offspring generally combines the mother's feeling of inferiority and the father's exploitive nature. This approach will not be elaborated on further here inasmuch as it was covered in Chapter 3 on ethnic identity and racial values. The structural-functional approach, which will be our present analytical framework, centers upon traditional Mexican values regarding three aspects of family life:

the extended versus the nuclear family, age grading, and sex roles.

Although Peñalosa (1968:685) declares that the once powerful extended family structure in Mexico is a thing of the past, historians give it prominence in explaining the informal cohesion of the peasant society in the hacienda system (which provided the majority of the Mexican emigrants to the United States). The hacienda system is essentially an estate system in which the *patrón-peon* relationship was reinforced through generations of inbreeding and in which there was virtually no geographical mobility. Most of the families of the hacienda were somehow related—through direct bloodlines, marriage, and godparent (*compadrazco*) relationships. However, in reality the informal communal patterns were probably more functionally important than the superficial genealogical network indicated above. When large numbers of peasant families fled from the haciendas, they brought with them those immediate members of the family who could relocate, leaving many more distant relatives behind.

A study of attitudes by Dworkin (1965:221) revealed that foreign-born Mexican Americans retained strong family ties in Mexico, whereas the native-born Mexican American denied having such ties. Samora and Lamanna (1967:30–37), studying the Mexican American enclave in east Chicago, found that *compadrazco* relationships extended family ties, and strong attachments to localities of origin in the Southwest or Mexico were critical factors in immigration to the area.

Studies of families forced to relocate from their Texas, California, or New Mexico hometowns, show that the constant movement and the complexities of urban housing and life in general debilitated the multigenerational family. In southern California urban centers, the traditional extended-family group is no longer found to any significant extent (Peñalosa, 1967: 413). The Mexican-American Study Projects in Los Angeles and San Antonio report similar findings. Only 3.5 percent of families in Los Angeles and 2.8 percent in San Antonio qualified as "extended households." A study on mobile Mexican American families by Ulibarrí (1966:363) confirms the fact that the extended family is disappearing. Even when these lower-class migrant families relocate to a permanent residence, they retain scars from former migrations. As suggested in a study of Mexican American aged in the Lubbock, Texas, barrio, the days when extended-family loyalties take precedence over nuclear family responsibilities are gone.

> Although the traditional family relationships characteristic of Mexican-Americans are still basically intact, anglicization is also taking place. This means that the traditional obligation of children . . . to care for dependent parents is weakening. Although slightly more than half of our respondents lived with children, many did not believe that the children had any obligation to provide for them in their dependency. . . . Until now, many Mexican-American old people . . . have had the feeling of security which goes with being involved in a meaningful group. With anglicization, this will diminish [Steglich, 1969:190].

One of the few areas where the institution of the extended family still persists to some extent is in a rural, isolated Spanish American village in northern New Mexico. However, even there the loss of younger villagers who migrate in search of work, are recruited to military service, or leave for other causes has to a large degree dissolved the extended family.

Knowlton (1969) attributes the dissolution of the extended-family structure in northern New Mexico to the collapse of the traditional village economic system, that is, the loss of land. Family heads seeking to provide for their families often traveled to other areas, leaving the family without its traditional, strong leader. Infrequent visits, letter writing, and financial aid from relatives working elsewhere took the place of the once close family relationship. Moreover, formal organizations began to handle law enforcement, dispense welfare and health care, and rent land for grazing, functions formerly handled in the family. Religious rituals, once centered in family shrines, were largely transferred to the formal church. Only through the stability and determination of those remaining in the village has even a vestige of the extended-family structure been preserved.

The emigrant to the United States, and especially to the

urban centers of the Southwest, has found that the traditional role of the father is functionally weakened by the younger generation's acquisition of skills that members of the older generation do not possess. One of the principal skills learned by Mexican American children that their immigrant parents do not possess is fluency in the English language.

> Few Mexican immigrants raised their children with English as the prevailing language at home. This implies that, in contrast to the experience of other nationality groups, the mother language largely remained the medium of expression between generations [Álvarez, 1966:485].

Thus, in the urban setting, the children attend grammar school and acquire in varying degrees the ability to read and write English. Having a monopoly on communications with the outside world and thus being the agency of cultural interpretation —the indispensable coordination unit—the child now shifts to a position of power in the family. Many current authors find that a minimum of serious conversation is taking place today between urban Mexican American parents and their children. This generation gap is especially evident between the militant Chicano youth and their parents and is a very important subject, in need of immediate research and clarification.

The disintegration of parental authority leads to new freedom in dating and in marriage in subsequent generations. In second generation Mexican American families, for example, the freedom to choose one's own mate is becoming accepted practice. There also seems to be more independence in family life, and in third generation Mexican American families a desire for fewer children is becoming evident (Francesca, 1958: 28). Compared with the first generation, the third generation Mexican American increasingly marries out of his ethnic group (Mittlebach et al., 1966:7–10, 45). The trend (in Los Angeles from 10 percent in the period from 1930 to 1950 to 25 percent in 1963) is not unlike trends among other immigrant minorities who have been assimilated into the dominant culture. Intermarriage among Mexican Americans in specific urban areas is thought to be higher for women than for men, though differences between the sexes are not substantial when considered in terms of sex ratio and marriage availability. Intermarriage between Mexican Americans and Anglo Americans is more prevalent among individuals of higher status; it increases through occupational and social contact with Anglos, especially those aspiring individuals residing within the barrio whose social world is outside. In conjunction with legal bans on segregation in housing, education, and employment, increased interaction between Mexican Americans and Anglo Americans of similar social class and with similar occupational interests will accelerate the present rates of exogamy. Intergenerational differences in values, language skills, and educational orientation will further deteriorate the patriarchal order of the Mexican American family, and increased geographical mobility to achieve upward social and occupational mobility will gradually obliterate the extended-family loyalties characteristic of rural Mexican and Mexican American families in the past.

Although many factors are involved in this transition from a strictly patriarchal type family structure to a more egalitarian type, the role played by language fluency in the new society is a major consideration in the case of women's expectations. As reflected in a study of Tucson Mexican American women, Spanish-speaking wives expected leadership from their husbands and only minor "togetherness," whereas English-speaking wives had greater expectations for a companionate relationship, with spouse intimacy linked to close family integration and togetherness. This difference in role perception is directly related to the degree of acculturation present and will accelerate with each subsequent generation.

The present stereotype of the Mexican American family presents the patriarchal order as persisting over time, that is, the aged male continuing to dominate his children and their children. However, as noted by Burma (1970:21), it is actually the concepts of home and family rather than the stability of conjugal ties that are strong in the Mexican American value system. Marriage, especially among lower-class Mexican Americans, is very unstable. A recent demographic analysis of Mexican American marriage and child-bearing patterns by Uhlenberg (1972), revealed that Mexican Americans marry relatively young: one-fifth of them are still in their teens and 43 percent are married by age twenty-one. Also, one-half of all

Mexican Americans have come from a family of seven or more children, and only 29 percent are from families with fewer than five children (among Japanese Americans, by contrast, 81 percent of the families have fewer than five children). Mexican Americans begin to have children very soon after marriage, but, by age sixty-four, only 57 percent are still married to their first spouse. In the lower classes, threat of desertion (the "poor man's divorce") is uncommonly high, whereas the legal divorce rate for Mexican Americans is lower than for other ethnic groups. Ironically, desertion does not violate the religious code of Catholics, to whom divorce is in most cases forbidden. In the Southwest, 13 percent of all Mexican American families are headed by females (as compared with 9 percent for the total population), revealing this as a relatively common occurrence. Compared with Anglos or nonwhite females who are divorced or widowed, few Mexican American females remarry. In Los Angeles and San Antonio, the Mexican-American Study Project reported that one-third of its sample families in the lower-income group had children being raised by one parent, and only a slightly lower percentage in the higher-income category. This situation questions the stereotype of patriarchal authority in the average barrio family, a stereotype upon which most federal government programs are based.

Recently in the Chicano movement females have become active leaders and have gained notice for their demonstrations of machismo. During the Delano grape boycott, for example, female protestors were among the first to "get busted," and participants proudly acclaimed their courage and leadership. In July 1971 a statement by the Black Berets of Albuquerque, Aztlán, in their paper, *Venceremos* 1, reads as follows:

We want equality for women. Machismo must be revolutionary . . . not oppressive. Under this system our women have been oppressed both by the system and our men. The doctrine of Machismo has been used by our men to take out their frustrations on their wives, sisters, mothers, and children. We must support our women in their struggle for economic and social equality and recognize that our women are equals within our struggle for Liberation. Forward hermanas [sisters] in the struggle.

Throughout the Southwest, and especially in rural areas, statistical evidence reveals a higher formal education level for Mexican American females than for males. Nevertheless, more highly educated Mexican American females, who are somewhat more self-sufficient and upwardly mobile, still seek to marry within their class, creating strain within the ethnic group and contributing to an increase in exogamous marriages. La Causa encourages women to increase their education and skills so that these can be used more effectively to preserve Mexican culture and its traditional institutions. It is ironic that this very drive for ethnic autonomy and pride in Mexican cultural heritage should produce such a marked departure from the traditional female sex roles of the past that it destroys the family structure—the very institutional form which La Causa is committed to preserve.

With increased educational achievement and increased economic opportunities, it is logical to assume that the Mexican American family will become increasingly heterogeneous, reflecting the more even distribution of Mexican Americans at all socioeconomic levels of American society. It is also logical to assume that acculturation will be reflected in higher divorce rates and other family pathologies characteristic of urban middle-class families in America.

Notes

[1] Many early Spanish colonists came from communities dominated for centuries by the darker-skinned Moors. Their "pure" Spanish heritage is more a result of a "bleaching" process by certain popular writers than an accurate measure of fair or swarthy complexion among Mexican Americans. (For a more accurate view see Mörner, 1967:13, 16, 55, 58.)

[2] As late as 1779, smallpox killed nearly 20 percent of the population of Mexico City. Another disease, presumed to have been a form of influenza or typhus, claimed millions in the two preceding centuries. In fact, the total number of Iberians who emigrated to the New World during the 125 years after Cortéz's conquest equaled the number of Indians who perished *every sixty days* during that same period (Cumberland, 1968:43, 50–51).

Chapter 5 ◉ Cultural Bridges and Barriers: Language and Formal Education

Language is a way of symbolically storing and subsequently transmitting culture. Parents and teachers socialize the young using the language familiar to the older generation. As traditions and cultural values become more standardized within an ethnic minority, they are reinforced through interaction within the family, clan, neighborhood, church, and other ethnic-dominated groups.

In normal interchanges using language, distortions and misunderstandings may arise. This is further complicated in a cultural setting such as the Southwest, where both English and Spanish are spoken. The acceptance of another language by the Spanish-speaking minority for relations with the larger society does create problems of differential language skill and experience. However, in such bicultural or multilingual settings, some system must be set up for the orderly interchange of information and sentiments between the various groups. The success of this interchange depends upon which language is selected as the common communication medium and what standards are used to determine the superiority of one language over another.

Since language serves more than as merely a medium of exchange—which is its primary function—its various other functions should be clarified prior to any further discussion of multilingual problems. A second function of language is as a repository of cultural values. Often when a concept is diffused from one culture to another, there is no word in the language of the receiving culture to convey its precise meaning, thus the "foreign" word is retained for its original connotations. Foreign words that persist in English such as *status quo, esprit de corp, laissez faire,* and the like are retained precisely because a literal translation into English would cause a loss of meaning. It is this aspect of meaning that is lost when one language is translated into another, especially if idiomatic usage is not taken into account. A third function of language is to promote group identity. The ability to speak Spanish or a specific barrio dialect may be a prerequisite for acceptance into the local *palo milla* (gang).[1] Barrio residents tend to accept leaders who speak in terms with which they are familiar.

When these three functions of language—communication, reflecting culture, and identifying groups—are mistakenly subsumed under the single heading of communication, resistance to, and problems with existent educational programs among ethnic minorities cannot be understood by the dominant society. The two latter functions of the Spanish language are what Mexican American leaders have been trying to convey to Anglo-dominated school boards for the past three decades. Within the past five years, militant Mexican Americans who resent the denigration of Spanish by Anglos have demanded that the language and those persons who speak it no longer be considered as culturally or intellectually inferior—or as "un-American." Top administrators in English-speaking schools have only recently been made aware of how traditional curricula and teaching methods, as well as measurement of intellectual ability, are heavily biased against ethnic minorities because English is the sole communication medium in the formal education process. Various alternate approaches to the English-only model in language training and formal education have recently become apparent. Some of these approaches will be briefly reviewed.

The *cultural-integration* model (also known as the Anglo-conformity model) was the one prominently accepted by both Anglo and Mexican Americans prior to the early 1940s. As perceived by Anglo governmental and educational functionaries, Anglo cultural values were those to which all "foreign groups" should conform. This approach implies that foreign languages and peoples are inferior simply because they are foreign.[2] Such an ethnocentric view perceives non-English cultures as having nothing uplifting to contribute to American culture: to embrace anything "foreign" would merely be to adulterate present American culture and make it "less pure." (Ethnocentrism is a process in which one's own culture is aggrandized to the point where anything foreign to it is considered inferior.) Until the post-World War II era, Mexican Americans felt compelled to accept this orientation as a consequence of American citizenship.

The *cultural-pluralism* model proposes that languages and ethnic groups should not be measured by the norms of only one group alone (for example, the Anglo middle-class or WASP), but that the cultural contributions of each distinct ethnic group be exposed to all other groups. The need for this approach became evident through the experience of Mexican American veterans of World War II, who found themselves suffering overt discrimination even after having acquired English language skills and Anglo middle-class values. Now it is advocated by the government to reduce discriminatory practices toward minority ethnic groups and to ensure equal opportunity and training for minority peoples so that they may fully benefit from the affluence of American society. In May 1970, in the new official guidelines from HEW, a four point plan was instituted to prohibit discriminatory treatment of children speaking languages other than English, and of different cultural backgrounds. It holds the local school district responsible for rectifying the language deficiency in English and prohibits the use of labels such as "Educable Mentally Retarded" or "Track" to classify and thereby discourage those with language problems, that is, minority students. It also requires that minority students' parents be notified in their own language about school activities.

The *cultural-segregation* model, originally employed by the dominant culture against ethnic minorities, is currently being extolled by the more radical minority elements as a prerequisite to ethnic autonomy and positive self-identity. By controlling the socialization process of the younger generation, radical minority leaders feel that a new positive self-identity can be developed. Since 1966 certain Brown Power extremists have advocated radical change or destruction of existing "racist institutions," suggesting that present educational institutions, even if partially modified, will perpetuate minority servitude. Therefore, from their point of view the only way to prevent further ethnic exploitation by the Establishment is to destroy the existing structures and to implement institutional development that will either guarantee minority equality or give minority members a dominant position from which to demand recompense for past indignities. However, such extremists do not explain what social structures will be employed throughout society at large in the interim to perpetuate societal norms until better institutions can be devised and implemented.

LANGUAGE AS A COMMUNICATION MEDIUM

Educators who are primarily interested in verbal and writing skills, correct pronunciation, and vocabulary mastery usually stress rote learning in their teaching methods. Such methods are expected to equip a Spanish-speaking student with the basic English skills with which to "compete effectively within the present American society [Manuel, 1965]." A study of the reactions of Mexican American first-graders to school clarifies this process.

> The first speech patterns of most Spanish-speaking children are formed in the home and neighborhood in Spanish with few secondary contacts with English-speaking people. Consequently, they first develop a small vocabulary of basic Spanish words and concepts directly related to these very restricted in-group experiences. Upon entering school, the first year in 1-C is devoted to teaching some of these same words and concepts in English as well as some preliminary first grade material. However, the present study shows that this year of initial contact with English language skills is only partially successful in removing the language barrier. Then the following year, with their minimal preparation in English, they begin regular first year work and are confronted with words and concepts in English for which they have no comparative terms in

Spanish. The result is that bilingual children can usually speak in their mother language with only a rather limited vocabulary learned in the home and neighborhood. When it becomes necessary for them to utilize a concept that they have learned exclusively in contact with "Anglo" culture, they have no alternative but to introduce English into their conversation [Holland, 1962:346].

Educators and language teachers have claimed that by increasing the English language skills of non-English–speaking students, interethnic misconceptions are greatly reduced (Manuel, 1965). As a result, a plethora of bilingual programs have been attempted in southwestern schools, some emphasizing both Spanish and English as the primary communication mediums, others, English as a second language, still others, language from a grammatical standpoint as well as for communication, and so forth. However, although administrators and educators profess to see the key to minority education in bilingual *instructional techniques*, some are incapable of objectively perceiving the value of bilingual *education* because they themselves are monoglots (i.e., can communicate in only *one* language). Like nine out of ten Americans who can speak only their own language, they regard a "foreign" language as a threat to 100 percent "Americanism" as they have traditionally perceived it (Anderson, 1969).

Spanish-speaking students enrolled in American grammar schools may be referred to as "bilingual," but in fact they are often "bi-illiterates"—unable to read and write in either their mother tongue or in English.

Many Spanish-surname children are put at a major disadvantage in their schooling because they literally have no real command of any language. Even their knowledge of Spanish often is limited to the spoken word, for they are not taught by their parents either to read or write it. The children generally have only a rudimentary knowledge of English, the language of instruction in the public school. . . . As a consequence, it is no wonder that their performance in school often is poor and retarded from the very beginning. Further, as a consequence, their sense of inferiority with respect to their Anglo classmates tends to widen rather than diminish over time. . . . Predictably, they are all too eager to seize the first opportunity to withdraw from school. Because these practices are so deeply embedded in family and peer-group structures, only a conscious and deliberate program to alter this pattern by going beyond the schoolroom will permit the needed substantial improvement in scholastic attainment of the Spanish-surname population [Browning and McLemore, 1964:64].

Depending upon to what extent language is assumed to be responsible for the present substandard attainment of Spanish-speaking students, various programs and techniques are being advanced to facilitate student adjustment to formal education in English.

The federal government's Elementary and Secondary Education Act (ESEA) of 1965 promotes two distinct orientations in compensatory educational programs to meet the needs of the Spanish-speaking community. The first of these, funded under Title I, is designed to provide English language skills without cultural overtones. In English-as-a-second-language programs (ESL) English is taught to non-English–speaking students in the same way as any other foreign language is taught. Rudy Cordova, Director of the Teacher Corps in the Office of Education, reported to a recent workshop of southwestern ethnic groups that after seven years, Title I compensatory education programs show few tangible results. The future is even bleaker. In most traditional school districts the most discernible impact of these government programs was in the increase in teachers' salaries and the acquisition of new school equipment, but little improvement was found in the performance of minority children. In those few schools in which new and innovative programs were attempted, far greater results were achieved.

The second approach of ESEA, called Title VII, emphasizes bilingual and bicultural education. In such programs, not only language but minority history, culture, and a total adaptation of school programs to the ethnic and socioeconomic background of the student are emphasized. Ideally, these are integrated with the regular, ongoing school programs so as not to segregate further the ethnic minorities, such as is now the case in the Southwest and especially in Texas. Since the objectives of Title VII are more diffuse than those of Title I, they are more difficult to evaluate from currently available criteria, but, according to educators working directly with students in schools with high ratios of minority students, the prognosis is good. Moreover, various auxiliary programs to assist bicultural education have been furnished through the Economic Opportunity Act of 1964, ESEA, the Higher Education Acts of 1956, and the School Lunch and Child Nutrition Act of 1966. They are summarized as follows.

Head Start provides educational, nutritional, and social services to poor children in an effort to expand the child's preschool experiences and thus enable him to compete with his economically more fortunate classmates. Follow Through supplements quality preschool programs with specialized teachers, teaching aids, and social services, according to local needs. The High School Equivalency Program (HEP) assists high school dropouts to adapt their potential occupational skills in vocational or academic programs that are equivalent to high school programs, but that are adapted to areas of special student needs. Talent Search is a recruitment program for disadvantaged youth who have been bypassed in traditional education procedures. It encourages the student to complete his secondary schoolwork and to go on to some type of higher education. Upward Bound is a program to motivate low-income students to attend college, to facilitate their entrance, and to provide supplementary allowances for college expenses. Special Services provides supplementary counseling and tutorial expertise for low-income students who are in college as a result of Talent Search and Upward Bound programs.

Supplementary grants designed to sustain these educational programs include Dropout Prevention, which provides grants to local public educational agencies to reduce the number of school dropouts; School Library Resources, Textbooks, and other Instructional Materials, which gives children and teachers greater access to high quality instructional aids; and Supplementary Educational Centers and Services, which facilitates the carrying out of programs for low-income children or children of different cultures.

Whether English is to be the communication medium in education or part of a bilingual program is still at the heart of the language-education controversy. G. Sanchez (1966:11–13) and others (cf. Cabrera, 1971:81) recommend that Spanish as spoken in the home and in the barrio be the medium of verbal communication in the schoolroom. Once this familiar medium of communication is handled with fluency, it becomes the means through which English can be learned as an alternate medium of communication. Meanwhile, the Spanish-speaking child is not penalized during these early years for his non-English–speaking background. This type of program, referred to as FLES (Foreign Language in Elementary Schools) seeks to reduce the strain of formal schooling on the Spanish-speaking child by eliminating the unfamiliar communication medium (English). Under FLES the change from Spanish to English as the language of communication in school would be postponed until the third grade or later.

Anderson (1969) criticizes the FLES program because of the traumatic changeover later from the Spanish to English, and he suggests instead that true bilingual programs be adopted in which all subject matter is taught in both Spanish and English. Pilot projects in San Antonio, Laredo, Del Rio, and Del Valle in Texas, in Dade County in Florida, and in New York City have shown that Anglo pupils taught standard subjects in both Spanish and English test as well in that subject matter as those taught in classes using just English. Moreover, they have the additional advantage of learning another language. Spanish-speaking students show a much higher achievement under these bilingual conditions than they do in the English-only classes, especially when Spanish-speaking, native teachers are employed. Such teachers often understand the meanings of certain language forms better than teachers who were trained in "school" Spanish. A brochure issued recently through the U.S. Commission on Civil Rights outlining bilingual and bicultural educational programs cites various successful bilingual programs that were begun at different grade levels. The therapeutic approach to Spanish-speaking students who are having difficulty with English is to provide remedial training of many sorts. Some therapists employ reinforcement techniques such as rote recitation of correct language forms, while others claim success in having the student consciously repeat the error to erase it as an automatic response reaction. An extreme therapeutic approach is to perceive Spanish-accented English as an indicator of speech pathology. Whereas organic and neurological difficulties in speech can be helped through therapy, there is less success in correcting a barrio-learned accent. The Spanish-speaking student hears those about him with whom he identifies speak "abnormal" English. Having this culturally learned trait regarded as a speech pathology provides him with a basis for resentment and defensiveness.

Not only does the Spanish-speaking student have difficulty switching from his native tongue to a foreign language such as English, but he must also overcome the additional problem common to *all* students—switching from informal barrio vernacular to the formal language deemed acceptable in the schools. In the school atmosphere, the Spanish-speaking student's inability to express his feelings adequately in precise English is more than a deficiency in vocabulary and grammar; it is compounded by the shift from barrio conversation to formalized information-transfer systems. This process is analogous to listening to a familiar TV jingle followed by a panel of erudite technical experts discussing the same product.

LANGUAGE AS A REPOSITORY FOR CULTURAL VALUES

The differences in language structure and word meanings from one part of society to another restrict the manner in which society members perceive the real world. Language, rather than being a neutral channel through which information and feelings are conveyed, is first an influence on cognition, which in turn affects perception. The language tools used in learning will either expand or reduce the uniformity and the dimensions of the real world, as a person seeks to become familiar with it.

Once the child has acquired language, the bulk of his knowledge of the world is conveyed to him through reports on what others have observed and learned. Even his direct learning in contact with physical objects is usually preceded by expectations based upon second-hand knowledge. For such knowledge the invisible but narrow limitations set by the categories of culture are profoundly important in molding its final form [Segall et al., 1966: 11].

Therefore, the amount, type, or degree of information gained through experience that can be conveyed to others outside one's group increases proportionately with the similarity of language structure and cultural background between the informant and the recipient.

Emigrants to the United States from countries with no immigration quotas can reinforce their position with regard to education better than those from countries where immigration is restricted. Thus Spanish, of the twenty-three major foreign languages spoken in the United States, has had the highest potential for becoming its second most common language. In 1940 Spanish ranked fourth among foreign languages spoken in this country, but by 1960 it was in second place, since constantly high levels of immigration have been a prominent factor in language maintenance (Fishman and Hofman, 1966:50).

Ethnic minorities seeking to perpetuate their distinct style of life may do so through informal and formal institutions of socialization. The language of one's people and of one's culture has deep personal meaning. The school's role in perpetuating native languages has been generally negative except in the case of special "minority schools," which are rapidly declining.

A major factor affecting Spanish retention today is ethnic concentration in residential areas, mostly barrios, where a high rate of Spanish usage has the indirect effect of lowering the level of English fluency. In the southwestern urban and rural barrios, Spanish is still the language spoken by a majority of residents. Since the barrio is in many ways an ethnic institution, Anglo designs for improving the housing, health, recreation, and living conditions there are often perceived as a threat to the survival of the barrio itself, that is, to the Spanish lan-

guage and Spanish customs. Functionaries from the larger society often interpret this resistance to change as obstinacy or
ignorance, not understanding the emotional attachment and
the security that Spanish culture and language within the
familiar barrio setting affords the Mexican American. To the
degree that Mexican American barrio residents are unfamiliar
with English or with middle-class life, and similarly, to the
degree that middle-class Anglos are unable to understand the
barrio experience, each group is unable (and unwilling) to
comprehend the richness and variations within the cultural
milieu of the other.

Moreover, Spanish as a cultural repository reduces the
acculturation rate of barrio children in English-speaking
schools. In addition to the normal trauma accompanying the
child's initial contact with formal schooling, the child whose
mother tongue is Spanish has a symbolic orientation toward
the world about him, usually discounted and even negatively
evaluated by English-speaking teachers or peers. He is less comfortable in social situations where English is used to explain
rules, to give instructions, and to grade him. Because school officials often interpret this lack of enthusiasm as an indication of
cultural poverty, the student who is *culturally different* becomes
stigmatized as *culturally deprived.* Brooks (1968) distinguishes
between these two classifications. The culturally different child
is a perfectly intelligent pupil who, because of non-English–
speaking background, has difficulty in communicating his potential to other people whose lingual skills are limited to English. When such a child is seen as a potential contributor to
the classroom experience, his different cultural background, if
properly directed, can enrich the scope of the others. The culturally deprived child, on the other hand, is one who has been
isolated from those experiences that other persons take for
granted—meaningful, personal contact within *any* cultural
ethos. This cultural isolation may have been brought about by
poverty, meager intellectual resources in the home, or incapac-
ity of parents to induce perceptual skills of personal and social
awareness in their offspring. Oscar Lewis (1966) argues that
people in economic poverty in all societies share a common experience that he terms "the culture of poverty." Thus in *any*

nationality, there are those few children legitimately classified as "culturally deprived" as a result of the poverty of their individual experience, but not of their racial and ethnic background.

LANGUAGE AS AN EXTERNAL CRITERION OF IDENTITY

With the possible exception of physiological attributes, the possession of a Spanish surname or an obvious Spanish accent is the most distinguishing characteristic of persons in the Mexican American category. A health study by Clark (1959:53) revealed that "language, more than anything else, isolates the Mexican-Americans of San Jose from their fellow citizens." In Castroville, California, Parsons observed that anyone speaking Spanish, or English with a Spanish accent, is identified as "Mexican," even if he doesn't have the appropriate skin color (1965:151). In a schoolroom, a Spanish surname or Spanish accent will bias the teacher in his evaluation of student ability and achievement potential. A study of Mexican American youth in El Paso revealed the feeling that Anglos use the criteria of language, skin color, and family name (in that order of importance) for identifying the ethnic group (see Table 4.3, page 81). Observers also declared that behavior patterns which would otherwise be considered characteristically lower class may be evaluated as part of the ethnic group pathology because of language deficiency.

Some years ago Tuck (1946) explained that by means of language rather than through overt discriminatory practices, non-English–speaking minorities such as Mexican Americans were subtly controlled. Goffman (1959) compares this process to what goes on in the theater. The producer-director controls the communication and information sources, withholding these from his audience. He is then free to assign the roles of hero or fool according to his own preferences. In a similar manner, negative minority stereotypes are perpetuated in situations wherein the information sources and images are reinforced by the existing power structure, which jealously guards its control over mass media and information it has concerning the minority, lest facts be revealed that destroy its scenario facade and, with it, its power base.

The myth that Anglos are superior to Mexican Americans may be easily maintained when comparisons between the two are limited to the one criterion of proficiency in English. The basic assumption that English is superior and, therefore, Spanish is inferior conveys inferior status upon the ethnic groups associated with the Spanish language. This becomes a perfect rationalization for disallowing "inferior" language systems to contaminate the "superior" ones. Such an ethnocentric viewpoint was the official educational policy of former U.S. Commissioner of Education Harold Howe II. He proclaimed:

> [Our society] equates Anglo American origin and Anglo American ways with virtue, with goodness, even with political purity. Other cultures are not only different; they are inferior. They must be wiped out, not only for the good of the country, but for the good of the child. Not only must he [the pupil] learn to speak English; *he must stop speaking anything else* [Montez, 1960:28; italics added].

This has been the underlying philosophy of many school boards throughout the southwestern United States until just the last few years. For example, in Brownsville, Texas, Mexican Americans have been fined for speaking Spanish in school. Corporal punishment has been meted out to students who break the "no Spanish" code. In El Paso even in the late 1960s, the speaking of Spanish on school grounds either before or after school, during classes, or even during the noon hour was prohibited. Violators were subject to reprimand, punishments such as staying after school, or even expulsion for repeated violations. This discriminatory treatment affected the Mexican American students to the point where they could not perform to the best of their abilities. Not until after a major student confrontation was the rule abolished, and then only with outside regional threats by a certifying body (the West Coast office of the NEA). Then, in a complete turnabout, El Paso began to include

Mexican American professionals in the school administration, and in the fall of 1972 initiated a program for complete bilingual instruction (English and Spanish) within five years in early elementary grades containing substantial numbers of Spanish-speaking students.

Universities throughout the United States require that a Ph.D. candidate master at least two foreign languages. Apparently, at this level more than one language is an indication of cultural broadening. Yet, in an elementary or secondary school student the ability to speak Spanish is regarded as an educational drawback, an insurmountable obstacle to the mastery of English. Within this public school milieu, there is little motivation for a Mexican American student to acquire English fluency, because he is ridiculed and embarrassed by Anglo peers who mimic his accent, by teachers who reprimand him for mistakes, and by Chicano peers who taunt him for speaking English *too well*. The student flounders between the identity demands of parents who speak Spanish, peers who demand that Spanish be spoken as a sign of Chicano loyalty, and Anglo school officials and teachers who reward only the ability to speak English correctly. These conflicting demands interfere with any degree of mastery or sophistication in either language. Parenthetically, this does not alter the fact that to individuals who do not master English the economic and status rewards of the larger society are inaccessible. But one need not assault the Spanish language as an inferior tongue in order to promote the effective study and mastery of English.

A person limited to communicating in one language fears the multilingual situation. In Europe it is not uncommon for children to speak one language at home and another at school. Since most European teachers as well as students are multilingual, it is quite inappropriate to consider one language (or ethnic group) superior or inferior. The widespread notion in the Southwest that Spanish and Mexican American peoples are inferior reveals more about the lack of self-confidence and cloistered fears of the unilingual school board members and teachers who express and support such attitudes than it does about the expressive value of Spanish as a teaching and conversational medium.

LANGUAGE AS AN INTERNAL CRITERION OF IDENTITY

Parents and sons from 133 Mexican American households in El Paso agreed that the criteria of language and Spanish surname were of greatest importance in determining ethnic identity (Stoddard, 1969:487). However, the stress on language as an identity factor differed from one generation to the next. For Mexican American adults born since 1900, American citizenship has been their major goal. The younger generation, native born and thus already citizens, have aspired more toward social acceptance, especially by their peers and in school-related social activities. Whereas parents had considered the mastery of English as a sign of good citizenship, in subsequent generations it was mastery of the language used by the Anglo teachers and administrators. The speaking of Spanish at home with parents or siblings has implications only within the family structure itself (other than in English practice time forfeited), but the use of Spanish in public suggests a rejection of English and any attempts to become Anglicized. Thus language becomes for the Mexican American a badge of ethnic loyalty.

As the Mexican American child grows up, he identifies first with one social institution and then with another. There emerges a sequential pattern in the acceptance and then the rejection of English. If Spanish is spoken in the Mexican American family, the young child learns Spanish during his preschool years. His first experience of any extended nature with English is in grammar school. During the first three or four years, his English usage increases and his vocabulary expands. Then, when the child reaches ten years of age or so, the use of English as the primary communication language decreases. The adolescent becomes reticent about speaking English informally, and in postadolescence he consciously rejects English usage except as formal situations demand. Unless relocation, military service, higher education, or occupation brings him into direct contact with the English-speaking world, he adapts once again to the language of the barrio—and to its poverty as well.

Even when the student from the barrio ventures into the larger society, his barrio speech patterns are evaluated negatively. Unless a Mexican American pupil wishes to repudiate the language of his people, advising him that his English is "abnormal" causes him some conflict in identity. If he continues to speak with an accent, his teachers are disappointed. If he adjusts to correctly spoken "school English," his peers may ridicule him.

If ethnic identity or peer-group pressures demand that the student speak Spanish to indicate ethnic loyalty, or if he can no longer compete academically in English with other students whose mother tongue is English, or if he is embarrassed by his accent, he will revert back to Spanish, the language with which he feels comfortable (Heller, 1966:30). However, with the spread of the Chicano movement the stigma attached to having a foreign accent has diminished and there is more willingness to speak Spanish with pride rather than merely for convenience or comfort. At any rate, in terms of ethnic identity the thrust of the Chicano movement during the last decade has been to glorify Spanish and to dismiss Anglo attempts to ridicule the accent of Mexican Americans speaking English. In this context, the deliberate nonuse of English does not represent lack of English fluency or a lack of motivation to become proficient in it. Rather, it is symbolic of the emotional resentment felt toward the dominant Anglo society for its unnecessary disparagement of the Spanish language and those people who speak it. Unless school officials are taught the difference between English and Spanish language *functions* (i.e., communication, culture, identity) within the educational milieu, crash programs in bilingual education and remedial English programs will merely accentuate rather than ameliorate present bicultural problems in the Southwest.

EDUCATION

Since many of the communication and perception problems dealing with educational attainment were discussed in the language section, here we consider the level of educational attain-

ment among the Spanish-surname population in order to ana-
lyze the influence of demography, family, peer group, and
school on educational achievement.

SPANISH AMERICAN EDUCATIONAL ACHIEVEMENT

The Spanish Americans of northern New Mexico appear to
have a distinct educational situation that differentiates them
from the rest of the Spanish-surname persons in the Southwest.
Their educational level is higher than that of the border-area
Mexican American, but this has not led them to a higher
income level or to greater occupational mobility than that of
their less-educated brothers. There are relatively few jobs,
skilled or unskilled, within the entire region, necessitating relocation to the urban centers of the Southwest and the West Coast
for those who would pursue economic success. The majority
of the older generation and many of the youth seem willing
to remain in their familiar surroundings rather than leave to
pursue economic success elsewhere.

Gonzalez (1969) considers as distinct groups the Spanish-
surname population in northern New Mexico villages (which
has a heavy dropout rate in high school) and the urban and
more middle-class residents of the metropolitan communities,
who make up a fair percentage of the college students graduating from New Mexican universities. It is well to remember
that in New Mexico, unlike Texas or California, Spanish-
surname families are distributed throughout the socioeconomic
strata rather than being concentrated almost exclusively in the
lower socioeconomic classes.

MEXICAN AMERICAN EDUCATIONAL ACHIEVEMENT

The latest available census data for Spanish-surnamed Americans indicates that Mexican Americans in the Southwest have
a very low level of formal education compared with Anglos.
Table 5.1 reveals that in 1950 most Spanish-surnamed individuals had gone only through the elementary grades and

*Table 5.1   Percentage of Spanish Surname and Anglo Persons
Completing Various Levels of Education: 1950 and 1960*

YEARS COMPLETED	ANGLO		SPANISH SURNAME	
	1950	*1960*	*1950*	*1960*
None	2.1	2.4	18.0	10.9
Grades one–four	6.6	7.0	27.3	16.7
Five–seven	14.8	14.6	20.8	21.2
Eight	21.2	17.8	9.5	12.8
Nine–eleven	17.3	18.7	9.9	20.1
Twelve	21.4	21.2	7.8	12.8
College one–three	7.6	8.6	2.1	3.8
Four or more	6.4	9.6	1.3	1.7
Unreported	2.6	—	3.3	—

SOURCE: U.S. Census, 1950 and 1960, *Educational Attainment* and *Persons of Spanish Surname.*

approximately 18 percent of the population had no schooling at all (the comparable figure for Anglos is just over 2 percent). The figures for 1960 indicate that more Spanish-surnamed individuals are now going on to high school. Nevertheless, although educational inequalities appear to be on the wane, this ethnic minority continues to be stereotyped as uneducable.

In 1950, one-half of the foreign-born Mexican males had not reached a fourth-grade level in school. This educational level was decidedly lower for immigrants from the rural interior of Mexico than for urban-based immigrants. Though America prides itself on being a land of opportunity, demographic data show that this opportunity is limited to immigrants from Western Europe and is not available to Mexicans (Peñalosa, 1969:488). It appears that language facility and rural or urban life styles combine in some manner to affect educational levels among Mexican Americans. The imposing of quotas on Mexican immigration should limit the number of Mexican families from rural areas entering the United States and thus raise the education level of the immigrant. This will also lower the ratio of foreign-born to native-born Mexican

Americans, thus further decreasing present educational differences.

Very different educational opportunities are afforded the Mexican immigrant, depending upon which of the southwestern states he chooses for his residence. If he chooses California, he will receive more years of schooling than if he chooses Texas. Among the younger immigrants in Los Angeles, for example, more than half had completed eight years of schooling. This is near the average for all United States residents and is double the education level for foreign-born Mexican Americans elsewhere in the Southwest (Álvarez: 1966:487).

Not only foreign-born Mexican American immigrants but all Spanish-speaking persons in the Southwest show similar variations in educational level. As shown in Table 5.2, Spanish-speaking persons from both California and Colorado have more years of formal education than do those residing in Texas. There are also variations according to sex and rural or urban residence. Spanish-surname males and females show similar education levels (the females being slightly higher overall) in both urban and rural areas. For male farm residents (with the exception of those in Colorado), however, the educational level is drastically lower than for all other categories. Except for farm workers, the level of education for the Spanish-surname minority is highest in California and Colorado. Texas ranks lowest of all of the southwestern states. The pathetic state of education in Texas is further illustrated by a recent study of two central counties in Texas (including San Antonio). The study concluded that the average Mexican American household head in the rural portion of this area had completed only three years of formal schooling. Even the heads of households in urban areas had completed only six years on the average. This was just half of the educational level for Anglos in that same area. In the category of persons with no formal education, there were 27.0 percent in Texas in 1950 as compared with 9.5 percent in Colorado. At one time, Texans could rationalize this situation by claiming to have more Mexican Americans within their boundaries than did the other southwestern states, but now that California has more Mexican Americans than Texas, even this petty excuse is gone.

Table 5.2 *Median School Years Completed by Persons of Spanish Surname in Five Southwestern States: 1960*

	MALE				FEMALE			
	Urban	Rural Nonfarm	Rural Farm	Total Population	Urban	Rural Nonfarm	Rural Farm	Total Population
Arizona	8.3	7.1	2.9	7.8	8.3	8.0	6.0	8.2
California	9.2	8.1	4.9	8.9	9.4	8.6	8.5	9.2
Colorado	8.7	8.1	8.1	8.5	8.9	8.1	8.3	8.7
New Mexico	8.8	8.0	6.9	8.4	8.7	8.2	8.0	8.5
Texas	6.7	5.0	4.1	6.2	6.4	5.2	5.0	6.1

SOURCE: U.S. Census, 1960, *Persons of Spanish Surname*, Table 3.

Inasmuch as certain regions with large rural populations have managed to maintain high levels of education among their Spanish-surname residents, it is important to note that it is not location per se but the factors associated with a particular life style that affect educational attainment. The educational level of Spanish-surname females in rural areas is not as low as that of the males, indicating that lower educational achievement is a combined product of sex (male) and occupational life styles (rural farms). There are also few educational programs for migrant and farm laborers of Mexican American extraction. However, for more than a decade the states of Colorado and New Mexico have had special programs to reach Spanish-speaking farm migrants and rural farm residents. These have boosted educational levels among Mexican Americans to almost those of the urban population.

There are wide variations in levels of education for Mexican Americans residing in metropolitan centers of the Southwest, too, as shown in Table 5.3. California communities show a rather uniformly high median level of formal education, and during the 1950–1960 decade this level rose by more than 1.5 years. On the other hand, Texas communities show an extremely low level of educational attainment. For example, in 1950 the cities of Lubbock and Midland had rates of only 1.7 and 1.8 years of schooling, respectively, for their Spanish-speaking populations. These families were nearly all migrants from the lower valley of Texas who since World War II had settled out of the migrant stream. Similarly, Brownsville, San Angelo, and Waco showed rates of less than 3.0 median years of education for Mexican American residents. Some improvements occurred during the decade from 1950 to 1960 in Amarillo, Dallas, Fort Worth, Galveston, and Waco, as shown by at least a 2.0-years-of-education rise among Mexican American residents. This trend, however, is not reflected generally throughout the state.

Although, in general, younger generation Mexican Americans tend to be better educated than their parents, there are still large numbers of Mexican Americans with no formal schooling at all. In Texas, by 1960, the figure for Spanish-surname individuals over twenty-five years of age and without any formal

Table 5·3 Median School Years Completed by Spanish Surname and Anglo Persons in Selected Southwestern Metropolitan Areas

STANDARD METROPOLITAN STATISTICAL AREA (SMSA)	1950		1960		
	TOTAL POPULATION	SPANISH SURNAME	TOTAL POPULATION	ANGLO	SPANISH SURNAME
Arizona					
Phoenix	10.6	5.3	11.6	12.1	6.1
Tucson	11.2	6.5	12.1	12.3	8.0
California					
Bakersfield	9.9	6.5	10.8	11.4	7.3
Fresno	9.8	5.6	10.4	10.7	6.1
Los Angeles–Long Beach	12.0	8.2	12.1	12.3	8.9
Sacramento	11.3	7.9	12.2	12.3	9.1
San Bernardino–Riverside–Ontario	10.9	6.7	11.8	12.1	8.0
San Diego	12.0	8.1	12.1	12.2	8.9
San Francisco–Oakland	12.0	8.9	12.1	12.3	9.7
San Jose	11.4	8.0	12.2	12.4	8.3
Santa Barbara	11.8	7.0	12.2	12.4	8.3
Stockton	9.1	7.2	10.0	10.7	7.5
Colorado					
Colorado Springs	11.7	8.4	12.3	12.4	10.1
Denver	12.0	8.0	12.2	12.3	8.0
Pueblo	9.1	6.3	10.2	11.0	8.1

New Mexico					
Albuquerque	11.7	7.7	12.2	12.5	8.7
Texas					
Abilene	10.1	n.a.	11.7	12.0	4.0
Amarillo	11.3	4.7	12.1	12.2	8.1
Austin	10.9	3.5	11.7	12.3	4.4
Beaumont–Port Arthur	9.7	7.0	10.8	11.7	8.7
Brownsville–Harlingen–San Benito	6.3	2.7	7.9	12.3	3.9
Corpus Christi	9.4	3.2	10.1	12.2	4.5
Dallas	11.0	4.4	11.8	12.1	6.4
El Paso	9.2	5.2	11.1	12.4	6.6
Fort Worth	10.7	5.4	11.4	11.9	7.7
Galveston	9.4	4.9	10.3	11.3	6.9
Houston	10.4	5.2	11.4	12.1	6.4
Laredo	5.4	5.2	6.7	n.a.	5.4
Lubbock	11.0	1.7	11.6	12.1	3.1
Midland	12.1	1.8	12.4	12.6	3.7
Odessa	10.4	3.9	11.4	11.8	4.6
San Angelo	10.2	2.9	10.7	11.5	4.0
San Antonio	9.1	4.5	10.0	12.1	5.7
Waco	9.4	2.9	10.3	11.0	5.5
Wichita Falls	10.3*	4.5*	11.4	11.7	6.3

* Complete data not available for Spanish surnames in one country (Archer).
SOURCE: Revised from Grebler, 1967: Table 6.

education was an astonishing 22.9 percent, as contrasted to only 1.1 percent for Anglos in that same age category. Among nonwhites in Texas, only 5.4 percent were without any formal schooling, placing the Mexican American at the bottom of the "no schooling" category (Browning and McLemore, 1964:29).

The future promises an improvement in educational levels achieved by younger Mexican Americans over those achieved by their parents. Grebler (1967) found that Mexican American youth under twenty-five years of age had a substantially higher median-education level than those over twenty-five. This is directly the opposite of figures for the Anglo population, which show that the older category has a higher level of education than the younger. In summary, although present educational levels of Mexican Americans are low in comparison with those for Anglo and nonwhite groups, the gap is decreasing rapidly.

MEXICAN AMERICAN SCHOOL ENROLLMENT AND ATTRITION RATES

A 1968 HEW survey of the nation's 2,002,776 Spanish-surnamed public school students indicates that more than 70 percent of all Spanish-speaking students are Mexican Americans residing within the five southwestern states. Mexican Americans also constitute the largest percentage of the more

Table 5.4   Mexican American Public School Population for Five Southwestern States: 1968

	Total Number of Pupils	Number of Mexican American Pupils	Percentage of Total Enrollment
Arizona	366,459	71,748	19.6
California	4,477,381	646,282	14.4
Colorado	519,092	71,348	13.7
New Mexico	271,040	102,994	38.0
Texas	2,510,358	505,214	20.1
Total	8,144,330	1,397,586	17.2

than 100,000 Spanish-surname students in urban areas of Illinois, Michigan, and other midwestern and western locations where Mexican American dropouts from the migrant stream became permanent residents.

The most recent information on rates for the five southwestern states shows the following data for Anglo, Mexican American, and black students at first, eighth, and twelfth grade levels, and those entering or completing college. The higher attrition rate for Mexican Americans is evident from this data.

Table 5.5   *Comparative Education Attrition Rates (by Race)*
at Selected Levels in the Southwest

Educational Level	Anglo (%)	Mexican American (%)	Black (%)
Grade 1	100.0	100.0	100.0
Grade 8	100.0	91.1	98.6
Grade 12	85.0	60.3	66.8
Enter college	49.3	22.5	28.8
Complete college	23.8	5.4	8.3

Generally throughout the United States the school enrollment rates for Spanish-surname students are increasing, and dropout rates are diminishing. Grebler (1967:221–226) presented a graphic description of their enrollment and dropout patterns based on an intensive analysis of 1960 census data for the Spanish-surname population. Although Spanish-speaking children enroll in school at an older age, their subsequent school enrollment patterns, until about age thirteen, are similar to that of the total population. From that point until age twenty or twenty-one the differential rate of lower enrollments in comparison with both Anglo and nonwhite students is clearly evident. Ultimately, about 12.1 percent of Spanish-surname persons are still attending school compared with 21.2 percent of all persons in the Southwest.

As more Mexican Americans become centered in urban areas and thus more attend public schools, it is entirely possible that a higher level of educational attainment will simply result from school officials "passing" minority students who have not mastered English. If this becomes true, it will cause an increased dropout rate during junior high and high school, with the most precipitous point occurring in high school or at the equivalent age level (cf. Grebler, 1967:Table A-5).

Carter (1970:28) suggests that prior to high school graduation the Mexican American dropout rate is about 60 percent in Texas and 40 percent in California and Colorado. The rate is lower in Arizona and New Mexico. One reason for the absence of exact figures is a lack of standardization in defining what constitutes a dropout. In some school districts, dropouts are persons within the legal age of compulsory school attendance, but not currently attending school. For others, just the pupils registering for school in the fall are considered the "school population," and only registered students who discontinue their schooling during the school year are called dropouts, while those who do not register during the semester are simply not counted.

Spanish-speaking peoples make up one-third of the population in New Mexico, one-sixth in Texas and Arizona, and one-tenth in California and Colorado. The ratio of Spanish-speaking enrollment to total enrollment at the major universities in these states varies from 5 percent in New Mexico to just over 1 percent in Colorado and California.[3] Most of these students are heavily concentrated in the few major colleges and universities listed in Table 5.6.

In terms of their numbers in the total population of the Southwest, Mexican Americans are more severely underrepresented in institutions of higher learning than in intermediate and high schools. A Ford Foundation report suggests that, in order to achieve the same proportional representation in college as they have in the total population of this country, Mexican Americans must increase their present college enrollment by 330 percent—or from approximately 50,000 to 215,000. Within the past few years, nearly all major educational institutions with large ethnic populations in their areas have endeavored to promote programs to increase the enrollment of minority students. Only recently have programs been stressed to help

Table 5.6   Mexican American College and University Enrollment at Selected Institutions in the Southwest (1968–1969)

Year	College or University	Enrollment of Spanish Surnames	Percentage of Total Enrollment
1969	University of Texas at El Paso	3,175	30.3
1968	Pan American College (Texas)	1,896	59.6
1968	Texas A & I	1,872	29.2
1968	University of New Mexico	1,711	11.7
1969	Highlands University (New Mexico)	1,211	51.0
1968	University of Arizona	1,116	4.9
1968	University of Texas at Austin	838	3.4
1968	University of California at Berkeley	496	1.9
1968	University of Colorado	249	1.3

keep them there. Some of these projects will be discussed later in this chapter.

Most dropouts occur during the freshman year. Winther et al. (1969:24,38), studying freshmen at the University of New Mexico, reported that in 1963, 69.5 percent of the Spanish-surname group dropped out compared with 61.1 percent from all other groups. Gonzalez (1969:151) indicates that the drop-out rate for Spanish-speaking students at the University of New Mexico in 1965 was proportionately higher than the over-all rate for the student body.

An institutional report containing a detailed analysis of the 1969 enrollment at the University of Texas at El Paso (which boasts the largest number of Mexican Americans of any university in the United States), showed that more than 50 percent of entering freshmen considered academically deficient had Spanish surnames. This suggests that their high school standing and/or entering test scores were not equal to those of incoming Anglo students. In spite of this apparent handicap, there was only a 15 percent differential in academic achievement between Spanish surnames and Anglos from the freshman to the senior year. The students with Spanish surnames who survived the first two years had academic records equal to, or superior to that of Anglo students.

Uhlenberg's (1972) penetrating comparison of Mexican American and Japanese American demographic patterns shows that low educational and socioeconomic achievement is related to early marriage, early childbearing, and large families. A pattern of late marriage, delayed childbearing, and smaller families among the Japanese Americans (and a very few middle-class Mexican Americans) enabled this group to give their children a better opportunity for higher education. Adams and Meidam (1968:238) have also accented the relationship between family size and income and educational achievement.

There is a great need for a comprehensive, long-range study of the enrollment and attrition rates of Mexican Americans in colleges. Some variables to be considered are the type of institution entered, high school background, family structure and size, parental or peer-group influences, income and social class, counseling available, work-study funds, scholarship grants, and minority student attitudes toward ethnic identity and educational aspirations.

SOCIAL FACTORS AFFECTING MEXICAN AMERICAN EDUCATION

Although higher education is generally necessary in order to pursue careers at the higher socioeconomic level, the seeds for ultimate success or failure are sown in grammar and secondary school. The individual pupil is subject to group pressures that cause him to want to do well. These are his reference groups and the student uses them to reinforce his attitudes toward educational attainment. Most important of the various reference groups influencing a student's attitudes are his family, his peer group, and the school functionaries. The Coleman report summarized the results of comprehensive investigations into the educational experience of Mexican American children throughout the nation, citing these factors, in the following order, as most important to higher educational attainment:

family background, teacher's characteristics, and social composition of the student body or peer group. Of less importance for higher educational attainment were the school facilities, curricula, and staff. Using this list as a guide we will discuss family and peer influences and then the impact of teacher and school on the success of the Mexican American in education.

From the period of the Mexican Revolution in 1910 until well after World War II, the overwhelming majority of Mexican American families in the United States were lower class. The family structure of this social stratum was parent-centered and authoritarian, dedicated to group survival rather than to competitive individualism and personal development of educational skills among its members. The parents had limited education and the constant economic pressures of acquiring the necessities of life demanded that children begin to work for the good of the family as early as possible. The orientation of middle-class Mexican American families was quite different; they *did* stress education for their children. But this class accounted for such a small proportion of the total Mexican American population that the system of parental domination in the lower class was mistakenly thought to be an ethnic value.

Parental domination is considered a major element in the development of individualism and personal competitiveness, the qualities so necessary for success in middle-class educational institutions. The conclusions of research by McClelland are illustrative of many similar studies by social scientists:

> The data . . . strongly support the hypothesis that achievement motives develop in cultures and in families where there is an emphasis on the independent development of the individual. In contrast, low achievement motivation is associated with families in which the child is more dependent on his parents and subordinate in importance to them [1953:328].

The relationship implied between parental domination and educational achievement is really spurious, however, inasmuch as the social-class position and value orientation of the parents would be equally as crucial to the motivation level of the child as the degree of domination exercised by them. Middle-class parents, either Mexican American or Anglo, who find educational experiences a positive asset for upward mobility will teach their children to accept and effectively utilize these skills within an achievement syndrome. Hence, the crucial issue for Mexican American families is not whether parental domination still exists, but rather what value orientation is held by the parents and relayed to the child.

In discussing the role of parental influence on the child's performance in school, Rosen (1959) distinguishes between the *type of training orientation* received in the home and the *amount of encouragement* supplied by parents to offspring. Though Rosen has been justly criticized for the application of his findings to specific ethnic groups (such as Italians), the concept itself has merit. However, it must be applied not as a total cultural attribute to all Mexican Americans, but selectively to those segments stressing the specific orientations outlined as determined by specific investigation. Two orientations that lead to success, according to Rosen, are *achievement training* and *independence training*. In achievement training, the parents impose standards of excellence upon tasks assigned to their children and simultaneously communicate their evaluation of the child's competence and their expectations for his eventual high achievement. In independence training, the parents indicate to the child the desirability of self-reliance while granting him relative autonomy in selected decision-making situations. Thus early in life he is given both freedom of action and responsibility for the success or failure of his ventures, thereby preparing him for later years when parental guidance will no longer be available. These two orientations outlined by Rosen are designed to teach children to do things well and to use their own personal initiative in finding solutions to these problems. They represent essentially middle-class values, however, and will not be stressed in lower-class families. Children with such training will be more self-confident in Anglo middle-class schools, which emphasize the development of problem-solving capabilities and individual resourcefulness. Children devoid of such skills will be relatively disadvantaged initially and, barring direct supervision and compensatory training, will not fully recover from their handicap throughout the remainder of their education.

Students do well in school when parental attitudes are positive toward education per se as well as toward specific educational achievements by their children. A student's own evaluation of his personal abilities and potential comes from what he perceives his parents think of him. Whereas Heller (1966: 39) reports that many of the Mexican American children studied from California complained that they lacked encouragement from their parents, a very extensive study of El Paso high school students reflects quite the opposite situation and directly questions the universality of parental nonsupport of education among Mexican Americans (without considering the socioeconomic position of the parent).

> It is rather significant that there appears to be little difference between Mexican-American families and other families with respect to the amount of emphasis on education that the child experiences in his home. This finding is in contradistinction to the traditional notion that parents of Mexican-American children place little emphasis on formal education [Anderson and Johnson, 1968:14].

Mexican American migrant parents are at the bottom of the socioeconomic structure. Although they may want their children to finish school, over one-third of all migrant children are considered "retarded" by the second grade, and three-quarters by the ninth grade.

A tangential factor is the physical and social milieu of the home itself. Typically, a Mexican American family in the barrio lives at near subsistence level. Nearly half of the Mexican American youth in five southwestern states are living in households with more than 1.5 persons per room, in contrast to less than one-tenth of all Anglo children in the Southwest who live in similar circumstances. Thus the household density factor becomes a major consideration in evaluating educational potential. In large families, older children must work long hours to help provide additional income for the family. Superimposed on physical fatigues are nutritional imbalances, lack of medical assistance, vision or hearing problems not recognized, and the lack of study facilities, adequate privacy, lighting, or resource materials to do large amounts of assigned homework. The aforementioned study of more than 3,000 Mexican American students in El Paso junior and senior high schools demonstrated that more than half of these students desired to do well in their schoolwork, but many had no place to study at home. Forty percent of these 3,000 students were working outside the home, and most of the others were engaged in household duties such as caring for younger siblings or helping with household chores while both parents worked outside the home.

The problems of "poverty culture" go beyond mere lack of money. Situational factors affect the slum dweller, preventing him from accurately perceiving his situation and thus trying to improve it. Therefore, upon gaining some knowledge of how to manipulate and control his destiny, he can neutralize many economic obstacles. However, this presupposes that there are available demonstrable successes from the ethnic group to reinforce the reality that his destiny can be altered by personal initiative.

The role of peer-group influences in the educational process is an important factor to be considered in understanding educational achievements. The peer-group orientation of younger Mexican Americans is an extreme departure from the traditional stereotype of Mexican American youth dominated by an authoritarian family structure. Although parents are initially the most important reference group, and parental training has been shown to have a major impact on attitudes and skills used for educational advancement, peer-group pressure is a major factor in explaining the educational behavior of Mexican American youth, especially males (TenHouten et al., 1971). A study among Mexican American youth in a barrio of San Antonio suggests that there is a shift of reference group from family to peer during the junior high school years. Barrio youths see the desirable aspects of dropping out of school and becoming financially independent. The youth who stays in school is still dependent upon adults (parents for support and school teacher for behavior standards), whereas the dropout who gets a job and becomes economically self-sufficient acquires a degree of autonomy and maturity measured by an ability to play adult roles (Farris and Brymer, 1965).

In a comprehensive study of El Paso high school students, it was found that the Mexican American's evaluation of himself in relationship to his peers is the most significant factor in predicting achievement levels in selected school subjects. Another study in the same community, comparing intergenerational, core ethnic values and educational aspirations, found a general disparity between parents' and sons' values and aspirations. However, there existed an unusually close agreement on priority ranking of values between the young male respondents and their peers. The shift of reference from family to peer groups that Mexican American youth normally experience during the junior high school years, and their comparatively early interest in the opposite sex are major factors causing pre–high school dropouts.

Most educational programs designed to reduce school dropout rates among Mexican American youth concentrate their efforts on the school structure, the student's personal skills, and parental influences. At that stage, little attention is directed toward the major source of motivation and values, the peer group. Even when the influence of youth culture is recognized by school officials, all students in a given grade or class are considered as a closed reference system, whereas in reality the group of recent school dropouts may be the peer group from which a student wishes to gain approval.

EDUCATIONAL ASPIRATIONS OF MEXICAN AMERICAN STUDENTS

The Coleman report suggested as one of its major findings that Mexican American children throughout the nation strongly desire to stay in school and be good students. Although they plan to go to college less commonly than do Anglos, they hold high occupational aspirations. Mexican American teenagers studied in southern California, East Lansing, and El Paso revealed similar high educational aspirations. Borup and Elliott's

(1969) study of older Mexican American college students in Texas found that their aspirations were higher than those of their fellow Anglo students. Yet, many other social scientists question whether these aspirations are in any way related to behavior motivation when they are "reality tested."

An intensive study of Mexican American youth in south Texas revealed that they had higher aspirations than either Anglo or Negro youth, but were far less certain of realistically attaining their goals than was the Anglo group (Kuvlesky et al., 1971). It might well be as Heller suggests, "that the school socializes the Mexican American boy in mobility values but fails to socialize him in mobility-inducing behavior." Or perhaps, as claimed by Mexican American critics of the Anglo Establishment, the barriers within the present system cannot be surmounted by members of this ethnic minority, regardless of the level of personal motivation.

Social and psychological factors related to the self-image of the Mexican American have been studied to determine their role in educational success. Cooper (1972), focusing on high school seniors representing four ethnic groups in fourteen New Mexico and two Texas high schools, found that Chicano and black students had the highest self-assessment scores, whereas Anglo and Indian students were lowest in this regard.

DeBlassie and Healy (1970) found that Spanish American youth seemed to be highly accepting of themselves as they were at the time. Compared with Negro and Anglo adolescents they had the lowest self-criticism scores and were the most accepting of the self they perceived. Anglos were the lowest in accepting the self they perceived, reflecting no doubt the constant pressure of middle-class success standards. It is apparent from these data that a positive self-image is not synonymous with confidence in the ability to change one's destiny. The latter is partially a function of acceptance by the larger society and equality of opportunity. Though the Mexican American student has high aspirations and is given high expectations for superior rating within his reference group, he is realistic enough to know that an equal chance may not be given him by the larger society. In the El Paso secondary school research project, students voiced these fears as follows:

Probably one of the most significant findings that has so far emerged from this study is the discovery that Mexican American children may have less confidence in their ability to successfully fulfill the expectations of their parents and the school than their contemporaries despite the high educational expectations of the child and his parents [Anderson and Johnson, 1968:16].

Córdova's (1969) research with Mexican American elementary school pupils demonstrated that their alienation from the larger social system was not due to a lack of motivation or desire for achievement but rather to a lack of realistic involvement in the larger society. The minority students felt that the material taught in school was irrelevant to their real problems in the barrio. The structural barriers that lead to exclusion of minority members from full experience in American social institutions is a key to the difficulties of both minority- and majority-group identity.

If a social system is defective in role casting, it becomes like a play in which most of the actors are dissatisfied with their parts; or, worse, extras standing around with no parts at all. If a social system is inadequate in feedback and symbolization, it cannot give individuals an adequate sense of meaning—of others, or of themselves [Klapp, 1969:14].

It is crucial for the future of Anglo society that the ethnic minorities are allowed to participate in the "play." Otherwise these groups will put all their efforts into creating their own society and, as a last resort, they may attempt to disrupt or destroy the society from which they have traditionally been excluded.

SCHOOL ADMINISTRATION AND MEXICAN AMERICAN STUDENTS

In large urban centers and in rural areas of the Southwest, Mexican Americans reside principally in highly segregated neighborhoods, or barrios. Within these enclaves the dominant cohesive element is the informal pattern of visiting cliques, friendship loyalties, and kinship relationships. These residents do not react well to the impersonalism of bureaucracy or to associations generally, and their previous experience with law enforcement, community agencies, government programs, and schools has been unsatisfying and often painful.

School boards are comprised of successful businessmen and members of established families who represent dominant middle-class interests and norms. Since education, more than any other institution besides the family, is concerned with formal socialization and transmittal of societal values from one generation to another, those who control the schools are likely to be those who seek to maintain the status quo. Conspicuously absent from representation on these boards, as well as from top administrative positions, are Spanish-surname Americans. Therefore, school policies rarely reflect the needs and wants of this disenfranchised minority groups.

In structures such as school boards, Anglo models of behavior are always preferred, and these are constantly displayed as the *only* respectable success models. Ethnic students do not conform to these nor do they resemble them, and hence, they are often considered deviant by the local school officials and may well be handled as such. At least three techniques are used by middle-class school administrators to "reduce the pressure" on ineffective but traditional teaching procedures and antiquated curricula. These are segregated districting, class "tracking," and special remedial classrooms.

Segregated districting is accomplished by manipulating school district boundaries to correspond with segregated residential areas. This allows school administrators to handle the problem as a unit. Although segregated districting to separate Mexican American from Anglo students has been outlawed in the Southwest, current legal battles show that it is still practiced. In California, in the 1946 case of *Westminister School District v. Mendez et al.*, separate Mexican schools were outlawed. In Texas, the 1948 decision in *Delgado v. Bastrop Independent School District* banned separate Mexican American facilities in that state. Yet, more than two decades later, in the case of *United States v. State of Texas*, neighboring school districts in Del Rio, operating under de facto segregation, were ordered to integrate. California school boards were advised by the decision of *Crawford v. Board of Education of the City of Los Angeles* that they could not knowingly plan and build schools to perpetuate Chicano and black segregation.

Even these legal directives, designed to aid minority groups and give them better access to quality education, promote segregation as they attack it. The case of *Cisneros v. Corpus Christi Independent School District* established Mexican Americans as an identifiable ethnic minority, subject to discriminatory policies and thus protected by the 1954 *Brown v. Topeka* decisions involving the abolishment of segregation. Then, in a thoroughly inconsistent move, a circuit court in Houston *(Ross v. Eckels)* declared that Mexican Americans are part of the "larger Caucasian majority" and allowed twenty-seven of their schools to be paired with black schools to achieve integration along racial lines.

An interesting turn of events can be seen in the rapidly changing attitude toward segregated schooling. Once a tool of the Anglo majority to maintain their educational superiority, segregation is now being advocated by Chicano barrio leaders as the only way to preserve the ethnic culture of the barrio. These local ethnic leaders resist integration of Mexican American and Anglo students because of the danger of Anglicizing the minority group. Another interesting consequence of complete ethnic integration in schools was reported in an intensive investigation of students and school dropouts in Waco, Texas. Within the triethnic milieu studied, integration resulted in a more favorable self-concept and higher educational achievement for Mexican American pupils while producing a lower achievement level among Anglo students. This raises the following moral question: Does the maximization of Anglo student achievement justify the continuance of an educational practice that minimizes the achievement potential of the ethnic minorities? Can a social institution be allowed to persist when its existence depends upon the destruction of human dignity in a disenfranchised minority? And would the side effects of implementing rigid national guidelines be more destructive in the long run than local multiethnic commissions with adequate minority representation and direct participation in school planning?

The second technique used by school functionaries in handling the problem of Mexican American pupils is the "track" system. In theory this is a means of limiting the range of student interests to allow the teacher to standardize his presentation. In practice it places a "grade ceiling" of "average performance or lower" on the pupils in the "slow tracks," regardless of individual performance. When a student is placed in a "slow track" because of a language barrier or a low score on an I.Q. test, this activates the "self-fulfilling prophecy" of failure. Language fluency and I.Q. scores are a measure of the cultural values built into the testing instrument and not the ability to learn (Garcia, 1972). Jensen's work (1961) in evaluating I.Q. tests that discriminate between fast and slow learners found that although they were moderately accurate for Anglo American students, they were inadequate for predicting performance by Mexican American students. Performance varied with I.Q. for Anglos, but it was constant for the Mexican American group irrespective of I.Q. scores. Hence, the ethnic students often would be placed in lower tracks on the basis of their I.Q. scores, even when these scores did not reflect their true performance potential. Tracks are often cover-ups for discrimination. The student may really be placed in the slower tracks on the basis of his skin color, or Spanish surname, or detectable SLAAC (Spanish Language Ability and Accent Coefficient), which has already isolated him within the school and determined what the school will expect from him (Arciniega, 1971b:6). The content curriculum of a "Mexican room" can be diluted so that students will be promoted from one grade to another regardless of performance, as is alleged to be the practice in some southwestern schools. A recent study of a midwestern high school documented the use of track placement, allegedly based on educational potential, as a cover for discriminatory practices.

Socio-economic and racial background had an effect on

which track a student took, quite apart from either his achievement in junior high or his ability as measured by I.Q. scores [Schafer et al., 1970:40].

A study of Mexican Americans in Milwaukee comparing the track method with a random placement system showed that when ethnic families were given complete residential and social mobility, they performed equally as well in school as Anglos. In the integrated school situation, the constant interaction with Anglo students allows the Mexican Americans to develop and polish those skills that are rewarded by middle-class–oriented teachers (Matthiasson, 1968:104).

The third technique used by middle-class school administrators to facilitate handling Mexican American pupils is the remedial classroom. Students are labeled under the following categories: special education, educable mentally retarded (EMR), or culturally handicapped.

With the support of HEW's Office of Civil Rights, a number of legal suits has been filed to end the practice of placing minority children in EMR (Educable Mentally Retarded) classes because of language differences. In California, the case of *Diana v. California State Board of Education* was settled out of court when the state agreed to accept bilingual and bicultural testing standards for EMR placement. In May 1971, the California legislature extended the procedures for EMR placement, requiring parental approval prior to the placement of any student. Moreover, all school districts must provide specific guidelines, including requirements for teachers assigned to EMR programs. Two other suits in southern California and one in Boston (affecting Spanish-speaking Puerto Ricans) seek damages for the incorrect assignment of Spanish-speaking and black students to EMR classes. The pressure has become so intense in Boston that no Spanish-speaking or black pupils are currently being assigned to EMR classes. Hopefully, procedures can be worked out to separate true EMR pupils from those with the potential for normal development in school but with language handicaps and administrative techniques that cause Mexican American children to be segregated and then neglected replaced.

CLASSROOM MANAGEMENT AND
MEXICAN AMERICAN EDUCATION

A classroom atmosphere, in addition to being affected by language differences and considerations of administration and student motivation, is affected by ethnic ratios, curricula, and pedagogical methods employed by teaching personnel. In 1968 only 2.1 percent of all white students were in classrooms in which they were in the minority; whereas, among Mexican American students, only 45.3 percent attended schools in which their ethnic group was dominant, leaving more than 50 percent of them in the minority in the classroom. If the teacher is a member of the dominant ethnic group, additional tensions are felt by the minority student that hamper his learning experience. But present solutions are seldom successful: a sudden policy change to reduce the stigma or an abrupt realignment of minority students to put them in the majority destroys the existing pattern of social interaction and creates far-reaching repercussions for both minority- and dominant-group students.

Present educational curricula in the United States have been developed under the direction of middle-class legislators, administrators, and educators. Reinforced by textbook materials that reflect the ethnocentric view of these key decision makers, standardized primary, secondary, and collegiate materials have become self-perpetuating even in an era of dynamic change. All states exalt their own images through required civics, history, and government courses that, throughout the Southwest, generally deny the cultural contributions of ethnic groups other than the more recently arrived Anglos. One of the principal objectives of the justifiably angry Chicanos has been to revamp school curriculum to include heroes and events with which they can relate and to present developments in the Southwest with more objectivity. Though their zealous efforts have reflected strong ethnic biases, they have forced educators to take a new look at the educational system—teacher training, classroom procedures, and curriculum content—and to become more aware of their own self-delusions and stereotypes.

It is obvious that most teachers today have learned only superficially about Mexican Americans and are not prepared to handle these minority students within their classroom. Córdova (1969) observed that when expectations set forth by the teacher were not met by the Mexican American students, the increased force applied by the teacher to gain compliance resulted in insecurity and frustration on the part of the student, which then precipitated an increased indignation on the part of the teacher. Thus a self-defeating, negative spiral of insecurity feeding on insecurity was set in motion.

Ramirez (1969) claimed that in a schoolroom atmosphere where interpersonal relations are stressed and Mexican American students are made to feel a personal concern for them on the part of the teacher, student performance will be higher than in the more impersonal milieu. A project designed to test the impact of such personalized, individual attention was carried out in an experimental and a control classroom, both of which contained Anglo and Mexican American students. At the conclusion, no significant difference between the experimental group and the control group was observed. At the beginning, in the middle, and at the end of the experiment, the Anglo students in both experimental and control groups were more advanced than the Mexican Americans, and to the same degree (Johnson, 1962). It appears then that personal attention from the teacher is not enough to compensate for ethnic and class inequality. Córdova's study (1969) of Mexican American sixth graders found that student alienation came from school activities that were unrewarding and intrinsically meaningless in their life outside the schoolroom rather than from lack of personalization displayed by the teacher. Perhaps the personal approach stressed earlier, if it means a trained sensitivity to cultural variations and multilingual learning situations, is the key to teacher effectiveness with minority students.

Teachers in elementary and secondary schools supposedly are trained and qualified for immediate teaching duties after being certified according to state requirements. However, departments of teacher training and administration are not noted for requiring a broad multicultural, multilingual educational background. Usually, school personnel are graduated as classroom directors within racial, cultural, and class biases and with little or no sensitivity to or awareness of sociocultural differences. Thrust into a classroom situation with students who do not manifest the typical "American" attitudes they have been taught to expect, new teachers will perceive the students as deviant from both the larger cultural system and the teacher's personal value system. Thus the teacher repudiates those characteristics that are not common or comprehensible within his or her own cultural experience or training. Pressure is brought to modify some of these "foreign" characteristics, which can be changed by the student only at the peril of losing his group and self-identity. Immediate student resistance is expected.

Specific programs to complement the standard courses for elementary and secondary school teachers and administrators have been devised in recent years to assist school personnel to recognize their middle-class biases and ethnocentric viewpoints. These are a welcome departure from entrenched teaching procedures, which have undergone few changes since the lecture technique was employed in the Greek academies. One such program in California, called the Claremont Project, was initiated with the cooperative effort of anthropologists and educators. The change in teachers' perceptions of themselves and of ethnic minorities, and the change in students' reactions to unfamiliar cultural cues were no less than amazing. Some results of the Claremont Project are summarized as follows:

> The assignment of work projects was designed to introduce teachers to practical uses of anthropological methods. These carried teachers into the homes and streets where pupils lived. . . . Through this work teachers became aware of the varied cultural forces acting in them and the effect these had on their pupils. They were also able to see these same forces operating in their pupils. This made them more sensitive to conflicts which occur as a result of different expectations reinforced by culture [Ramirez, M., 1969:17–18].

Other similar programs have more recently been inaugurated in west Texas and throughout New Mexico. Administrators, teachers, librarians, and counselors were given cultural-awareness seminars and cross-cultural training by this author. In these programs, teachers and school functionaries were introduced to cultural concepts that will enable them to comprehend and recognize not only the distinct value orientations of their students but also their own; they have learned how the family and other societal institutions act to pass on ancestral beliefs. The minority-group participants possessed steretoypes that were just as rigid as—though different from—those of the Anglo participants. Whereas the Anglos were finally able to see from the perspective of the minority students, the latter group was desensitized to bureaucratic functions, which they had previously seen as existing for the sole purpose of causing ethnic discomfort.

Teachers who are not trained in cross-cultural skills operate much like the Vista volunteers and secondary staff in Indian villages, whom Murray and Rosalie Wax referred to as the "enemies of the people." Seeing the poverty conditions of a Mexican American barrio, it is not unusual for an Anglo teacher to feel guilty about these conditions and to react to this guilt by assuming a do-gooder or helper role. Thus, on the one hand, the ethnic minority is trying to divest itself of a dependency role, on the other, the untrained educator is forcing his assistance upon it in a vain effort to improve the deplorable conditions. Though often the poor Mexican American family receives such help gracefully, there is great loss of pride in such a transaction. The Mexican American would much rather be an active participant in the modification of his environment (though less technically qualified than the outside helper) than a spectator, who watches those who come to root out his culture of poverty and replace it with their superior ways.

The hiring of school counselors to supplement classroom teaching is regarded by some administrators as a positive aid to minority students. Educational psychologists warn of the built-in biases of middle-class professionals, usually Anglo Americans with little or no training in cross-cultural understanding and no sophistication in dealing with lower socioeconomic groups. The counseling interview itself contains underlying demands that are incongruous with the barrio experiences of lower-class Mexican Americans. Moreover, previous experience with majority professionals has created as under-lying distrust in the minority pupil. He expects the counselor to *do* something *for* him and, when he does not, perceives this as a lack of concern that further reifies the image of the formal school as a barrier rather than a helping friend. Mexican American students as a group are advised by counselors to seek vocational training in manual, craftlike occupations, often with little or no testing of individual abilities. Paul Morín, Julian Nava, and Armando Rodriguez are but three documented cases of Mexican Americans who received such counsel but ignored it, and instead went on to successful professional careers. These men, known for their writing and educational leadership, acquired college educations under the G. I. Bill and were able to demonstrate a high level of intellectual and lead-ership ability. It is fortunate that all Mexican Americans have not been diverted into manual labor by inadequately trained counselors, but it is tragic that so many Mexican Americans are never given direction to fulfill their true potential because of superficial labeling that guides the typical counselor.

Teachers and counselors set the emotional tone for criticism or acceptance of minority culture, of language differences, and of racial distinctions between students. Whether these factors are seen as personal threats or an exciting challenge that pro-vides the milieu for a multicultural interchange will depend largely upon the training in cultural values that has been given to the teacher. Whereas his or her past experience may be entirely within a middle-class framework, some scientific knowledge concerning the minority with whom he or she is working is a prime requisite for making the classroom become a place for minority students to develop rather than keeping it a courtroom in which minority cultures are on trial.

Notes

[1] *Palomilla* refers to a social institution in which small numbers of young Mexican American males have close social relationships on a specific street corner or at a given *cantina* (Rubel, 1966:101–118).

[2] "Americanism" has not always been synonymous with English-speaking ability. In the twelfth century, natives of this hemisphere spoke Mayan, Toltec, Eskimo, or the Aztec Nahautl, depending upon where they lived. In all probability Spanish Americans felt that English interlopers in the nineteenth century should have been required to speak Spanish, Walapai, Comanche, Papago, or Yaqui—or forced to "go back to where they came from." Even some colonists protested when the Congress selected English as the official language of the newly liberated country.

[3] As of March 1971, in the eight campuses in the University of California system, there was a total enrollment of 76,133 at the undergraduate level, of which only 2,462 (3.2 percent) students were Mexican American. Over 70 percent of these were enrolled primarily because of the Educational Opportunity Program (Rochin, 1972).

Chapter 6 ◉ Money Trees and Social Ladders: Income, Occupation, and Social Mobility

Most Mexican Americans residing in the southwestern United States have incomes that place them at poverty level (by federal government standards, below $3,000), with many at an even lower, "subsistence" level. Mexicans endured exploitation, despotism, pillage, and economic instability during the conquest and colonization periods in Mexico, so their experience with poverty did not commence with their arrival in the United States. Many of the early Mexican immigrants entered the United States in flight from economic upheavals in the Republic to the south and seeking a land of opportunity, where they, too, might share in the prosperity. Yet of all the many immigrant groups in the United States, Mexican Americans alone have been unable to achieve economic, social, and occupational mobility in subsequent generations. Why have Mexican Americans as a class failed to achieve success in the land of opportunity? This chapter will describe the evolution of economic conditions among Mexican Americans, and the present factors that promulgate poverty among them.

MEXICAN AMERICANS—A LEGACY OF POVERTY

After Cortéz found gold in the New World, the mining of precious metals became the basis of the Mexican economy. However, though the Indian peoples provided the labor, only their Iberian overseers and the Spanish crown shared in the wealth produced. When the mines flourished, the Spanish nobility was pleased, but when production was lower than expected, vengeance was meted out upon the hapless natives of New Granada.

Economic privation, among other things, engendered support for the Popular Revolt of 1810—a final demonstration of the smoldering discontent from the past. During that abortive revolution, mine owners and technicians were among the hated *gachupines* indiscriminately slaughtered. The mines, a symbol of servitude, were destroyed, and this, combined with the general pillaging of the countryside, led to an extended period of poverty among the masses following the quashing of the revolt.

The official policy of the Díaz regime was to continue to keep the masses in economic servitude. By around 1880 economic stability had been restored. Although the rule appeared to be one of benevolent despotism, it was economically beneficial only for the elite. Governmental leaders were convinced that

the mass of the population . . . could not and would not work efficiently. They were dirty and vicious and lazy; they had to be taught obedience; they would not save money because they were drunkards, and whatever wage they received was probably more than their productivity deserved. The only salvation for Mexico lay in attracting Catholic European immigrants whose industry and intelligence would transform the land [Cumberland, 1968:191].

Following the turn of the century, peasant discontent with the exploitive, militaristic government manifested itself in sporadic strikes and local uprisings. In 1905 the entire economic base of the nation was severely threatened when the move to convert from the silver to the gold standard caused a severe devaluation in Mexican currency. Subsequent inflation resulted from the printing of money to cover governmental costs. Sharp declines in metal production and in agriculture brought widespread suffering, and by the 1920s it was reported that "the poorer classes had less corn to grind and fewer tortillas to go around than at any time during the past two centuries." Capricious taxation brought additional burdens. Even the nationalization of mining did not seem to help the economy. Transportation and labor difficulties were only partially ameliorated by an expanding petroleum extraction industry, which was largely controlled by United States and British investments. It was no accident that the largest wave of Mexican immigrants to the United States occurred during this period.

The Great Depression of the 1930s affected the entire world. In the United States, American citizens were given job preference, and Mexicans found little incentive to go northward. In fact, a great reverse migration, back to Mexico, occurred among recent Mexican immigrants to the United States even though poverty was rampant in both countries. According to Cumberland, "The average peon ate measurably less in 1936 than in 1896, and the low real wage paid to him in 1910 would have looked magnificent in 1934."

It was not easy for Mexican Americans to survive in the United States during the Depression decade. In San Antonio, Texas, families barely survived by working as pecan shellers, work that on the average grossed a family $251 per year with all family members working. Individuals worked for $1.50 to $4.00 per week; although wages were depressed throughout the entire United States, this was scarcely a living wage. In order to survive, more than 88 percent of these families had to receive additional assistance from church and labor organizations. A 1938 study of 512 Mexican American families who worked as pecan shellers revealed that 40 percent had been doing such work for at least eight years and that four out of five paid an average rent of $4.49 per month. Others lived with relatives or stayed in abandoned shacks. The concern for their welfare expressed by the pecan company that employed them is reminiscent of the attitude of the Díaz regime in Mexico some decades earlier. Shapiro cites the following official's statement as an example:

If the shellers made 75 cents by three o'clock, they would go home for they did not care to make much money. They were satisfied to earn little, and besides, they had a nice warm place to work and could visit with their friends while they earned [1952:232].

In San Antonio Mexican Americans had little chance to move up the economic ladder during the prosperity period following World War II. The heavy concentration of Mexicans, Mexican Americans, and Negroes enhanced the chances for advancement among the smaller number of European immigrants, no doubt because of discriminatory practices based on skin color. Overt discrimination against recent Mexican immigrants was extended to include all peoples of Mexican extraction, regardless of citizenship or date of arrival. Even the direct descendants of the Mexican American patriots who had liberated Texas were treated as "undesirable foreigners." Mexican Americans, uneducated and numerically plentiful, remained heavily concentrated in unskilled occupations, at the lowest pay rates and doing the menial tasks required by the community. Similar circumstances were common in urban areas throughout the Southwest.

Among immigrant families who had settled in the rural areas of the lower valley in Texas, seasonal field labor was the prime source of income for the uneducated and untrained. It became a family pattern to join the migrant stream, from truck and cotton farms to beet and tomato fields and on to cherry and apple orchards. Mostly, migrants returned home for the winter months and prepared to begin the seasonal cycle all over again. Occasionally, a family made a temporary residence in one of the urban centers encountered in their travels. During the decade following this, the accelerated rate of settlements among migrant families in communities along the way such as Lubbock, Texas, Tacoma, Washington, and Traverse City, Michigan became apparent.

During World War II and the years following, Mexican Americans increasingly relocated in urban centers. There, some manual, clerical, or service-connected occupations were available. But Mexican Americans provided the large pool of unskilled labor that did the hard physical work in the Southwest at extremely low pay. Their dependency ratios were high, their education was limited, and both parents often had to work to support a large family. They were unskilled because of discriminatory practices in education, job-training programs, and business in general. This ethnic minority was trapped at the bottom of the economic ladder. Thus, although the Mexican migrant had raised his income and level of living upon coming to the United States, his children, no longer applying Mexican standards to their economic and social standing, despaired at the barriers between them and economic success. Though their physical labor helped to produce the wealth of the region, they were effectively excluded from participation in the prosperity. The stage was set for ethnic activism during the 1950s and 1960s to break through these exploitive work patterns and demand equality in the pursuit of economic goals.

MEXICAN AMERICANS AS A POVERTY CLASS

In all regions of the United States, Anglos in the poverty class outnumber the Spanish-speaking poor. However, in terms of population ratios, Spanish-speaking persons in the Southwest are twice to three times as heavily represented as Anglos in the poverty category. This economic disparity is closely related to state of residence and occupational profile (i.e., background training and type of employment for which one qualifies).

According to Mittlebach and Marshall (1966:21), California is the state with the lowest percentage of Mexican Americans in the poverty class (19.1 percent). Colorado (35.0 percent) and Arizona (31.8 percent) reflect a median ratio, and New Mexico, with 41.5 percent, follows closely. In Texas, 51.6 percent of the Mexican American families have annual incomes below $3,000, giving that state the dubious honor of having the largest number of ethnic poor. The low average income for Mexican Americans, which varies from $1,500 to $4,100 (see Table 6.1) results in part from the occupational skills they possess and the type of work they do.

In 1950 Spanish-surname persons in the five southwestern states were more heavily concentrated in lower-paying manual work categories compared with the larger Anglo population. For instance, the ratio of Anglos to Spanish-surname professionals is about four to one (10.8 percent to 2.7 percent), and in management it is again Anglos by a three to one margin (11.5

Table 6.1   *Median School Years and Median Income*
of Spanish-surname Males for Five Southwestern States,
by Residence and State: 1960

	Median Years of Education	Median Income
Urban	8.4	$3,197
Rural Nonfarm	6.9	1,871
Rural Farm	4.6	1,531
Arizona	8.3	$3,269
California	9.2	4,179
Colorado	8.7	3,283
New Mexico	8.8	3,170
Texas	6.7	2,297
Average	8.1	$2,804

SOURCE: U.S. Census, 1960, *Persons of Spanish Surname.*

percent to 4.4 percent). There are more white-collar Anglos than Spanish (21.9 percent to 10.0 percent), but in the manual occupations there is a larger percentage of Mexican Americans than Anglos, and in the poorly paid farm worker category the ratio of Anglos to Spanish-surnames is about one to six (Dotson, 1955:162). In sum, in urban areas only 17.6 percent of the Spanish surnames, compared with 44.2 percent of the Anglo working population, was employed in nonmanual-type occupations.

The statistics haven't changed much. By 1960, Fogel (1965: 20) reported that only 19 percent of Mexican American males in the urban Southwest were employed in nonmanual occupations, with few of these in a high-wage category. In contrast, 47 percent of Anglo males in the same region were in nonmanual categories, and more than half were in managerial and professional classifications. The Mexican American male labor force is highly concentrated in factory work, mining, construction work, farming, clerical work, and domestic service, while Mexican American females are employed mostly in domestic service, clerical work, or sales, with a few in such professions as nursing or teaching. Mexican American males have an unemployment rate of 8 percent compared with a 5 percent rate for Anglo males, and the rate for Mexican American females is 10 percent compared with a 5 percent rate for Anglo females. Only Negro males have a higher unemployment rate than Mexican Americans of either sex.

The low median income for both male and female Spanish-surname persons (Table 6.2) shows that urban dwellers have an annual income that is twice as high as rural nonfarm and farm families. A recent study of the agricultural labor force inn New York reveals that local or *intra*state Mexican American workers there had little or no unemployment, but the *inter*state migrant had a 6.8 percent rate of unemployment. Even more revealing was the fact that 64.3 percent of the interstate migrants were not actively seeking work through unemployment agencies.

In sum, the median incomes of both male and female Mexican Americans are low in comparison with other immigrant groups of the same generation and extremely low in comparison with Anglo incomes in the southwestern United States or in the United States as a whole, while their rate of unemployment is far above the national average.

EXTERNAL FACTORS ASSOCIATED WITH MEXICAN AMERICAN POVERTY

Controls exerted by the external society contribute to Mexican American poverty. Higher salary and positions of policy are allocated by powerful members of the majority society, and only a very limited number of Mexican Americans are ever considered for them, despite qualifications and training. Such traditional barriers directly affect the minority individual's personal motivation—he will anticipate unfavorable treatment even when his training and proficiency level is equal to competing Anglos. Thus, few characteristics that retard upward mobility among Mexican Americans are purely external or internal; most are a combination of both, and it is difficult to

Table 6.2 *Median Income of Spanish-surname Persons in Five Southwestern States, by Place of Birth, Parentage, and Sex (1960)*

NATIVITY CLASS	TOTAL	URBAN	RURAL NONFARM	RURAL FARM
Male				
All classes	$2,804	$3,197	$1,871	$1,531
Native of native parentage	2,689	3,071	1,890	1,495
First generation of foreign or mixed parentage	3,345	3,650	2,152	1,892
Second generation of Mexican or mixed Mexican parentage	3,114	3,426	1,971	1,648
Foreign born (total)	2,307	2,742	1,610	1,423
Foreign born (in Mexico)	2,158	2,602	1,564	1,374
Female				
All classes	$1,065	$1,202	$1,000*	$1,000*
Native of native parentage	1,036	1,194	1,000*	1,000*
First generation of foreign or mixed parentage	1,184	1,325	1,000*	1,000*
Second generation of Mexican or mixed Mexican parentage	1,095	1,243	1,000*	1,000*
Foreign born (total)	1,000*	1,033	1,000*	1,000*
Foreign born (in Mexico)	1,000*	1,000*	1,000*	1,000*

* Less than $1,000.
SOURCE: U.S. Census of Population, 1960, PC(2) 1B, Table 6.

arbitrarily blame either the minority for its own ineptitude or the larger society for its rigidity.

Within the larger society skin color has been held as the physical characteristic that triggers discrimination. Yet empirical evidence suggests that this factor, in isolation, cannot explain present Mexican American poverty levels. For instance, residents of Bakersfield, California, when asked about their attitudes regarding skin color indicated that Negroes were not accepted as readily as were lighter-skinned Mexicans (Pinkney, 1963:354, 358). Nevertheless, in that community the Mexicans were positioned castelike at the bottom of the occupational ladder, below Negroes. Other factors such as better mastery of English, success models from their own group, and organized political power had given blacks the advantage in the occupational world. Studies done in Racine and El Paso reveal similar conditions. The situation is summed as follows by Miller, in his survey of poverty in America:

> There are those families who are poor even though they do not seem to suffer from any of the obvious factors that cause poverty. Many of these families are Puerto Ricans and Mexicans, who are technically white but do not get the advantages that "whitehood" brings [1964:69].

Along the United States–Mexican border areas, native-born Mexican Americans are confused with Mexican nationals by members of the Anglo majority. Moreover, commuting Mexican workers are an employment threat to United States citizens of Mexican descent. So Mexican Americans resent not only Mexican nationals but also those Mexicans who commute to work in the United States, thereby undermining the local wage scale, reducing union effectiveness, and increasing the surplus of unskilled workers. In the twelve highly urbanized United States–Mexican sister-city complexes along the border, feelings of the Mexican American lower-class residents against "alien commuters" are perpetually hostile.

Smaller numbers of an ethnic or racial minority may be absorbed into an educational or political system without fear of minority group takeover felt in regions of higher ethnic concentrations. Although the function of numerical concentration is not clearly resolved, it, combined with other related factors, seems to affect the economic opportunities available to minority group members. A high ethnic concentration combined with Spanish usage, for example, appears to be a major barrier to economic success in the larger society. As Mexican American families use Spanish exclusively in the barrio, the children have little opportunity for learning English prior to entering school. This absence of English usage in the early years of life serves as a barrier to subsequent educational and economic achievements within the presently constituted monolingual school systems.

However, although language differences are usually cited as the obstacles to gaining higher-paying jobs and better incomes, a recent study of Cuban refugees (Portes, 1969) suggests that similarity of *class* behavior patterns and skills is more crucial to economic success and social acceptance in the United States than are language differences. During the early years of the Castro regime, the traditional upper-class leadership, considered to be a threat by the revolutionary movement, left Cuba, carrying with them an intense desire to return eventually and to resume their former elite positions in Cuban society. These refugees were highly educated and had occupational skills and middle-class attitudes similar to those of the Anglo middle class. Therefore, they were able to gain immediate acceptance, employment commensurate with their training, and the corresponding social and economic rewards. However, later waves of lower-class Cubans with less education and few marketable skills were unable to integrate themselves into the American economic and social system, and their adjustment problems are more akin to those experienced by the lower-class Mexican immigrants.

Another class-related factor affecting occupational placement is the ability to occupy higher corporate positions and effectively manipulate the impersonal relationships characteristic of bureaucratic structures. When Mexican American and Anglo employees in a large banking chain were investigated, the particularistic orientation of the Mexican American employees alienated them from those skills demanded of banking executives, and they did not exhibit a great deal of upward mobility within the corporate structure (Zurcher et al., 1965). This finding would be more meaningful if the effect of class background had been controlled when the comparisons between ethnic groups were made. Also, unless upper-echelon corporation personnel were receptive to Mexican Americans, the lack of occupational mobility could well have resulted from discriminatory practices.

Factors other than class behavior are also determinants of occupational opportunities for economic betterment. Provincial groups such as the Spanish Americans in New Mexico have a much higher average educational level than Mexican American border residents. Yet demographic data on those persons remaining in that region show that in spite of these educational attainments these New Mexicans have lower incomes than Spanish-surname groups in California, Arizona, and Colorado, and a similar disparity exists in comparisons between Mexican Americans as a whole and Anglos from the same region. A lack of industrial development in New Mexico limits the number of high-income positions available. With limited occupational choices available in the local village, high school graduates usually must relocate to find decent paying jobs. Often the urge to remain with their family in familiar surroundings is stronger than the urge to seek wealth and success. Moreover, it is difficult for Spanish American youth, reared in an atmosphere where resentment over Anglo takeover of ancestral lands and Anglo discrimination is rife, to set out in that very society expecting fair treatment or even a realistic hope for eventual success.

INTERNAL FACTORS ASSOCIATED WITH MEXICAN AMERICAN POVERTY

In this section we will seek to discover the sources of Mexican American economic failure in terms of the culture, institutions, and value motivations of the ethnic group itself, independent of barriers encountered in the larger social structure.

Cultural values as the source of poverty among Mexican

Americans have been emphasized by many social scientists. Madsen gives a representative explanation of their limited motivation in terms of value orientation.

> Acceptance and appreciation of things as they are constitute the primary values of *La Raza*. Because God, rather than man, is viewed as controlling events, the Latin lacks the future orientation of the Anglo and his passion for planning ahead [1964:17].

Kluckhohn and Strodtbeck (1961:207) describe rural Spanish Americans as being dependent and lacking in long-range planning ability by Anglo standards, but they do suggest that Spanish Americans are not lazy by their own standards. Mead (1955:164) goes so far as to say that they regard work as a necessity but have a strong aversion for it.

Such writers, by focusing mainly on one group of Mexican Americans—the poor—have had a hand in perpetuating a stereotype. The truth is that attitudes toward work differ markedly between lower- and middle-class Mexican Americans, just as they do in the Anglo population. Lower-class Mexican Americans surveyed by the UCLA Mexican-American Study Project averred that they have to work harder than other Americans (89.6 percent in San Antonio and 68.0 percent in Los Angeles). There were proportionately fewer middle-income Mexican Americans who felt that they had to work harder than other Americans (54.7 and 50.2 percent, respectively, from the above-named cities). The upper-income group in San Antonio reported only 44.1 percent who felt that they have to work harder than other Americans. Although these data may reveal an attitude toward work itself, the more plausible explanation is that class position dictates the amount of physical labor required for performance of work and that these responses accurately describe reality in the world of work today. Since Mexican Americans are heavily concentrated in manual-skill jobs, they are more frequently relegated duties involving hard physical labor, and their income is proportionately smaller than those of workers doing other types of jobs. All lower-class workers share this same fate, having to do more physical labor than middle- or upper-class persons. Therefore, many comparisons of work styles between Anglos and Mexican Americans might be comparisons of class work behavior and attitudes rather than ethnic reactions.

Work attitudes among lower-class Mexican American youth today do not reveal a picture of apathy and fatalism. In a funded social-action program in the barrio of South El Paso, it was discovered that the barrio youth touched by the program were very concerned with finding jobs and often initiated requests to projects workers for assistance in locating work. In a separate research project in "Smeltertown," a geographically isolated Mexican American enclave in El Paso, males, age twelve to twenty-one, were asked their priorities from a list of five salient values: popularity, obedience, self-mastery, helping others, and hard work. These youths selected hard work as the single most important value, whereas their parents, when asked the same question, rated obedience as most important and relegated hard work to a median position among the five. Observation of urban Mexican American youth indicates an awareness of their deprivation and a desire to share in the privileges of the system, though they are still lacking basic knowledge of the workings of the system in most cases.

Many poverty-related programs of federal, state, and local agencies fail because they are operated on the premise that Mexican Americans are lazy and incompetent and need to be motivated to achieve upward occupational mobility. Frequently, the problem for Mexican American youths is their lack of knowledge and experience to convert aspirations to realistic achievements and their difficulty in being accepted as equals in society. The stereotype of the Mexican American seeking a "welfare dole" is ridiculous and misleading but generally believed. This author's experience in disaster relief studies has been that Mexican American families, more than other ethnic groups, would subject their families to starvation rather than accept relief from persons they do not know or cannot trust. A rent subsidy study in a Texas metropolis indicated that Mexican Americans who did not receive rent subsidies were more satisfied with their housing arrangements than those who were currently receiving assistance. They considered the acceptance of the dole as an indication of their inability to provide for their families and thus a blow to their feelings of self-sufficiency. Much of their so-called dependent behavior may well have its genesis in the social structure and in demands made by the dominant Anglo functionaries rather than in the culture of Mexican Americans per se.

Whatever combination of external and internal factors contribute to the present low-income level among Mexican Americans in the Southwest, it is quite evident that the solution, like the problem, involves both segments of society. A change in attitudes and practices in both the minority and the dominant group will be the only effective means to abolish poverty among the Mexican American lower classes. As Julian Nava's comment illustrates, the present question is appropriately *"Quo Vadis* (where are you going) American?" whereas it once was "Where are you going Chicano?"

MEXICAN AMERICANS AND THE SOCIAL CLASS SYSTEM

In America, social class may be determined on the basis of different criteria. However, income and prestige accruing from one's occupation are the single most important factors in determining style of life, values, and social rank. Since Mexican Americans are heavily concentrated in areas of semiskilled and unskilled labor, most of them have lower median incomes and are classified as "lower class." Many behavior patterns manifested by members of this ethnic minority that are attributed to ethnic heritage may well be characteristic of all lower-class people, regardless of ethnic background.

Being part of the lower classes in the United States is nothing novel for most Mexican immigrants: they were part of the lower class in Mexico also. At one time, Mexico resembled a medieval society, with its own small, select elite of clergy, lords, knights, and royalty. Iturriaga (1951) describes the early rural Mexico class structure as 1 percent upper class, 2 percent middle class, and 97 percent *clase popular*, or lower class. Urban Mexico, he goes on, is 1 percent upper class, an expanded (compared with the rural structure) 23 percent middle class, and the always numerous 76 percent *clase popular*, which have come from the rural areas to relocate in the urban poverty enclaves. However, lest this larger middle class be taken to mean that class lines have been broken down during the period of rapid urbanization, a very recent research study in Monterrey (one of Mexico's most progressive metropolitan centers) verified the continued existence of a rigid class system.

Social rank is passed on from parents to children in Mexico. Even after relocating to a country with a more democratic social system, small enclaves such as the Canary Islanders of San Antonio seek to preserve their elite status among the Mexicans and Mexican Americans about them—as did the Manitos, the Spanish Americans of northern New Mexico. Mexican poverty-level families similarly bequeath their own low status to their offspring who emigrate to the United States. Inasmuch as nearly all United States immigrants from Mexico originate from *la clase popular*, it is not surprising that a lower-class Mexican life style would be mistaken as ethnic heritage. Again, because poverty establishes Mexican immigrants as lower class in Anglo society, class values become confused with ethnic characteristics.

MEXICAN AMERICAN IDENTITY— SOCIOECONOMIC CLASS OR ETHNICITY?

This confusion of social-class origins with ethnic values continues in subsequent generations. Casavantes (1969) describes this dilemma and attempts to more clearly separate Mexican American culture from the United States culture of poverty by segregating those structural-demographic attitudes that are distinctly Mexican American. First, separating out those class norms characteristic of peoples living within the "culture of poverty," be they Negro, Anglo, Oriental, Indian, or Mexican American, he lists the following Casavantes, 1969:Tables A and B): (1) life within the context of an extended family and particularistic involvements; (2) nonjoiners of voluntary association; (3) preference for the old and familiar reticent to negotiate with strangers; (4) a marked antiintellectual orientation with little admiration for school officials or for their own children's school activities; (5) machismo, or demonstrations of physical and sexual prowess among males; declining involvement in activities associated with the feminine role such as housework, tending babies, etc.; (6) an inability to postpone gratification—intensity of short-range goals and few provisions for long-range objectives; (7) the use of physical force in disciplining children and in settling adult disputes of various kinds; (8) extremely fatalistic world view, feelings of little control over nature, institutions, and other elements that have power over their destinies. Cavasantes then lists those characteristics that truly separate most Mexican Americans of any class from persons of other ethnic groups: (1) the majority are from Mexico or have parents or grandparents from Mexico; (2) they speak the Spanish language, and many have a distinguishable accent; (3) they belong to the Roman Catholic church and much of their personal behavior is guided by church dogma; (4) many have darker skin, dark hair, and brown eyes that distinguish them from white Anglos; (5) they live in the five southwestern states of the United States; (6) the average educational level is less than eight years of schooling for those over twenty-five; (7) between 30 and 40 percent of the families earn less than $3,000 per year; thus, they may be said to be living in the culture of poverty.[1] Whereas some characteristics ascribed to Mexican Americans in the latter list equally describe certain other minority peoples, such as Irish-American Catholics or American Indians, the point is made that Mexican Americans themselves must distinguish between their life style in the barrio and their real ethnic and cultural heritage. If this is done, their ethnic culture can be maintained as future generations ascend the socioeconomic ladder.

Some researchers have compared various ethnic and national groups in the poverty class to determine which were class and which were ethnic differences. Cohen and Hodges (1963) compared Anglos, Mexican Americans, and Negroes of the lower, blue-collar level and found no significant value differences among them. A study of values corresponding to upper-, middle-, and lower-class levels in Lima, Peru, and

Chicago, Illinois, indicated that at the poverty level similar values seemed to prevail over national differences. But with each step upward on the social-class ladder, cross-cultural value differences became more pronounced (Theresita, 1968). It is doubtful that this would be true for the elite classes. However, these data do question the contention of some radical Chicano groups that only lower-class Mexicans are continuing the "pure" Mexican way of life and that by elevating themselves to middle-class level they automatically become cultural traitors to their Mexican American heritage. It may be entirely possible that Mexican heritage will be preserved more by middle-class Mexican Americans than by those presently living in poverty.

Many middle-class agency workers, religious volunteers, school teachers, and public officials currently insist that Mexican Americans have the right to be proud of their heritage and then proceed to designate the "romanticized" traditions in which Mexicans should take pride. Meanwhile, the minority groups insist on the right to define Mexican heritage for themselves. This dilemma is not entirely resolved even by those of Mexican ancestry who are trying to separate the Mexican heritage from lower-class norms. For example, Ralph Guzman, a Mexican American scholar, has made the following exhortation:

> I feel that it helps to know what to be proud about. . . . If we are to help youngsters to be proud of their Hispanic/Mexican heritage, we are wisest in giving them specific elements about which they can be legitimately proud. . . . How can we ask our children to be proud of being terribly poor? Even if it could be said that some individuals feel proud of being from humble homes it could not be said that this arises out of the fact that they are Chicano. This would have to be an individual matter, not an ethnic one. Or, one could be proud to be from California or from Texas, but this again would not be tied to being Chicano. These two elements are independent of each other. But, *to speak Spanish well, to enjoy Mexican music and Mexican food, to periodically recall the customs and ways of life of Spain and of Mexico, these are truly Chicano* [Quoted in Casavantes, 1969:6].

A further consequence of mistaking lower-class cultural patterns for Mexican heritage occurs when aspiring barrio leaders became caught in the "crawfish syndrome,"[2] in which internal factionalism results in a continuous and rapid loss of ethnic leadership. Beneficial projects spearheaded by barrio leaders who have influence with community leaders can do much for conditions in need of change. Unfortunately, suspicion and factionalism often neutralize this source of external economic, political, and social support. Guzman continues:

Unless Mexican Americans *themselves* came to distinguish clearly between ethnicity and social class, a Mexican American youngster might well be ostracized by some peers when he tries to live the life of a middle-class Mexican-American. As matters stand now, far too often the feeling is that any Mexican American individual who tries to be middle class in his style of life is "not a true *Chicano* [Casavantes, 1969:7–8]."

At the present time much of the criticism by Chicanos of Anglo insensitivity to minority problems is directed against the middle-class Anglos' refusal to accept lower-class ethnic individuals unless they shed lower-class customs. This is not unlike the problem faced by the lower-class Anglo slum youth, who must decide whether to live within the world he knows and understands (but which contains few economic opportunities) or to risk an attempt at success *à la* middle-class life style (and with expanded economic potential goes a high possibility of failure).

The presence of a strong Mexican cultural tradition allows the Mexican American a familiar base of operations, complete with rules which he understands, and rewarding personal associations to which he is accustomed. When and if this traditional culture is placed off limits without his having mastered the new roles and standards within the American system, he is caught in the frustration of anomie—unable to retreat, and without the social skills to move ahead and compete in the newly joined U.S. society. Without the stabilizing background culture, a break with the past calls for desperate measures [Stoddard, 1970c:12–13].

When a Mexican American from the lower class seeks to adapt to middle-class ways, the personal strains and traumas of identity are lessened if agencies or individuals worthy of his trust are available to facilitate the transition. And if external agencies are to reach the people residing in lower-class neighborhoods, they must establish the same confidence and trust which was available to them from barrio patrons in former days.

Barrio leaders often interpose themselves between the ethnic residents and social agencies in an attempt to maintain the internal cohesion and stability of the lower-class barrio culture. Often, barrio norms are glorified as the only pure test of Chicano loyalty—a test in lower-class standing rather than in ethnic beliefs and practices—and middle-class Mexican Americans are cited as ethnic sellouts. Actually, the differences are mainly in class values rather than in ethnic loyalties.

MEXICAN AMERICANS AND UPWARD MOBILITY

Americans are proud of their country and the opportunities open to each citizen on the basis of hard work and ability. After Mexican Americans have done hard work for two or three generations without reaping the promised rewards, however, they feel a sense of "relative deprivation" in comparison with ethnic minorities from Western Europe or with Anglo Americans. Mexican Americans find it burdensome and difficult to feel pride in a heritage of poverty, unemployment, illiteracy, and social stigmas, which are the lot of the lowest socioeconomic levels in this country. Are the dreams of the first-generation Mexican Americans for an increasingly higher standard of living for their children realized in subsequent generations? The data say *not*. A higher income level occurs among the first generation of native-born Spanish-surname children, but income level is lower for both the immigrant generation and the succeeding generations of Mexican Americans. In other words, after the initial surge resulting from immigration, Mexican Americans show negative economic advancement.

For the immigrant from Mexico, lower-class conditions in the United States might still be considered an improvement over conditions in Mexico. Thus, using a former style of life as a criterion for comparison, immigrants may regard their present conditions as an economic improvement. However, in succeeding generations, native-born Mexican Americans will measure their income and class level by American standards and will generally be disappointed by their economic position. An intensive comparison of intergenerational mobility among Mexican Americans in Texas hypothesized that an index composed of educational attainment, employment, and income level would reveal the foreign-born at the lowest, those of mixed foreign-born parentage next, and those of native-born parentage highest. The findings of the study did not support this view:

> The foreign-born group is significantly below the other two. The prediction fails, however, in the ordering of the other two groups . . . either there is virtually no difference between them [native-born of foreign or mixed parents vs. native-born of native parents] or as in the case of income, the natives of mixed or foreign parentage are demonstrably superior to the natives of native parentage [Browning and McLemore, 1964:65].

A replication of this intergenerational analysis in California by Peñalosa and McDonagh (1966:503) produced similar results. But in both of these studies, even the mobility occurring within the first generation could well be a reflection of measurement bias that ascribes higher status to urban occupations than to rural ones.

The single positive element in this otherwise gloomy economic picture for the Mexican American minority is contained in Renner's (1969:11) examination of income and occupational prestige. From a detailed demographic analysis of 1960 Spanish-surname census data, she concludes that the income loss among subsequent Spanish-surname generations corresponds to their leaving better-paying "dirty work" for lower-paying "clean work" occupations; thus, a higher prestige level accompanies the lower median income. Other studies have confirmed that Mexican American youths genuinely aspire to higher positions than those held by their fathers. In fact, high school Latinos in a two-county area in the lower valley of Texas demonstrated a stronger intensity of aspirations than either Negro or Anglo youths from that same area.

Even so, the Mexican American's realistic appraisal of his chances for fulfilling these hopes showed an abnormally strong goal deflection, probably resulting from the dismal channels of educational and occupational mobility available to him (Kuvlesky et al., 1971). An attitude study conducted among freshmen students at Texas A & I showed that Mexican Americans ranked higher than their Anglo cohorts in occupational, social, and personal aspirations (Borup and Elliott, 1969).

All comparative studies attempting to measure aspiration and achievement must deal with the methodological pitfalls of standardized measurement and the inference of causal factors. The lower educational achievement of rural Mexican Americans has been erroneously equated with low aspirations, whereas in fact it could be related directly to a limited access to educational facilities. This has been complicated by the fact that educational attainment of Mexican Americans in rural areas is unduly influenced by the extremely low median level of education among farm males (see Tables 5.2 and 6.1).

High aspirations in Mexican Americans may produce undesirable results if no channels are available through which to implement them. When an increasing disparity is perceived between present circumstances and the levels to which they aspire, frustration, bitterness, and disappointment are the natural outcomes (Love, 1969). If their economic situation is a result of an inability to handle middle-class norms and procedures, the solution is a complete realignment of mobility channels, which are presently monopolized by Anglo Americans. But if it is in fact the result of a lack of middle-class skills, Mexican Americans must acquire the necessary skills to develop a positive self-image within the existing socioeconomic structure. Excessive moving about such as characterizes migrant seasonal labor must be avoided and the learning of English (without sacrificing an equal fluency in Spanish) is a prerequisite for educational training. In this society, English fluency is a requisite for obtaining increased rewards within the economic system. However, regardless of training or motivation of the minority group, without a corresponding change in discriminatory employment policies in the dominant society, future confrontations with the powers-that-be are inevitable.

Most Mexican American barrio dwellers grow up with a rather distorted idea of how the larger society functions. They are not experienced in the formal procedures of the courts and of government. They know little of civil service examinations or how to apply for community services or scholarship programs. When they are in junior high school they do not think about becoming a doctor and thus they do not plan to study high school biology and chemistry in preparation for a pre-med course in college. Upon graduating from high school, they may encounter the possibilities of a career in medicine, but at that stage it is difficult to gain acceptance to a college or university without the required high school subjects. They admit wanting to attend college, but they have very little idea of what a four-year college program entails.

Public social action programs tend to work *on* rather than *with* Mexican Americans to solve their economic needs. Quite often these programs have goals that are inconsistent with the real situation in the barrio. They are often designed to raise minority-group motivation levels, which only serves to create an even greater disparity between presently high aspirations and unattained goals. Future programs for minority-group betterment must shift their orientations to two vital areas. First, they must realize that local members of the minority group must be involved in the planning of the program, must participate in its initiation, and must provide criticism of the ongoing program if it is to be accepted by the target society. Second, the preparation of minority peoples for upward mobility will accomplish little other than frustration if advance planning has not concentrated on opening channels for future careers. Government can provide information and economic assistance, but it must be sensitive to the element of trust and the need for minority-group participation in the planning of the future. When programs for the betterment of the Mexican American minority are planned without any group participation, this implies that members have a limited capacity for action and destroys their personal initiative. The following is an excerpt from a poetic appeal by Abelardo Delgado, delivered in 1967 to a predominantly Anglo group attending a Mexican American Conference in San Antonio, where Delgado was a self-appointed, and uninvited, representative of the barrio.

> Hold conferences and fool each other; but for God's sake, do not hold them in the name of the Mexican-American unless [you] are going to give him a voice and make him a participant in solving his own problems and not hurt him any more than he is hurt already by giving him one more tranquilizer . . . a middle class we cannot reach, ashamed of being Mexicans and sure of not becoming Anglos. . . .
>
> I have no intention of letting you walk out of here satisfied . . . I close with the last remark in my own language. . . .
>
> *"Mas de nosotros somos imigrantes a esta nación, primera o tercera generación. Decidimos un país para mejorarnos, porque carecía de oportunidades; venimos a éste que profesa ser rico en oportunidades. Mis abuelos y yo no las hemos encontrado . . . Quizá . . . Mañana* [1967:137–138]."*

If we wait until *mañana* to rearrange our economic priorities, to allow more opportunities for Mexican Americans, *mañana* may be too late *for us all.*

---

* An English equivalent of Delgado's message is "Most of us are immigrants to this country, from first to third generation. We selected this nation in which we might better ourselves because it claims to be rich in opportunities and there was a lack of opportunity in our own country. My forefathers and I have not yet encountered these opportunities . . . perhaps . . . *mañana.*"

Notes

1 Although Casavantes discourages others from equating class with ethnicity, some of his items inadvertently perpetuate the stereo-

type that "Mexican American stands for poverty," which he vociferously attacks.

2 Two crayfish, when placed in a shallow bowl, will fight to prevent each other from leaving, each preferring to perish rather than allow the other a privilege it does not itself have. In like manner, intraethnic hostility and factionalism in determining "who represents us" causes internal power struggles as a barrio leader becomes more acceptable and influential in the larger society. Forced to perpetuate his lower-class values to maintain barrio support, he must at the same time emulate middle-class life styles to gain external approval and external resources to effectively assist in the barrio. Thus the barrio leader is trapped. (See Watson and Samora [1954] for a fuller explanation of the ethnic leadership dilemma.)

Chapter 7 ◉ From Conquest
to Confrontation:
Mexican American
Organizational Development

Contrary to popular belief, Mexican Americans have a history rich in organizational development. To give the student a more objective view of this, a time-frame model of five periods will be used here to emphasize the distinctive organizational thrust characteristic of each time period. These major time periods have been designated as follows: (1) the conquest and colonial period, extending from 1519 through the Popular Revolt of 1810 and up to the Mexican Revolution of 1910; (2) the period of cultural accommodation and stress on "100 percent Americanism," from the Mexican Revolution through World War I and the Great Depression and up to the years just preceding World War II; (3) the period of ethnic separation, from the beginnings of United States involvement in World War II through the Korean conflict and up to the early 1960s; (4) the period of ethnic autonomy and radicalism, beginning with isolated political and social protests in the early 1960s and culminating with the Chicano movements, which peaked in 1969; and (5) the period of strategic penetration, a shift from radicalism to a more precise and calculated use of existing institutional structures, which began in 1970 and is still emerging.[1]

Admittedly, each of these periods has more variation of organizational history within it than is evident from the name. However, the underlying philosophy characteristic of each era distinguishes it and reveals the salient value orientations of the Mexican American generations pertaining to each period and leading from an image of subordination to one of independence and autonomy.

THE CONQUEST AND COLONIAL PERIOD (1519–1909)

The conquest period was one of violence and military subjugation. Each new conqueror dominated the empire and forced his own social, religious, economic, and military institutions upon it.

From pre-Spanish codices written in Nahuatl, a Uto-Aztec language, we find that the organizational heritage from the Aztec empire era is anything but monolithic and dictatorial. Over the period from 300 to 1100 A.D. the cultural center was gradually shifted from the urban ceremonial site of Teotihuacán to the city of Tula. Their decendants, forced to abandon their city by the Chichimecs, went south and west into the fertile valleys of Mexico and founded city-states around the lakes in the present valley of Mexico. These became the cultural centers during the new historical era.

The Aztecs, who migrated into this valley in the middle of the thirteenth century, were a wandering and persecuted people who had been forced to establish their capital city on a small, barren island in Lake Texcoco. They were in bondage, paying tribute to the Tepanecs of Azcapotzalco, the powerful city on the lakeshore opposite their island. King Itzcoatl, with the aid of his brilliant advisor, Tlacaelel, threw off the oppressive yoke of the Tepanecs. He created a military aristocracy by granting titles of nobility to distinguished, successful soldiers and taking land expropriated from his subjugated enemies and dividing it among the new nobles, himself, and the traditional elders of the city. He then set about to destroy the records of his people and write a mythical version of their history, as they would have wished it. King Itzcoatl's aim was the creation of an empire-state. By using the religious practice of human sacrifice as an instrument of political terror and creating political and military alliances with Tlacopán, Tlaxcala, and other surrounding Nahuatl-speaking powers, he and his successors achieved a Confederation of Republics composed of a highly stratified class society (León-Portilla, 1960:8–12).

The Spaniards, who arrived in the sixteenth century, superimposed upon the subjugated indigenous peoples of Mexico the institutions of the Iberian peninsula. These were not unlike those of the Aztecs except for differences in politics and theology. Cumberland's comments on the weaknesses in the Aztec and Spanish empires (both of which proved to be less effective in actual operation than in theory) are insightful:

> Both Spanish and Aztecs created social and economic systems based upon false assumptions, and neither Spaniards nor Aztec could envisage a society with any underlying precept other than rigidly drawn and legally enforced class lines [1968:42].

The Spanish crown took measures to ensure that the indigenous, Nahua-speaking leaders were not educated or instructed in the Spanish language, which further weakened the administrative system of the Aztecs. Catholic monastic orders, which had begun to educate the Indian populations, were enjoined from continuing their efforts. Church doctrines, rituals, and leadership from the Iberian social hierarchy were reconstituted in the New World to bolster the Society of Castes (Mörner, 1967:44, 53ff.). As a result of the conquest and the spreading of Old World diseases, the Indian population was decimated, which caused the few white elites in power to become further entrenched. A conquest psychology prevailed, coloring the attitude of the Iberian elite toward both the pure-blood Indian groups and most of the Mestizos (who were by this time the numerical majority).

> The original assumptions that the native would not work for personal profit, that he was childlike and could not learn the skills necessary in a complex economic system, and that he could never achieve an intellectual sophistication equivalent to the European gave birth to the *encomienda*, the *repartimiento* and to debt peonage [Cumberland, 1968:83].

Long after the servitude of the *encomienda* and the *repartimiento* had officially ended, until the Mexican Revolution of 1910 and even afterward, the vast majority of Mexico's people were still in debt peonage. Following the revolution, efforts were still being made to force Indians to become loyal Mexicans by adopting Spanish and being educated in the classical Spanish tradition. Not until 1940 in Mexico was there a departure from the traditional conquest psychology to one that regarded the indigenous cultures as worthy of preserving (Aguirre Beltrán, 1953:48).

Following the colonial period in Mexico came the revolts, paving the way for independence. The leadership for the numerous uprisings and rebellions was drawn almost exclusively from factions of the elite who were out of power at the time, and from the educated local clerics. Thus, Creoles rebelled against the "pure-blood" peninsulars in their quest for equality in the New World, and local priests championed the needs of their parishioners against the stifling proclamations of the church. The principal revolts of the impoverished masses were engineered and directed by local clergy who had spontaneously assumed the roles of military command. Although the indigenous peoples were willing to support reform movements, they were dependent on traditional Spanish institutions and Spanish-trained leaders to provide them with unity and direction to articulate their goals.

SPANISH-AMERICAN ORGANIZATIONS Most Anglos perceive the colonial period as the beginning of southwestern history, whereas in reality much preceded it. During the early colonization period, the social hierarchy of the Society of Castes in Mexico had been transferred intact by colonizers to the northern frontier of New Spain near present day Santa Fe, New Mexico. Both the pure and hybrid descendants of the dominant families of the early Spanish society retained leadership in the New Mexico territory, even after the Society of Castes in Mexico had begun to deteriorate.

A great number of ethnic-dominated organizations developed in the Santa Fe region and continued to persist even in the face of a visible shift of power at the time of annexation from the old-core Spanish families to the newly settled Anglo administrators.

In northern New Mexico, following annexation to the United States, the associations that developed consisted largely of *confradias* (religious brotherhoods), auxiliaries to the Catholic clergy such as Our Lady of Light, the Poor Souls, the Blessed Sacrament, the Rosary, and the Third Order of Saint Francis (Gonzalez, 1969:87–93). Los Hermanos Penitentes, a religious order founded centuries earlier in Spain, was brought to Mexico first and then to New Mexico in 1828 when the Franciscan friars were expelled. The isolation of the Spanish Americans in northern New Mexico made them logical caretakers for the somewhat altered secret order, characterized until recent years by extreme religious ceremonial forms such as flagellation and even crucifixion (Burma, 1954:188–198).

Secular associations such as mutual aid societies, so evident among immigrant groups during the early colonial days, also were organized in New Mexico. Some, such as the Caballeros de Labor (1890), Sociedad Cervantes, Sociedad Española de Beneficiencia Mutua, and Fraternal Aid Union, were still operating as late as 1915. Officer, in his treatise on ethnic sodalities of New Mexico, mentions that one of the earliest non-religious associations in this area, which functioned as a burial society, was the Alianza Hispano-Americana, founded in 1894 (1964:53). Broom and Shevky (1952:155–157) point out that unlike other foreign immigrant groups, Mexican Americans and Spanish Americans did not shift their early mutual aid societies into formal organizational entities. They preferred instead to sustain them as an extension of the informal kinship system. Even the livestock-marketing associations and water-irrigation groups of northern New Mexico were more familial or communal than bureaucratic.

The basic power structure of northern New Mexico consisted of two economic systems. In the larger cattle- and sheep-ranching areas of southern and eastern New Mexico, the patrón-peon system, with the accompanying debt peonage so characteristic of the Mexican haciendas, was common. Some of the patrónes were descendants of the original Spanish nobility, some were lawyers, and some were laborers of Indian ancestry who, either through land manipulation, mining, or merchant trading, had achieved wealth and patrón standing.

Since wool and woven cloth had become profitable exports, sheep-grazing lands were sought to the east, but such efforts were blunted by the expansionist campaigns of Anglo cattlemen in Texas. In the resulting militant encounters, vigilante groups and extralegal organizations such as La Mano Negro (Black Hand) and Gorras Blancas (White Caps) were organized locally by Spanish Americans to protect livestock and property when legal means were no longer available. With the acquisition of grazing lands halted, the maintenance of large herds produced overgrazing, which resulted in economic disaster for many small herdsmen. These herdsmen then became either marginal farmers or migratory laborers. Moreover, the reduction in grazing lands through legal land seizures indirectly cut down the spinning and weaving production as well.

The other economic system in northern New Mexico centered in the village, with its patrón. Prior to 1880 many of these villages had a communal ownership, land-grant society. However, when the U.S. Surveyor's Office refused, except in rare cases, to accept this type of land ownership as legal, the individual villagers had either to take out a claim in their own name, or legal means would be used by outsiders to acquire the land title. In some cases these land grants were transferred by the federal government to the public domain for subsequent disposal through homesteading, through outright sale, or through designation as national parks and forests. In the villages that survived this ordeal, independent, self-sufficient landowners chose one of their number to represent them as spokesman. This respected man became a broker between the villagers and the larger community. This pattern of local bossism has persisted to this very day, and currently forms the basis for political patronage and power in many of these northern New Mexican villages.

Following the formal annexation of the southwest territory during the mid-nineteenth century, recently arrived Western Europeans were so preoccupied with marauding Indian bands that they had little time to devote to the settlement of that region or the exploitation of its natural resources. Around

1887, with the appearance of railroads in the region, it was discovered that immense fortunes could be acquired through legal exploitation and seizure of the lands then under the stewardship of indigenous land-grant owners.

The rapid spread of Anglo associations, based upon legal provisions unknown in New Mexico in the past, spelled disaster for the Spanish American familistic-type organizations. Power and wealth shifted to the new Anglo elite; the Spanish American elite who could not adapt to the new order lost power and the deteriorating social structure based upon the old Society of Castes disappeared.

MEXICAN AMERICAN ORGANIZATIONS Elsewhere in the Southwest, Mexicans immigrated singly or in fragmented families. At the time of the annexation of the Southwest territory, these immigrants were located mainly along the border or close to former administrative/military outposts of the Republic such as San Antonio. During the late nineteenth and early twentieth centuries, when the great bulk of Mexican immigration occurred, immigrant families were absorbed into the lower strata of quasi-estate societies in California, Arizona, and Texas. The only difference between their position in the United States at this time and their position in former societies was that their rulers were Anglo rather than Mexican, Spanish, French, or Aztec.

Moore (1970b) analyzes three forms of Mexican American subordination that emerged in various regions of the Southwest. A pattern of "traditional colonialism," characterized by the superordinate-subordinate relationship between Spanish American elite and other Spanish Americans, prevailed in northern New Mexico. An "economic colonialism" emerged in California and portions of Arizona, based upon wealth. Those who lacked economic resources were subjugated by those who controlled enterprise, and although most of the economic barons were Anglos, this was not exclusively so, as evidenced by the Californios, who until the end of the nineteenth century owned large ranching operations in these areas (Pitt, 1970). Mexican American workers, subordinated under economic colonialism in California and Arizona, became dissatisfied periodically and would strike or protest in the mines, in the fields, or on the range. But these protests were poorly organized and faded rapidly. In general, worker rebellions were dealt with severely, and few organized efforts at changing economic, social, and political conditions emerged during the colonization period.

In Texas, the castelike social structure based on "conflict colonialism" prevailed. Mexican Americans were viewed as a conquered people, devoid of any rights in the superior Anglo hierarchy. Any attempts at political involvement by Mexican Americans were perceived as "slave uprisings" and a threat to the Anglo power monopoly, to be met with intimidation or direct force. These methods effectively protected the dominant society from any direct political challenge by resident Mexican Americans, and in time a tradition of total withdrawal from former political, social, and economic participation developed among Mexican Americans in that state. Thus for nearly a century, ethnic labor was used to literally "carve out the Southwest" but because of the economic systems that simply dismissed minority rights, Mexican Americans were denied the economic and social advantages of the dominant Anglo society. This was particularly the case in Texas.

THE PERIOD OF CULTURAL ACCOMMODATION (1910–1941)

During the cultural accommodation era there was a general acceptance by the minority group of the dominant society's values and institutions. Since this demanded no modification of Anglo life styles and implicitly sustained the superiority of Anglo culture to all others, relations between Anglos and Mexican Americans were relatively smooth. This Anglo-conformity pattern of acculturation stresses the learning of English and includes the downgrading of non-English languages and peoples. Racial and cultural superiority of Caucasian or Nordic types (whites) is further enforced by legislative support in the form of immigration quotas that favor Anglo-dominated countries.

Popular writings in Western Europe espousing the doctrine

that Nordic peoples were genetically and culturally superior stimulated various nationalistic movements in the United States at the turn of the century. American authors and statesmen took up the cause to "preserve Americanism"—not least among them President Theodore Roosevelt. With the advent of World War I, Western European immigrant groups suddenly became "enemies of our country," and there was a concerted drive among Italian, Romanian, German, and other immigrant groups to become "100 percent Americans." While Mexican Americans were not primarily involved in this nationalist problem brought on by World War I, as "foreigners" they were categorically caught up in the Americanism and patriotism moves. During this period Germany wooed Mexico as an ally, promising to give back to Mexico all of the southwestern lands that were formerly hers when victory was won. But Mexico was not interested and still remained loyal and friendly toward the United States.

Two organizational patterns are apparent for Mexican Americans residing in the border region during this era. On the one hand, there was a middle-class emphasis on the need to assimilate into American culture; on the other, a reaction from the working class characterized by intermittent local revolts and brought on by unbearable economic exploitation in mining, railroading, agriculture, and ranching. First, let us briefly concentrate on middle-class organizational efforts. In order for persons of Mexican descent to achieve American identity, organizations were founded that stressed the responsibility of Mexican Americans to obtain American citizenship and develop loyalty to their new country. Among them were the Order of the Sons of America (San Antonio, 1921), the Order of Knights of America, and the League of Latin American Citizens. In February 1929, these merged to form the League of United Latin American Citizens (LULAC), which stressed conformity to traditional American values, trained members and poorer immigrants for citizenship, and presented a solid front against vigilante groups such as the Ku Klux Klan. In the same spirit of loyalty, women's clubs emphasizing cultural and intellectual activities, such as the Pan American Round Table and the Good Neighbor Clubs, were founded. Such organizations were evidence of the desire on the part of Mexican Americans to acculturate to Anglo values even though they were operating under an apartheid system that shut them out. This social schizophrenia prevailed until after World War II.

Among the working class, many successful and some not so successful attempts at protest, strikes, and work demands occurred before the turn of the century and again before the mid-1930s. Field laborers, railway workers, pecan shellers, coal miners, and sheepherders made their complaints known. Moore (1970a:23–24) documents local uprisings of sugar-beet workers, miners, and railway workers in California and Arizona from 1903 to 1920, most of them led by local, charismatic leaders who lacked long-range organizational skill and who were usually removed by local authorities "owned" by the companies. Long-range leadership skills were mainly developed through external organizations such as labor unions. Under the supervision of the Confederación Regional Obrera Mexicana (CROM), an industrial union associated with the AFL, the Confederación de Uniones Obreras Mexicana was formed in 1928, with about twenty locals, but it lost strength sharply during the Depression. Also in 1928, the Unión Trabajadores del Valle Imperial, with support from CROM, struck during the cantelope harvest. The strike was immediately broken by local law enforcement officers representing the grower's interests, who arrested the leader and harrassed the strikers. Results from such protest movements were often oppressive rather than ameliorative. In 1934 in New Mexico, the Liga Obrera de Habla Español (League of Spanish-speaking Workers) was formed by miners and farm laborers, but an effective smear campaign accusing it of being Communist caused it to lose support and wither. Working-class protests were generally ineffectual in influencing legislation or long-range policies. Their impact was immediate and, according to local circumstances, brought either immediate relief or repression.

During the Depression years, the alien Mexican national in the United States may well have received better protection than the United States citizen of Mexican ancestry (Taylor, 1931: 238), although both Mexican Americans and Mexican nationals in the migrant stream were, though tolerated, exploited.

These conditions are graphically portrayed in the federal report on migratory labor in American agriculture, which notes the relationship of the migrant to local community organization and the absence of organized protection for the migrants:

> Migratory farm laborers move restlessly over the face of the land, but they neither belong to the land nor does the land belong to them. They pass through community after community, but they neither claim the community as home nor does the community claim them. . . . The migratory workers engage in a common occupation but their cohesion is scarcely greater than that of pebbles on the seashore. Each harvest collects and regroups them. *They live under a common condition, but create no technique for meeting common problems.* The public acknowledges the existence of migrants, yet declines to accept them as full members of the community. As crops ripen, farmers anxiously await their coming; as the harvest closes, the community, with equal anxiety, awaits their going [U.S. Government Printing Office, 1951, italics added].

In the isolated Spanish American villages of northern New Mexico, there was change perceptible during the later nineteenth and early twentieth centuries. Institutional changes of that period occurred mostly as a result of the catastrophic shifts in the economies of these villages, resulting from the loss of grazing lands and subsequent decisions on the part of villagers to give up livestock (mostly sheep) and either go into farming or join the migrant stream.

The events leading up to the involvement of the United States in World War II brought a general economic prosperity to urban centers, which attracted large numbers of Mexican Americans. Wartime military service, defense project employment, and jobs in reopened mines resulted in the out-migration of from 50 to 70 percent of the males ages fifteen through sixty-five from New Mexican villages (Loomis, 1942). Sizable numbers of these Spanish Americans, along with Mexican Americans from small rural hamlets along the Rio Grande and from the middle-sized cities and the larger metropolitan areas such as Los Angeles, were suddenly in direct contact with affluent urban society in the United States.

· During World War II many Mexican Americans became aware of their former subordinate status and exploited energies. Following the end of the war, they and their children spearheaded the organizational impetus to disengage from institutions fostering Anglicization and committed themselves to a doctrine of cultural pluralism, within which their ethnic identity, as determined by themselves, could be realized.

THE PERIOD OF
ETHNIC SEPARATION (1942–1962)

This period, arbitrarily designated as beginning during World War II, was concomitant with geographic shifts in the Mexican American population as well as in the American population as a whole. The economic surge during the early war years drew large numbers of rural residents to the cities, many of them Mexican American families. Likewise, many Mexican Americans were inducted into the military service and experienced there treatment and privileges based on military rank and not on race, which had been their experience back home. They tasted the fruits of first-class citizenship and, as veterans returning to their homes and neighborhoods, they were unwilling to relinquish this for the second-class status that had formerly been accorded them. They had a new feeling of self-identity—of self-confidence and autonomy. No longer were they convinced that all things Anglo were superior and that all things Mexican were inferior. They were beginning to distinguish between the goals of acculturation (acquisition of economic goods and services and improved technology), which they desired very much, and assimilation (social amalgamation, ethnic identity loss, and full acceptance of Anglo institutions), which they would decline when it was offered on the basis that Mexican Americans were inherently inferior. As one observer describes it:

Among them, a general questioning of Anglo American values and institutions is taking place. They tend to reject the facile acculturation and assimilation of their parents. They feel that their parents paid too high a price in feelings of self-hatred and group rejection for the social and economic positions that were gained [Knowlton, 1967a:3].

Mexican Americans returned home from military service to find that the class barriers were still there, excluding them from social clubs and professional associations, fraternal orders, and veterans clubs. The occupational opportunities of those not enrolled in colleges under the GI bill were limited mostly to manual labor. Resentment became directed not only at the institutions of the dominant Anglo society that considered Mexican Americans inferior but also at those ethnic organizations (such as LULAC) that had been founded upon the principle of "being a good American" Anglo-style.

A legal case involving blatant discrimination against Mexican Americans in south Texas provided fertile ground for open defiance of existing ethnic barriers. Mexican American veterans of World War II began applying through local veteran chapters in their hometowns for membership in national veterans' organizations. They were either denied membership or placed in "separate Mexican units" sponsored by the Anglo organization. The final indignity occurred when a Mexican American war hero from Corpus Christi was denied burial in the local military cemetery because of ethnic background. With their war records as evidence of their "patriotism" and their pride in their ethnic lineage as a rallying point, veterans organized the American GI Forum of the U.S. and carried their fight for equal rights (in this case, military burial rights) through federal channels—and won! Under the leadership of Hector García (who later became the first Mexican American to serve as a member of the National Commission on Civil Rights), their organization spread rapidly, boasting of more than 160 units throughout Texas and New Mexico in the first year. Later, it spread to California and other states. Just two decades later, its national president, Vicente T. Ximenes, was appointed first director of the federal Inter-Agency Committee on Mexican American Affairs, the highest U.S. government appointment held by a Mexican American up to that time.

Following World War II, Ignacio Lopez, publisher of a bilingual newspaper in Pomona, was instrumental in developing the Unity Leagues in California. These were organized for the purposes of getting ethnic voters registered, unifying the campaigns of Mexican American candidates for local boards of education or local governmental offices, and supporting candidates who would be friendly to Mexican Americans. As a result of organized action on the part of the leagues, the separation of Mexican American and Anglo students in elementary and secondary schools was declared illegal in California in 1946 and in Texas in 1948. Further activity won Mexican Americans a more permanent ethnic voice in local government and education. A committee formed to support Edward Roybal as a candidate for the city council of Los Angeles was unsuccessful in 1947, but succeeded two years later. The politicization of Mexican Americans had begun in earnest.

The polarization that arose during this period produced many cultural "marginals" who could not find identity either as Americans or as separatists. These individuals would provide future support for the more radical movements to come forth a decade later.

The middle-class leadership of the Sol Alinsky–inspired Community Service Organization (CSO) promoted voter registration drives. Finding that many Mexican Americans had not completed requirements for citizenship, the CSO began language and citizenship classes, fought for better old-age pensions for resident noncitizens, and assisted with problems of laws and customs (Briegel, 1970:168–169). In 1952 its director, Fred Ross, was introduced to a man who became a CSO worker and eventually chairman of various locals in the San Joaquin Valley—César Chavez, one of the most successful leaders of La Causa during the 1960s.

The grass-roots organizations of the American GI Forum and the unity leagues did not meet the additional needs of Mexican American veterans who had acquired a college education through the GI bill. These veterans required an organization with more professional sophistication, and so in 1954 in Los Angeles they formed their own Council of Mexican-American Affairs (CMAA). The CMAA lacked internal unity, however, and even during its formation the fight over standards for determining representation produced deep internal divisions not totally perceptible to admiring Anglos on the outside. Although the organization was doomed to failure, the issues and thrust of its education committee became the basis for the formation of the Association of Mexican-American Educators in 1965. This association has offered support, ethnic success models, and direction for grass-roots political goals, and has been instrumental in assisting Chicano student groups to compile El Plan de Santa Barbara, the model plan for Chicano studies.

Earlier ethnic organizations had supported political activity only indirectly. The first overt effort to establish an ethnic organization specifically designed for public political participation came in 1958, with the formation of the Mexican American Political Association (MAPA) in California and two identical organizations, the Political Association of Spanish-speaking Organizations (PASO) in Texas and the American Coordinating Council on Political Education (ACCPE) in Arizona. These were originally planned as a single powerful regional organization to cover the entire Southwest, but the heads of the three groups could not agree on a common name.[2] The Texas Mexicans did not want the Mexican American label and the California group did not like the euphemistic "Spanish-speaking" term. They also differed in that MAPA demanded purely Mexican support, whereas PASO sought external alliances with middle-class Anglos, labor unions, and black pressure groups to achieve its political objectives. MAPA had been quite unsuccessful at the polls during the 1960 campaign, but it did benefit from the Viva Kennedy clubs. In the 1962 election in California it endorsed one national congressman and two state representatives who were subsequently elected, after which internal dissension debilitated its efforts in that state for a time. At the same time both MAPA and PASO had been concentrating their energies in the lower valley of Texas, in communities where Mexican Americans were clearly in the majority, An election in Crystal City, Texas, drew national attention and became a springboard for national recognition of the success of ethnic politicization. One side effect of this was to bring many latent ethnic prejudices to the fore in Crystal City, when the power was no longer wielded by the white minority.

In Crystal City PASO leadership had withheld active support from the Mexican American slate, whereas MAPA had actively endorsed it and supported its efforts. Local PASO affiliates in Texas, indignant about the lack of support, declared their independence from the national office of PASO. On election day, Texas Rangers had been sent into Crystal City by the governor of Texas, ostensibly to maintain order during a highly emotional conformation but actually because local politicians requested them, to discourage a heavy ethnic voter turnout. Documented charges and countercharges of harassment and brutality are available, but the significant point is that *for the first time in Texas, Mexican Americans had been victorious in selecting their own ethnic candidates through the prescribed political process.* Subsequent victories by the MAPA-sponsored candidate José Angel Gutierrez, running on the Raza Unida party ticket, gained political impetus from Crystal City and nearby communities, which served as a spearhead for political power in the lower valley of Texas and eventually a political rallying point for Mexican Americans throughout the Southwest. After decades of political disenfranchisement and intimidation, at last there was evidence that a united Mexican American voting bloc could be victorious. This symbolic victory would spark an increased activism in the decade-and-a-half to follow.

Meanwhile in Arizona, ACCPE had acquired 2,500 dues-paying members by 1962, as well as chapters in all but two of Arizona's fourteen counties (Martinez, J., 1966:54–55). However, its visible accomplishments have had little impact beyond local political races, and this impact has been more inferred from voting patterns than from organizational power.

During the same period an occurrence in California was also having an important effect on increasing political power of ethnically based organizations. César Chavez had redirected much of the CSO's organization to labor inequities, and had, by 1960, received direct support from the AFL-CIO in the form of funds to expand its activities to include legal aid for persons seeking old-age benefits or public welfare. Moreover, it had become an active force in dealing with police brutality and harassment toward Mexican Americans in southern California. In 1961 the somewhat conservative CSO board refused to support direct farm labor demands, and Chavez left the organization to become personally involved in the farm labor movement in his wife's hometown of Delano, California (Matthiessen, 1969).

Though an increasing sense of ethnic pride was no doubt a positive factor in the militancy of the post–World War II era, yet another dynamic process was in operation, too. In the past, the Mexican Americans had accepted the mandate of being "good losers" as a means of making Anglos feel superior—but at the expense of their own self-image. However, as Mexican Americans developed more pride in their own race and more sophistication about Anglos and their society, they became aware that sometimes the game is played with rigged rules. Thus, though they separated themselves from the exploitive situation during the era of Ethnic Separatism, they went further and sought to change the rules of the game in the era following.

THE PERIOD OF ETHNIC AUTONOMY AND RADICALISM (1963–1969)

The period from 1950 through the early 1960s was marked by political and social activism in the United States. Early movements focused on the plight of blacks but soon spread to other minorities. In order to increase sensitivity among whites over the plight of blacks, student activists and black leaders began organizing public protests. Peace marches, acts of civil disobedience, and mass confrontations followed. Among Mexican Americans this general awakening found its voice in the Chicano movement, which gained publicity through the activities of its militant wing.

Sena Rivera correctly argues that there has not been a single Chicano movement but rather many specific collective actions within the overall movement—which is not unlike the pattern of any other emergent social force. He distinguishes three dominant ideologies in Chicanismo which range, politically speaking, from far Left anarchists to far Right reactionaries. The small group to the Left are those proclaiming cultural nationalism, the vast majority in the middle represent the various degrees of cultural pluralism, and the small number on the Right call for total acculturation to Anglo society. Rivera further contends that, ironically, the concessions wrung from the dominant society are obtained through the sacrifices by the militant group, but generally benefit the Right, which has remained personally secure by "playing it safe" and not getting involved. There is some evidence to support the contrary notion that the Right is strategically rather than militantly involved and gets the rewards because, in terms of organizational prowess, they deserve them.

Even within the militant segment of the Chicano movement there are such varied bases for organization as to make coordination of these several thrusts a major dilemma. Merkx's and Greigo's (1971) analysis of ethnic activism in northern New Mexico delineates three distinct groups that represent completely different social, economic, and educational goals, all of which are identified with Spanish American activism. First, there is the Alianza, led by the dynamic Reies Tijernia and consisting of a loose coalition of rural Spanish Americans and Indians seeking to regain their ancestral lands. Second, there is the Brown Berets, manned by urban ghetto youth seeking to improve their present status through radical methods. And third, there is the United Mexican-American Students (UMAS), a student organization that seeks through organizational expertise and educational attainment to establish a power position for articulating its ethnic demands upon the existing social system. Though all these factions support one another, the diversity of objectives, methods, and priorities diffuses their efforts and creates functional divisions within the overall Chicano movement.

Inasmuch as the major organizational thrust of this period of ethnic autonomy and radicalism was spearheaded by the militant Left of the Chicano movement, our analysis concentrates mainly on this. But it should be remembered that reform-ideology groups, not characterized by radical confrontation techniques, are also active in the Chicano movement, devising and initiating strategies that they expect to use in providing relief for Mexican Americans.

A case study of political action in Crystal City, Texas, over a six-year period (1963–1969) clearly illustrates the shift in emphasis from separatism to militant radicalism. Crystal City, a community of 10,000, is 75 percent Mexican American and 25 percent Anglo. During 1962 a poll tax drive was initiated to vote out of office the local Anglo elite, which had never been opposed politically because threats of economic retaliation had kept Mexican Americans from registering to vote. Since a large number of the Mexican Americans in 1963 were union members and by recent court ruling were protected against losing their jobs for political reasons, support of the union organization served as a protective shield for them when they became politically active. The Mexican American candidates for the five council positions were all working-class persons. As potential victory for these candidates became apparent, support from PASO was extended. The stage was set and the Mexican Americans won by a landslide. Unfortunately, the victors, unseasoned in political life, made errors and became factionalized. They lost the subsequent 1965 election but later gained back some strength in 1967 and 1971.

Though much had been accomplished by separatist political action through the established political processes, a more militant element provided the leadership for more rapid social change within the local school system. When administrative appeals for stamping out discrimination in the high school had been exhausted, local Chicano leadership organized student confrontations. The reactionary stance of the school board activated Mexican parents to rally behind their high school children. The high school students, with support from parents and from the Mexican American Youth Organization (MAYO), were victorious. Direct confrontation, in causing traditional Anglo power figures to overreact, welded together the Mexican American community. From then on, school boycotts and similar strategies brought about institutional changes that even the Anglo administrators confessed *would not have happened without the extreme means adopted.*

Although the origins of Chicanismo as an identifiably organized national movement are somewhat obscure, Cuellar (1970) suggests that the formalized organization grew out of a group of conferences held at Loyola University in Los Angeles in the summer of 1966. These conferences, originally conceived by the Catholic sponsors as a middle-class Mexican student gathering, attracted others who were *not* students and not middle class but who nevertheless were drawn to the ideology of La Causa. Another suggestion is that it began less universally with the nativistic religious leadership of Reies Tijerina in northern New Mexico and subsequently became articulated through the civil rights movements in the United States.

Chicanismo was heavily influenced in its direction and tactics by strong, charismatic leaders who early emerged as symbols of ethnic pride and courage. Three men stand out among these many fine Chicano leaders: Reies Lopez Tijerina in New Mexico, César Chavez in California, and Rudolfo "Corky" Gonzales in Colorado.[3] A short biography of each one will reveal his contribution to the overall Chicano movement.

Many writers have given detailed histories of Reis Lopez Tijerina, the fiery leader of the Alianza land-grant heirs in northern New Mexico, and the famous episode of the "courthouse raid." Particularly notable is the account by Gardner (1970), which begins with the birth of this dynamic Chicano leader, on September 21, 1926, on a heap of cotton sacks in a one-room adobe shack outside Falls City, Texas. His mother, a very religious woman, instilled a strong religious fervor into Tijerina in his early years. His father, a share-cropper, kept alive in young Reies the memories of land seizures by Anglos and gringo atrocities. Even in his preschool years, Reies was a visionary child. Later, at age fifteen, when his family was working in Michigan, he received a copy of the New Testament and read it from cover to cover. At nineteen he entered a Texas bible school run by the Assembly of God. Although he was later expelled, he nevertheless began his ministry in California and was eventually given his license. Tijerina experienced wild, cyclical moods in which he would leave his family and seek isolation for the purpose of purifying himself; twice, at a sudden urge, he gave away his automobile and clothing and lived for a time as a penniless recluse. He was a persuasive orator.

With seventeen families who followed him as their spiritual head, he established the Valley of Peace in the Arizona desert. In 1958 he arrived in northern New Mexico to assist the forty-year-old Abiquiu Corporation of Tierra Amarilla in its fight for restoration of land-grant rights. Tijerina believed that God and justice were on his side. His presence there was felt to be the fulfillment of the legend that had promised of strangers from the East who would afflict Mexican Americans and a leader from the people who would arise and make the conquerors return to their homes crying (Gonzalez, 1969:99).

In January 1960, Tijerina went to Mexico to study firsthand the land-grant documents. There he found an old volume, authorized in 1570 by Philip II of Spain, which was a recompilation of basic policies pertaining to Spanish colonial laws, including land grants. Using this as his law, and in defiance of the existing laws of New Mexico, he was ready to pursue his fight for reparations to land grantees, who had lost more than 1 million acres of land.

On February 2, 1963, he formed the Alianza de Las Mercedes and boldly proclaimed in power and emotional oratory that the millennium was near. Although violence would come first, members of the Alianza would enter this period living on their own land. Thus, Tijerina's early thrust was as the leader of a nativistic religious movement, whereas his subsequent explosive appearance as a national Chicano hero was part of a civil rights movement.

The Alianza held its second convention in August 1964, still unnoticed by the mass media. During this year Felix Martinez, a leader in the movement, visited Watts and Delano. He returned with the evaluation that the slow, peaceful methods of César Chavez did not cause the larger society to become aware of the problem as rapidly and forcefully as had the riot in Watts, adding that "revolution speeds up evolution." The Alianza was rapidly gaining membership, mostly converts brought in by the persuasive and charismatic Tijerina, or "King Tiger" as he was affectionately known. The membership declared a preference for the old Spanish laws that had formerly governed their land-grant acreages. Individual cases of arson, fence cutting, and even stealing stock were common. Stolen items were returned only upon payment of fees equal to those charged by the Forest Service for grazing privileges on U.S. government lands. On July 4, 1966, the Alianza faithful marched from Albuquerque to Santa Fe to present their grievances to the governor. While momentarily exciting, the march produced no results. Then in its fourth convention in September, Alianza established an independent city-state called the Pueblo de San Joaquin del Rio de Chama, free from the governments of New Mexico and the United States. It proclaimed a dedicated Anglo lawyer, a trusted friend of the Alianza leaders, as Don Barney Cuarto Cesar (King Emperor of All the Indies). Immediately following, documents were issued with the proclamation that the U.S. Forest Service had been notified of the intent of the true owners to claim the land that was theirs by right of inheritance. Subsequently, decrees were issued demanding that present illegal owners vacate the lands or face expulsion. In October 1966, hoping by a majestic assumption of authority to settle the question of land-grant ownership without forty years of litigation, Tijerina and his followers headed a one-hundred-car motorcade into the Echo Amphitheatre, a camping area within the Carson National Forest and on the ground included within the original Tierra Amarilla land grant. Little occurred that was not of a festive nature. One week later, fifty vehicles came to challenge the U.S. Forest Service, the caretakers of the land. Rangers without weapons had been posted to collect the dollar entrance fee and to note license plate numbers of those refusing to pay. However, anxious Alianza leaders "arrested" the rangers and, under the laws governing their independent city-state of San Joaquin del Rio de Chama, proceeded to hold a trial and convict them of trespass. Their trucks were impounded, but later the prisoners were released along with their vehicles. Tijerina and his followers camped over the weekend, building fires and securing local game for food. By Wednesday, when federal and forestry officers moved in, there were only a few persons left including José Salazar, the *alcalde* of the newly proclaimed independent city-state. Why had there been such a flagrant violation of federal laws? Tijerina answered:

Publicity. This time the whole world will know of our dilemma. This time they will have to charge us with tres-

> passing and take us to court, and then we will see whose
> land it really is (Gardner, 1970:132).

Instead, however, the federal officials carefully prepared charges against five Alianza leaders for putting government property to personal use, assaulting forest rangers, and preventing them from carrying out their duties. There were no charges for trespassing this time or any subsequent time during Tijerina's campaign.

In April 1967, Tijerina met with Governor Cargo, and soon a political war between the Republican governor and the Democratic district attorney Alfonso Sanchez emerged, the latter demanding immediate, forceful restraints against the Alianza and the governor seeking to take a more moderate approach. As illegal incidents of arson and fence cutting and public proclamations of defiance increased, the district attorney obtained a court order to force Tijerina to reveal his entire Alianza membership. Public charges had been made that the act of trying to take land by force was similar to Castro's tactics in Cuba and that Tijerina was therefore a Communist. The John Birch Society issued similar statements and printed massive numbers of handouts linking Tijerina to Communism. Upon receiving the order in May 1967 to make his membership and contribution lists known, Tijerina disbanded the Alianza and resigned as president, thus protecting his loyal supporters from embarrassment (for example, a twelve dollar contribution by the governor's wife was made public later). The setting for the courthouse raid was being prepared.

In June, Tijerina made plans to have a meeting of land claimants in Coyote, New Mexico, and to reorganize the Alianza as a Confederation of Free City-States. There, they would plan new strategy for getting their land claims into court. Tensions grew. Unknown persons began fires in land-grant forests, more fences were destroyed, and both landowners and claimants began to carry firearms. Alfonso Sanchez sought to have a restraining order served on Tijerina, banning the proposed June third meeting in Coyote, but he could not locate him. Finally, Sanchez made a statement on radio that all persons who intended to go to Coyote for the meeting would be arrested, and he arbitrarily banned all public assemblies. In the ensuing arrests of members arriving in automobiles, organizational records, along with firearms and ammunition, were seized. Sanchez again publicly branded Tijerina as a Communist because he had tried to secure the land by force. The Alianza leadership was pushed to the wall. The former occupation of National Forest Lands episode had not gotten their claims into a court of law, and this arbitrary abridgement of the right to peaceful assembly was one more sign of the right of the authorities to violate constitutional laws when it furthered their purpose. Radical methods were the only means left to preserve their honor and their cause. Alfonso Sanchez became their target, and they planned to make a citizen's arrest of him and charge him with unlawful conduct in exceeding the authority of his office. It was voted at Canjilon by the Alianza faithful to go to the Rio Arriba courthouse on the morrow. There would be no shooting, but arms would be carried for defense. It did not work out as planned.

On June 5, twenty men in five vehicles quietly eased into Rio Arriba, and, surprising the law officers, judges, and workers inside the courthouse, looked for Sanchez (who was not there). Pent-up emotions burst forth and counter-offensives brought quick retaliation on each side. A state patrolman named Sais was shot in the lung and the jailer Eulogio Salazar wounded in the head as he dove through a window to escape (Salazar was mysteriously murdered months later). Another deputy was knocked unconscious. Alianza members Baltazar Martinez and seventy-two-year-old Baltazar Apodaca took two hostages, deputy sheriff Pete Jaramillo and a reporter, Larry Calloway, back to Canjilon in a pickup truck, but they later escaped. The manhunt began! Five hundred men, including the National Guard (with two tanks), the FBI, state police, New Mexico Mounted Patrol, and the Apache Police, combed the mountains for the courthouse raiders. Alianza members' houses were searched and left in a shambles. A detachment of troops was dispatched to the Alianza camp at Canjilon, whose thirty-nine men, women, and children were held hostage at the points of bayonets for twenty-four hours in inclement weather. By Wednesday morning, eleven of the twenty raiders were in custody, and on Saturday morning, the last of the leaders, "King Tiger" Tijerina, was apprehended.

With the national spotlight on him and his followers, Tijerina had become increasingly more radical because he felt that only by combining his fight with other Chicano leaders and those of other disenfranchised ethnic groups could a solid and powerful front force the land issue to be resolved. Released on bond after a few weeks, he became ever more militant in his demands for a court hearing on the land grants. He proclaimed that the leader of the "Santa Fe Ring," Thomas L. Catron, was really a Jew. In a further foray into racism, he announced the "New Breed" of people—the Indo Spanish—who would rule over their own lands in the northern New Mexico area. Corky Gonzales and Bert Corona praised his bravado. Tijerina superficially embraced the Black Power movement with Martin Luther King, James Forman, Floyd McKissick, Ron Karenga, and Ralph Featherstone, as well as the cause of Tomas Banyacya of the Hopi nation and other Indian leaders. The power base gained through pledges of mutual support was more than neutralized by antiblack feelings among his "New Breed" followers. This strategy had backfired and his support declined markedly. Later, in 1967, he became a codirector of the Poor People's March on Washington, hoping that the plight of his people would be given a national spotlight. Instead the problem of land-grant ownership was shoved to the background, and the salient issues of his criminal charges and court battles, backlash from the Poor People's March, and growing lack of financial and moral support spelled a further decline in Tijerina's mass appeal. In 1958 he had attempted to revive his power base through political means, but the chance was now gone. Because of his court record his name could not be on the New Mexico state ballot as a candidate for governor. The personal appeal that had gained him followers could not be transferred to the lieutenant whose name appeared in his place.

A year later, Tijerina, now somewhat tired and despondent, gave up the Alianza leadership declaring that "there were too many old debts to pay." His voluntary abdication meant the loss of their "prophet" and that the legends of Indo-Hispanic greatness were yet to be fulfilled. Whether the illegal tactics of a frustrated and hostile minority are contrary to the spirit of American freedom or to law and order, as claimed by northern New Mexican officials, is subject to question. Whether a Tierra Amarilla land grant in 1832 to Manuel Martinez "and those who should wish to accompany him; the forests, roads and watering places to be kept free, according to the customs prevailing in all settlements [Gardner, 1970:52, 67–68]"—which was reaffirmed by the U.S. government in the Treaty of Guadalupe Hidalgo in 1848, a treaty that accepted such grants as legally binding—takes precedence over 1970 federal and state property rights, has never been settled in our courts. But one fact remains: with the loss of Tijerina's bold and courageous leadership, the American dream of ethnic equality and justice for all died a little.

The child of migrant parents, César Chavez, too, had experienced poverty and had learned the necessity of organized protest through the example of his father and uncle, who backed labor union organizations. He was introduced to Fred Ross, director of the California-based Community Service Organization (CSO), through Father Donald McConnel, a mutual friend, and he rose through CSO ranks, mastering in the process the skills of organization and delegation of power (Matthiessen, 1969). After more than a decade of service in CSO, part of the time as director of the San Joaquin Valley locals, Chavez became appalled by the lack of concern on the part of the organization over the plight of farm and urban laborers. When his activities on behalf of CSO championed the causes of labor, newly attracted professionals and white-collar leaders of the CSO board balked. He then severed his affiliation with CSO and went back to Delano, California, his wife's hometown, to organize farm workers at the grass-roots level. Chavez felt that workers should have the power, through organization, to improve their economic life.

Late in the summer of 1965, Philippine field workers in California, under AWOC leader Itliong, decided to walk out on the vine growers unless they were given a more humane wage. On September 8, when demands were not met, they did walk out, and on September 16, Chavez was proclaimed as the strike leader for both the Philippine and the Mexican American workers. The weeks of the strike dragged on, and the little money that had been raised was spent. Nevertheless, the farm workers stood behind Chavez, even though their families were in dire need of basic necessities. Just prior to Christmas, when events looked blackest for the impoverished strike families, Walter Reuther of the AFL-CIO declared his organization's support of the National Farm Workers Organizing Committee (NFWOC) strike against the vine growers. With a nationwide boycott against table grapes and California wines, Schenley Industries settled, in the late spring of 1966, and after that the big growers signed one by one until the fall of 1970, when the last major vine grower met the union's demands for a minimum wage. The story of the worker marches has since been retold in narratives, in documentaries, and in drama (most notably by Luis Valdez and his El Teatro Campesino troop).

Uniting educated Anglo and Mexican American college students with uneducated farm laborers in a common cause showed the organizational genius and personal dedication of Chavez. Steiner (1970:237–238) suggests that with this movement came the first break in the traditional barrier between lower-class Chicanos and middle-class Mexican Americans. Chavez also proved that long-range goals can be reached without violence, through effective organization and legitimate procedures.

As the word spread about *la lucha* (the struggle) from the vineyards of California, another more extreme movement was in the making. Noting the economic and political gains of the Black Power movement, some Chicano leaders began to question whether legal procedures were an effective means for gaining equal rights for Mexican Americans and for correcting past injustices. Symbolic of this more radical organizational viewpoint is Rudolfo "Corky" Gonzales.

Gonzales was at one time a well-known purofessional boxer. A local barrio hero in Denver, he served as a political go-between for almost every federal poverty program in the area. In his capacity as ethnic representative, he took an active role in the expanding number of conferences on Mexican American problems, but he finally became disgusted with what he considered to be the ineffectiveness of that role and resigned all his positions in 1969, declaring that those who cooperate with federal programs are guilty of "sell-out tokenism." An accomplished writer of plays and poetry, he expressed his symbolic rejection of Anglo success in his highly publicized poem "I am Joaquin."

Observers see Joaquin as an autobiographical persona, expressing Gonzales' most intimate feelings as he has lived and practiced them, not as he has observed them in others. Joaquin pours forth his soul as he explains the complex world in which he lives, where he is scorned by Gringos who dominate his society and whose rules are confusing to him. Although his forebears lost the economic struggle with Anglo society, he has won in that which matters most—preserving his culture. He must now make a fateful choice between the constrictions of an empty stomach and a full soul or acquiesce to Anglos and, with full stomach, become emasculated "in the grasp of American social neurosis." He despairs as he watches his children rising to mediocrity in a society which forces them to forget not only their noble traditions, but him! Yes, anyone reading the poem will know that "Joaquin" is Corky Gonzales. To the Mexican American Gonzales is the popular folk hero who has rejected Anglo success *to be with his people* (Steiner, 1970:378–392).

Gonzales first came into the national spotlight in 1965, when he renounced his role as Anglo go-between and proceeded to organize the Crusade of Justice in Denver as a "pure ethnic movement." This organization grew out of a civil rights battle involving legal discrimination against Mexican Americans. Gonzalez was an avowed separatist, and his writings were widely circulated by UMAS organizations and MAPA leadership. By the spring of 1968 he claimed a membership of 1,800 in his Crusade for Justice and was recognized as a separatist leader within the overall Chicano movement. In his declarations at a UCLA symposium (1968), with delegates from twenty-five Mexican American groups, Gonzales advocated a Brown Power approach to gain a place for Chicanos in Anglo society. "Integration is an empty bag . . . it's like getting up out of the small end of the funnel. One may make it, but the rest of the people stay at the bottom." Gonzales went on to renounce Chicanos who worked for Mexican American betterment through the institutions of the larger society, bitterly complaining that the young Mexican Americans were being siphoned off to stabilize a racist society in the United States rather than to assist in tearing it down to start over on an equalitarian basis. "All the new leaders we developed a year ago are now working for the poverty program. They were bought out. They are not provoking a revolution [Torgerson, 1968:286]."

Gonzales was supported in his declarations by Tijerina, free on appeal from jail. Tijerina, with Gonzales, had recently joined with Black Power leadership to further the work of black and brown peoples as a single power bloc. Bert Corona, head of the successful MAPA, also attended the symposium, as did Luis Valdez, representing César Chavez (who was currently on a twenty-five day fast and unable to attend).

Probably the zenith of the Brown Power surge occurred in 1969 in Denver, on Palm Sunday. At a national Chicano Youth Liberation Conference on that day Gonzales declared La Raza to be a separate and independent nation.[4] Of these three outstanding leaders of the Chicano movement, Tijerina was the fiery prophet and Chavez the intellectual organizer who reached the campesino and college student alike, but Corky Gonzales was its poet, with a strong right arm raised in defiance.

CHICANISMO AS A SOCIAL MOVEMENT Scholars have identified certain stages within social movements: the initial stage, marked by traumatic birth pains of emergent ideologies, the middle stage of explosive experimentation, and the culminating stage of increased stability. Chicanismo exhibits such a pattern. First comes the awareness that Chicanos themselves can do something about their present subjugation if they unite to combat ethnic discrimination. Next emerges a motivational stage, characterized by explosive rhetoric, anger, and self-purification, which may lead to a feeling of extreme ethnic nationalism. A final cooling off stage begins with contemplation and new insight. Earlier outbursts are recognized for what they were—tools, a means for breaking away from dependency on

Anglos. This final period consists of positive planning and application of tactics and strategies designed to accomplish self-determined ethnic goals, which is an indication of organizational maturation.

The awareness phase, in which pent-up frustrations are released, is illustrated in this widely publicized letter from a Mexican American high school girl, reflecting on her experience in the Anglo world:

> I am a Mexican-American. I was not always one. Once upon a time I was just a human being who had happened to be born in the United States. Sometime during the process of receiving my education I became a Mexican-American. Perhaps it was during my primary years when a teacher with blue eyes told me "Wash your hands . . . *you people* always manage to be filthy . . ." or maybe it was the teacher who told me "We don't want to hear you speaking *that language* here again. . . ." Somewhere along the road I learned that "*you* people" meant Mexican American and that "*that* language" meant Spanish. . . . They taught me many things and they taught other Mexicans, too. We learned our lessons well. Some of us majored in Hatred, which we stored up in our hearts until the day we could use it. Others took up Bitterness, which we engraved upon ourselves in forms of distrust of any Anglos . . . I am a Mexican-American. I want my people to have their rights . . . I want to become more than a second-class citizen . . . I want to be proud of what I am [Rodriguez, 1969].

The explosive self-purification phase, with its emotional reactions and awakening identities, brings forth angry and often vituperative outbursts such as those printed in the Chicano press or chanted at rallies of *La Gente* ("The People"). Appeals for ethnic support and unity are exemplified in this excerpt from a college newspaper.

> Many *Chicanos* on this campus still manifest a feeling of inferiority—even the more militant ones. But *Chicanos* must now comprehend that they are not inferior and in fact are superior in some ways. *Chicanos*, do not believe

that the *gabacho's* [slang for Anglo] life, values and culture are better. We have a rich heritage. . . . Once you are secure in your identity as a *Chicano*, you can function better in the Anglo world. Be proud of what you are and demand what you have coming [Garcia, 1969].

Radical groups, in their desire to maintain their Mexican heritage, functionally destroy many basic Mexican institutions by the very tactics they have employed in their organization. For example, the equality of role among male and female protestors in leadership positions runs counter to the traditional dominance of male over female in Mexican society. Nevertheless, among the militant Chicanos an overwhelming ethnic pride has emerged, and regardless of any other accomplishments of their organizations, the emphasis on a positive, self-determined identity has been a major contribution to ethnic unity and self-reliance. As Briegel notes:

Although the militants have yet to make a noticeable contribution to the economic or social situation of the Mexican-American community, they have increased the awareness of their problem in the larger community. The militants have created the greatest potential for change of any group of Mexican-American organizations [1970: 178].

In retrospect, it appears that the Chicano movement gained most of its support by maintaining an anti-Establishment position (a reflection of lower-class membership) rather than by emphasizing Mexican heritage. Yet, interestingly enough, the militant Mexican American leaders are very much a product of Anglo society, more Anglo in their attitudes than many of their fellows, and much more aware of their rights as Americans.

The constructive planning phase, in which effective tactics for accomplishing Chicano goals have been altered sufficiently by the national decline of radicalism generally, can be considered as an entirely new period of organizational development. The Chicano generation have their "identity phase" behind them for the most part. They are ready to use this newly discovered ethnic unity as an efficient instrument for acquiring other social and economic goals. Rather than proceeding along the route of ethnic autonomy, they have redirected their thrust toward a strategy of penetration and power within existing social institutions. This will be discussed subsequently as the fifth and last organizational period.

CAMPUS CHICANISMO AND ETHNIC STUDIES   Commensurate with the growth of the Brown Power movement in 1966 and 1967, many college and university students, especially those originally from the barrios, sought identity through campus Chicano organizations, among them the United Mexican American Students (UMAS), the Mexican American Student Association (MASA), the Mexican American Student Confederation (MASC), and the Movimiento Estudiantial Chicano de Aztlán (MECHA), all in California; and the Mexican American Youth Organization (MAYO) and the National Organization of Mexican American Students (NOMAS), both in Texas. Some of these had as their primary aim the politicization of the barrio or the radicalization of Mexican American high school students. Others worked principally to alter the campus atmosphere to provide a more favorable and equitable educational experience for the Chicano college student. It was due mainly to the organized insistence of these student groups that Chicano and ethnic study programs were adopted as part of higher education. In support of these student-led organizations were the small number of isolated Chicano faculty members, plus the organized strength of the Association of Mexican-American Educators (AMAE), the intellectual reservoir of ethnic scholarship. This formal organization became increasingly more activist-oriented as it succeeded in modifying curriculum and obtaining staff concessions. In 1969 at the annual AMAE convention members criticized specific corporate enterprises, local governments, and select federal agencies for their discriminatory practices.

Another source of educational assistance for campus organizations and ethnic studies came from the regional Cooperative Education Laboratories, federally supported research and information centers. The one located in New Mexico is especially sensitive to Chicano problems. In June 1966, with the assistance of the dean of education at the University of New Mexico, the Southwestern Cooperative Education Laboratory, Inc. (SCEL) was formed. It is heavily subsidized by the U.S. Office of Education, and its efforts bear heavily on the problems of bilingual education, training teachers for bicultural awareness, and fostering research activities that will destroy negative ethnic stereotypes.

College or university-based ethnic studies programs were designed to promote ethnic cohesion and pride among Mexican American students. To do this, Chicano studies sought to substitute for Anglo-biased history, literature, art, and social science that reflected more of Mexican American culture. To the Mexican American, the story of America does not begin with the Pilgrims at Plymouth Rock. This event is of relatively recent origin in terms of the Mexican's Indian and Spanish heritage, which spans nearly 1,000 years. Although curricula were developed to assist the Chicano student to know his own heritage, these same courses were a boon to non-Chicanos who wanted to know more about the group and its historical, social, and cultural legacy. Amado Padilla reported to a recent sociological gathering that in the introductory Chicano studies courses at the University of California in Santa Barbara, more than 50 percent of the enrollees are Anglos—an indication of the popularity of these offerings among nonethnic students.

On each campus, the variations in local resources, historical development, and ethnic student population dictate a different approach to Chicano studies programs. After a comprehensive survey of Chicano personnel and programs, Rochin describes the variations he finds in the eight-campus University of California system.

Not all campuses have a Chicano Studies Program *per se*. Berkeley has a Chicano Studies Division which is within a Department of Ethnic Studies. Davis functions with a Chicano Studies Program with faculty members teaching Chicano courses out of the traditional academic departments. Irvine has a Comparative Cultures Program with a Chicano sub-component. The Los Angeles program relies on a Chicano Studies Center which serves principally as an academic research center. Riverside has an interdisciplinary Mexican-American Studies Program with faculty members teaching out of their respective departments. Santa Barbara functions with a Department of Chicano Studies and a Chicano Research Center. Santa Cruz is just developing a Chicano program within a new Urban Studies College. And San Diego's Chicano Studies is a sub-component of its Third College. Of the eight campuses, Berkeley, Irvine, Riverside and San Diego offer majors in Ethnic, Cultural or Chicano Studies [1972:2].

Extensive comparisons of structural-functional similarities in Chicano studies programs are difficult, inasmuch as many of the programs are in different sequential stages of development, from recent inception to full-fledged, mature, permanent programs. As an analytical tool for investigating Chicano studies programs, W. Kennedy (1972) outlines the major stages through which the program at San Diego proceeded. The first phase was concerned with securing permission for its establishment; it was funded and became operational when recruitment started. The second phase consisted of the actual functioning of the program: recruiting more cadre and students and coming to grips with a dependence on the Anglo structure for economic support. In the third stage the program was well underway, its participants chiefly concerned with program autonomy and with university service to the barrio population. This phase is often possible only after continuous institutional support has been secured. The final stage of maturation in the Chicano studies program was represented by a full acceptance of the program by outside agencies.

A too successful Chicano program that produces a sudden large following creates problems. An increased number of students to be served will result in an increasingly bureaucratized organization and a more complex network of relationships with external organizations. This dissipates the close personal ties of a small struggling Chicano contingent. Chicano leadership at this point becomes concerned with the loss of revolutionary zeal and fears co-optation of its program as it becomes more stabilized.

At the University of New Mexico the ethnic studies program until recently was an older working program emphasizing curriculum and identity integration for the Mexican American student. Specific instructors and departmental offerings were investigated to determine the extent to which Mexican culture and identity were presented correctly. Approved course offerings and instructors were then recommended to minority students as being consistent with identity and scholarship goals for the Spanish American students there. These minority students selected a college major in an established academic discipline, and the ethnic studies operation became an auxiliary program to balance out the negative effects of Anglo-biased history and literature courses and to provide a coordinated voice for ethnic dissatisfactions. This approach dealt more rationally with the problem of getting employment for Mexican American graduates and considered the primary goal of college training in preparing students for a good-paying occupation. The fact is that there are few job openings for a graduate who has majored in Chicano studies, whereas traditional majors can readily compete for positions within the present economic system. A San Diego professor notes this dilemma:

> Although the proponents of Aztlán suggest that such a compromise is corrupt, they offer no solution to how one supports one's family. Thus, there is some question as to the literal or symbolic solidarity to be found in the concept of Aztlán [Kennedy, 1972:7].

A realistic evaluation of Chicano studies programs focuses on the short-range goals of ethnic autonomy, ethnic pride, and group identity compared with the long-range goal of economic and social independence from the dominant society. Whereas majors in Chicano studies will be well prepared in the first, only Mexican American students who have competed in traditional studies will acquire economic and social skills that can be employed in advancing the overall Chicano movement.

A beginning objective in the plan for Chicano studies is the hiring of native, ethnic faculty members to become models for Chicano youth—that is, teachers with whom students can identify with pride. However, the limited number of Mexican

Americans with formal academic credentials has created an overload of responsibilities for the few who are available. To illustrate, on the eight campuses of the University of California are employed 5,730 assistant, associate, and full professors, of whom only 30 are Mexican American. Of these only 9 have tenure. At the untenured level of instructor, associate, and lecturer, there are 25 more Mexican Americans, making a total of 55 throughout the entire system (Rochin, 1972:6–7). Likewise, at the University of Texas at El Paso there are 314 assistant, associate, and full professors, of whom only 13 are Mexican American. Only 3 of 246 tenured members of that faculty are from the Spanish-surname group. An additional 8 Mexican Americans are a part of the group of 66 instructors on campus, mostly in specially funded programs. Yet the salary schedule and prestige of the University of Texas at El Paso, though the school claims nearly one-eighth of the total undergraduate Mexican American students in the United States in its student body, is insufficient to compete with UCLA, Notre Dame, Yale, or the University of Texas at Austin for Chicano faculty members. There is continuous pressure on departments and administrators to employ more Chicano professionals, but their scarcity puts them at a premium. When these demands force an institution to hire a Chicano poorly suited by way of background experience and credentials to replace a non-Chicano with superior qualifications, it is not unusual for the Chicano studies or related program to suffer in efficiency and planning what it gains in obtaining a Chicano "success model." When Chicanos are brought into the campus with little prior academic experience, they know little of the "rules of the game." Often their innovative (and sometimes unorthodox) methods cause administrative overreactions, and this constant bickering is a poor basis for establishing a lasting program. Moreover, in extreme cases, as a defensive reaction to Chicano program failures, other academic departments are assaulted with unwarranted accusations, often the very departments which pose a threat to the "totalitarian methods" of Chicano leaders because of the quality of professionalism exhibited therein.

At some institutions, radical activity and notoriety have brought direct repressive measures from regents and adminis-

trators, government agencies, and private foundations, resulting in a discontinuance of funds for Chicano projects. The first
programs to be cut during the general tightening of the national
economy were marginal, innovative ones. Although Chicano
studies suffered because of these budgetary restrictions, the
often overlooked result was that those which survived did so
with a promising future under the direction of skilled Chicano
professionals.

As stated above, the supply of Chicano academicians is
extremely limited, and the drive to enlist Chicanos into Chicano studies majors leaves none for the traditional disciplines.
Though current data do not furnish a complete answer to
how many Chicano professions (especially those with the
Ph.D. or its equivalent) are currently available, it is generally
known that modern languages (especially Spanish), humani-
ties, and the arts have a large representation of Spanish surnames, though many of these are European or South American
rather than Mexican. In the various social sciences the Mexican
Americans with doctorates are few indeed. Rochin (1972)
claims that only three or four Chicanos in the United States
have Ph.D.'s in economics, of which he is one. In the political
science field, Carlos Muñoz of the University of California in
Irvine surveyed 943 schools and reported a total of eight Chicanos with Ph.D.'s in that discipline. It is thought that there
are about the same number of Chicano psychologists—though
this is not certain. Although there are about two dozen Spanish-
surname persons with Ph.D.'s in sociology, the Chicano Sociologist's Caucus at national meetings of sociologists claimed a
core membership of fewer than a dozen, with decreasing activity
by senior sociologists in radical policies. Spanish surnames are
probably better represented in the professions of law, medicine,
and dentistry, but as practitioners, not as teachers. Spanish-
surname faculty members are fairly numerous in the various
education departments of southwestern universities, no doubt
partially a consequence of the former practice of filling the
ranks with high school principals and school superintendents
who have had practical experience.

Since the few available ethnic faculty members are spread
so thinly, individual Chicano faculty members face major prob-

lems. According to Rochin (1972) and Estrada (1972), during the first year of university activity, the Chicano teacher must make a decision on priorities—whether Chicano interests or those of his discipline are to be paramount. Those who commit themselves to advancing the Chicano cause feel duty bound to work directly with ethnic students in an attempt to resolve their personal as well as their academic problems. School administrators will assign their few Chicano professionals to an abnormally large number of campus committees, sometimes to meet an "ethnic quota" and sometimes because they legitimately desire their ideas and input on committees concerned with sensitive campus policies. The professional Chicano has some responsibility to his discipline and his colleagues, but this may be dissipated by the constant demand for his personal support and assistance to Chicano students. If he is the titular head of a Chicano studies program, he is torn between attending formal ceremonies and accepting social invitations as a representative of his minority group while at the same time designing and developing new curricula suitable for achieving Chicano goals. It is not easy to become an overall expert in history, linguistics, education, political science, economics, sociology, and psychology and also to set up courses in these areas—particularly with the paucity of unbiased readings in each field. Further, some directors feel a compulsion to form a liaison with local barrio leaders, and this by itself becomes a highly demanding, sensitive operation. So, the Chicano teacher becomes more and more the scapegoat for failures; he is criticized by impatient, headstrong Chicano students, by disapproving colleagues, by vested interests that fear an upset in the status quo, and by the barrio leaders, who regard his middle-class life style as an Anglo sellout. It is little wonder that under the circumstances Chicano studies directors frequently succumb to these attacks and eventually return to their discipline.

OFF-CAMPUS CHICANO ACTIVITIES   During the years from 1965 to 1969 many new barrio-based ethnic organizations emerged. These represented tenement dwellers seeking to protest arbitrary rent increases, homeowners uniting against zoning changes or devastating urban renewal plans, barrio-member purchasing and credit cooperatives, legal aid groups, groups formed to seek improved community services or recreational facilities, mutual aid or relief societies, and those dedicated to educational reforms. Often begun by Vista, government social-action programs, or local churches, clubs, and brotherhoods, these barrio organizations would prosper when the leadership was finally assumed directly by local ethnic residents.

A major support for local barrio organizations has been direct or indirect financial support of private foundations and the federal government. In a recent directory of Spanish-speaking Community Organizations, one of the few national organizations listed is the Southwest Council of La Raza, presently with headquarters in Phoenix, Arizona. It was originally established by means of a large Ford Foundation grant and has since operated with supplementary funds from church and labor union contributions. Coordination of resources for the welfare of Mexican Americans is its primary aim. It works on target Anglo structures, locating or creating Chicano programs for betterment in a broad spectrum of content areas; in San Antonio and Oakland the Southwest Council has successfully provided legal protection for minority groups there. It is also attempting to create strong social bonds within the Mexican American barrios, especially when these are attacked through urban renewal, model cities, or urban rehabilitation programs. Its officials are aware that economic and social resources outside the immediate membership group itself must be tapped, various levels of power identified, and local programs for ethnic betterment unified politically (Cabrera, 1971:34–36). U.S. Representative H. B. Gonzalez in a recent report stated that a side effect of these grants is to equip local militant ethnic groups with the economic support to print materials that advocate violence, racism, hate, and fear, but pretend that they are building ethnic pride.

The direct involvement of Chicano social scientists in barrio affairs has created some hostility and stress within local barrios. Even former barrio residents who have achieved prominence within the larger society are viewed with suspicion. A Chicano professional who brings new ideas to the barrio thus pursues a dangerous course. He is vulnerable both to rejection by Chicano residents and to repressive measures by local power figures if he is successful in organizing the barrio. Often, only by renouncing his position in the Establishment can he become fully accepted as a Chicano. At this point, he gains favor and support in the barrio but loses his influence among Anglo leaders.

These barrio-based operations have filled a need, and their effectiveness in creating a spirit of collective identity among Mexican Americans is well documented. For instance, in Chicago during the summer of 1966, after the Puerto Rican riot, the Latin American Defense Organization (LADO), led by Obed Gomez, was organized to protect Mexican Americans of that community from their neighbors. In San Antonio, the Mexican American Nationalist Organization (MANO), comprised of 300 exconvicts of Mexican descent and under the leadership of Alberto "Beto" Martinez, rallied together to curb police brutality on San Antonio's west side.

In Los Angeles the Brown Berets, under their youthful leader, David Sanchez, who dropped out of college to assume leadership of that organization, coordinated units of uniformed barrio youth—in the style of the Black Panthers. Their goals were spelled out by Carlos Montez, minister of public relations for the Brown Berets.

> Gang fights are going out. We're getting kids from all the different gangs into the Brown Berets. It's going to be one big barrio, one big gang. We try to teach our people not to fight with each other, and not to fight with our blood brothers from the South [Torgerson, 1968:281].

Especially strong in lower-class barrios, the Brown Berets rejected Establishment programs such as OEO and the like. The organization claimed to restore and preserve the dignity of the Mexican Americans without violence, except in self-defense, although its selected activities were those in which police violence was anticipated. Operating principally in California, it now has small units in all major urban centers of the Southwest.

During the last few years of the confrontation era, activities of the militant arm of the Chicano movement were well publicized in the mass media, although the waning of ethnic interest has been highly visible. A close investigation of many of these confrontations discloses varied reasons for their activism. It also lays bare the difficulties in maintaining peaceful internal goals with short-term planning while dealing with overreacting Establishment representatives. Take for instance some of the school boycotts that occurred during the years from 1968 to 1970.

In the spring of 1968, a school "blowout" (walkout) occurred in Los Angeles. A local ethnic organization, the Brown Berets, was accused of being instrumental in causing the school walkout. David Sanchez, the Brown Beret leader, saw the organization's function in minority protection, to intervene between the students and police in case of Establishment reaction to the protest. He stated:

> We were at the walkout to protect our younger people. When they (the law officers) started hitting with sticks, we went in . . . put ourselves between the police and the kids, and took the beating [Torgerson, 1968:282].

Sanchez's claim was supported by a report of the Civil Rights Commission, prepared by the California State Advisory Committee in 1970. Investigators found that the demonstration had occurred in an orderly manner and that calm prevailed when police were absent. The people became ugly *only when police were present.* This grew out of a past history of disillusionment with the police as an effective, fair channel for gaining justice or redress for ethnic inequities. The walkout itself was the culmination of frustrations and bitterness festering over a period of time.

In retrospect, the Los Angeles walkout erupted prematurely and spontaneously, separate from the well-laid plans of student-protest groups. When students at Lincoln High approached a social science teacher, Sal Castro, about a blowout to protest lack of bicultural education opportunities, he told them to organize instead. With the aid of UMAS and nearby college personnel, blowout committees were established at each of the four east Los Angeles schools and coordinated through a central committee. Castro explains how their plans were preempted by spontaneous student reaction to school administrative decisions.

The original plan was to go before the Board of Education and propose a set of changes without walking out—to hold that back to get what they wanted. Then, at Wilson High Friday (March 1), the principal canceled a play they were going to do as unfit, and the Wilson kids blew out. It was spontaneous. Then Roosevelt and Lincoln wanted to blow, too. Garfield, too. Later on (March 8) Belmont, which was never in on the original plan, came in, too.

These blowouts in the other schools, like Venice and Jefferson, weren't connected with the Chicano blowouts, but they may have been in sympathy. Some of the kids from schools uptown asked us to send representatives to tell them how to organize. What do you think of that! The Anglo schools asking the Chicano kids to help them organize. They should've told them "Ask your dads how they organized to oppress us all these years" [Torgerson, 1968:283].

With this confrontation between an emotional, radical ethnic movement and a rigidly repressive society have come the multitude of news stories of riots and mass violence. Have these stories restored law and order or have they merely precipitated further violence? Following the Los Angeles walkout, Ralph Guzman of UCLA, observing the police efforts to subdue the overexuberant participants, remarked:

They've given these people a real revolutionary experience. No Marxist could do better. They're making rebels. When they see police clubbing them, it's the final evidence that society is against them—that existing within the system won't work [Torgerson, 1968:282].

During the Denver riots of 1969, police reacted similarly, and during that year in many metropolitan areas, cities, and towns, apathy and disgust turned into overt dissent, protest, and confrontation. As a result, student-led walkouts have continued to occur throughout the Southwest in recent times.

In Los Angeles, for example, there was still anger two years after the arrest and indictments by a grand jury of the thirteen participants in the Los Angeles school blowout of March 1968. Much of the smoldering distrust between the community and the law had spread from teenagers to parents. Peaceful student demonstrations in the spring of 1970 were met with police force, student beatings, and jail, which again brought into question the function of the local police force (to protect the people or repress them?). The California State Advisory Committee reported in 1970 that following a publicly declared Chicano moratorium, various events occurred that created a further polarization. An east Los Angeles National Chicano Moratorium March of 7,000 Chicanos to protest United States' involvement in Vietnam and decry the high percentage of Mexican American battle casualties, led to a confrontation in the streets and at Laguna Park, where the crowd included Chicanos, Anglos, and blacks—adults, teenagers, and children. Bottles were thrown at police vehicles, tear gas was fired profusely, and violence finally resulted in some deaths, including that of the most eloquent Chicano spokesman of the Los Angeles press, Ruben Salazar. More than 400 demonstrators were jailed. Although this event was organized by Rosalio Muñoz, a former UCLA student-body president, and was endorsed by nearly all Mexican American organizations in the Southwest, its multipurposes (to protest the Chicano casualties in Vietnam, to promote a feeling of Chicano identity, and to protest police brutality) produced varied reactions toward what occurred that day.

Even though radicalism generally cooled throughout the Southwest after 1970, there were events occurring significant enough to suggest that the radical era of the movement was far from quieted. For instance, on June 13, 1971, at Albuquerque's Tijerina Park, a mixed group of hippies and Chicanos were checked by police for alleged drinking. Strong claims are made that police harassment was the underlying motive, but bottles and rocks thrown by park participants forced a call for reinforcements, and what had started out as a confrontation between police and park inhabitants became an ethnic confrontation. After a park rally the following Monday, sponsored by the Gorras Negras, at which the lieutenant governor and attorney general had agreed to speak, the hippies wished to continue the antipolice move, but Chicano leaders, sensing that their people would bear the major brunt of the ensuing battle, attempted to make the people go home. Roving bands created disturbances on campus and downtown, and some 283 more persons were arrested. The barrio newspaper *Venceremos I* blamed the entire event on the police, but, obviously, the initial move to clear the park area provided the means to act out (on both sides) the underlying hostilities previously felt between the police and Chicanos.

Unless some positive measures are taken to increase the dialogue between the community, Anglos on the police force, and denizens of the barrio, Anglo and Mexican American blood will probably be spilled in the ghettos of Los Angeles, San Antonio, Houston, Flint, Oakland, Denver, and Albuquerque within the next few years. Police confrontations that are completely unrelated to ethnic problems will become violent, and when barrio reaction to police harassment runs high, it will provide the spark for interethnic violence, even though the events themselves are not initiated by ethnic hatred. Repressive police tactics and arrogance on the part of minority leaders who are attempting to "save face" provide fuel for riots, and with increasing tensions, totalitarian-type barrio leaders become ethnic spokesmen. Such conditions further increase the danger of open hostility and mob violence. Ignoring the problem in hopes that it will resolve itself will only allow the underlying frustrations and hostility to fester and gather momentum for these periodic outbreaks. In most cases, local police officers and many Chicano protestors are the pawns of both the dominant and minority leadership in their efforts to blame the other side for a very sensitive and uncomfortable interethnic situation.

THE PERIOD OF STRATEGIC PENETRATION (1970 TO THE PRESENT)

The events of the militant period just past have affected even the more traditional ethnic organizations. Gonzalez (1969: 188) reports that the LULAC membership in northern New Mexico have agreed to be included in the overall category of Mexican American rather than to try and maintain their isolation as Spanish Americans. The LULAC organization has been accommodating to the more aggressive GI Forum, and it is cooperating in the sponsorship of SER, Inc. (Service-Employment-Redevelopment), to provide barrio-centered manpower retraining opportunities for needy Mexican Americans. But the extensive coordination of the various political, social, and cultural organizations representing the different Mexican American orientations just discussed in this chapter is the first requirement for success in a strategic penetration period. The first national La Raza Unida party convention in El Paso in August 1972, was a vivid demonstration of a focused penetration into the heretofore "untouchable" political arena.

Whereas in former years radical confrontations were instrumental in focusing attention on the severity of ethnic poverty and discrimination, these methods no longer create the same favorable public interest they once did. Even in the Chicano studies programs, which have suffered some reverses in recent years, the more realistic adaptations of those that survive indicate that the final phase of maturity for the Chicano movement has been reached. Once self-identity has been firmly established within the ethnic group itself and has been accepted to some degree by the dominant Anglo society, then penetration of dominant institutions can be effected, eventually leading to more considerations of Chicano interests.

There are presently two dominant orientations within the Chicano movement, one emphasizing pragramatism and the other ideology (Kennedy, 1972). The pragmatists sense the change in mood in America and feel that penetrating the existing institutional structures will yield the best results now. Their immediate goal is the placement of Chicano professionals in strategic political, economic, and educational positions, which will secure and validate Chicano gains and promote ethnic pride through achievement and competition in the larger society. This appears to be the strongest force in the Chicano movement today and is admirably suited to integrating the Chicano's desire for ethnic autonomy (i.e., self-identity) with his need for some outside help to solve his problems.

The ideological orientation is more of a romantic approach, typified by the creation of Aztlán. In practice, an Atzlán would have to function somewhat like England's royal family—as a figurehead but without organized power. In any other sense, it is an unrealistic goal.

The humanist component of the ideological orientation seeks further development of Chicano art, music, poetry, and literature, and more nearly approximates the efforts of the pragmatists. However, the social scientists who seek an ideological solution to current Chicano problems are searching for alternatives to the institutions presently existing within American society. One Chicano spokesman warns that these alternate structures must not be just Chicano-dominated replications of existing Anglo institutions (Muñoz, 1970). As Sena Rivera put it:

> Truly distinct approaches are needed to solve Chicano problems, not just models duplicating existing Anglo structures. Thus, a Chicano institution of higher education should not be one with Chicano President, Chicano Deans, Chicano Department Heads and Chicano Faculty but an original structure which truly represents the interests of the Chicano student [1972].

It is difficult to foresee what will be the outcome of the Chicano movement, because it, like everything else, is influenced by affairs outside its sphere of influence. This includes Vietnam, hostilities in the Middle East, national spending policies, and election trends. Also important is the way in which Mexican American leaders trained during the 1960s adapt to new strategies and tactics appropriate to the 1970s: whether they trigger further backlash reactions through rash confrontation and threats or coordinate and unify their constituency for penetration and manipulation of the system for long-range results.

CHICANISMO AND
OTHER CONTEMPORARY MOVEMENTS

The Civil Rights Movement of the sixties initially appeared to be strongly allied to the Chicano cause. In order to publicly display the inequities suffered by Mexican Americans, Chicano leaders needed a power base from which to demand changes. On the other hand the ethnic cause was a useful tool for Civil Rights leaders to initiate mass demonstrations that would have popular appeal. Some positive gains accrued in the short run from this relationship. However, once the plight of the minority had been exposed, the confrontation tactics required a follow-up plan of strategy to secure further gains. Since radical protest leaders maintain their power position only within a milieu of tension, race polarization, and social ferment, when these leaders could no longer use the ethnic issue to generate dissent, ethnic concerns were replaced by other sensational appeals. When reform-minded ethnic leaders suggested reducing tension through cooperative efforts with external agencies, the power base of the radical protest movement was threatened, and radical leadership had to decide whether to forego ethnic support or undermine the traditional ethnic leadership. Choosing the latter, they accomplished their goal by labeling moderate Chicanos as ethnic sellouts, or *malinches*.

These same radical protest leaders made use of certain functionaries within the dominant society whose rigidity, fear of losing power, and general overreaction to radical tactics gained much sympathetic support for protest groups. In such cases, protest leaders became self-appointed spokesmen for the Mexican American minority, and their charges of "Establishment repression" were subsequently taken up by educators, welfare workers, police officers, politicians, and others in reaction to strong confrontation tactics. As Moore correctly notes:

> In recent years it has become plain that the fate of America's distinctive groups depended upon the reaction of American institutions more so than upon any institutions the group may have generated within itself [1970a: 96].

Ethnic nationalism was another approach to gaining a higher living standard for Mexican Americans. Radical Chicanos, using the Black Power movement as their model, formed Brown Power organizations. It was supposed that if the efforts of the two disenfranchised minorities were coordinated, each would have a better chance to break down ethnic barriers. As the years went by, hindsight showed that a common distaste for Anglo-dominated institutions and ethnic stereotypes was not a strong enough bond to overcome the vastly different objectives and areas of major concern among Blacks and Chicanos. For instance, English is the native language of American Blacks, and they are never questioned about their United States citizenship. What they seek is to restore their multicultural heritage, which was lost during the decades of slavery. The Chicano, on the other hand, has not really lost his Mexican heritage, but must fight the "foreigner" label and the discriminatory results of having Spanish, not English, as his mother tongue. As benefits from the coalition between the two movements accrued disproportionately to blacks, Brown Power support weakened. As so often happens, minority members were more negatively oriented toward other minorities than were members of the majority group.

Tijerina and Gonzalez, with leaders of the 20,000 member Mexican-American Political Association (MAPA), are the architects of a coalition with militant black organizations of the West Coast. Presumably there is a united front made up of their three Mexican-American organizations and chapters of CORE, SNCC, and other black militants . . . the coalition is at times more verbal than actual, more mutually protective than jointly decisive, more crisis-oriented than comprehensively strategic. The Black and Mexican-American rank and file consider the arrangement a tactical necessity for situations of special duress. . . . The fact of the matter is that Blacks and Mexican-Americans barely know each other [Lara-Braud, 1970:13].

There is a tendency by some to view ethnic dissent as unjustifiable disruption of a "good system," fomented by agitators paid to carry out the goals of the "Communist conspiracy." Such ridiculous stereotyping places the stigma of illegitimacy on the actions of a minority that is attempting to gain that legal, social, and economic equality of opportunity supposedly guaranteed to all Americans. After patiently tolerating decades of benign neglect, sheer desperation has forced this group to adopt radical methods of making its grievances known. But these actions, rather than being perceived as legitimate displays

of ethnic indignation, are regarded by Anglo reactionaries as a
carefully contrived, pernicious scheme fostered by a few dedicated, Communist-inspired revolutionaries. These actions may
be unlawful or deleterious to society, but those criteria hardly
constitute a solid case for labeling them Communist.

The John Birch Society in New Mexico had already effectively used the label "Communist" to smear the Alianza movement. This process was far less effective, however, against the
Brown Berets during the Los Angeles school walkout. Carlos
Montez, minister of the Brown Berets (whose uniforms resemble that of the late Ché Guevara but whose ideology is quite
dissimilar), refuted this charge in the following statement:

> Communism? That's a white thing. . . . It's pretty hard
> to mix Communists and Mexican-Americans. Ché [Ché
> Guevara] doesn't mean a thing to the guy in the street.
> He's got his own problems [Torgerson, 1968:281].

To be anti-Establishment does not automatically make one pro-
Communist. This is an essential point often missed by Anglo
leaders, who feel threatened by those questioning the fairness
of certain practices in our present society.

Occasional hippie support for minority issues on college campuses has caused some observers to assume these groups have
a perspective in common with protesting ethnic groups. However, Chicano leaders have openly ridiculed the "do-your-own-
thing" doctrine as damaging to the Chicano movement. To
establish effective solidarity and self-identity as La Raza Nueva
demands ethnic loyalty and unity, not individualistic, sometimes aberrant behavior.

Even the peace movement has become linked with the drive
for Mexican American autonomy. In El Paso, Chicanos had the
full support of the peace movement liberals until the fall of
1970, when, during an organized rally to protest the war, Chicano leaders introduced local demands that diluted, it was felt,
the impact of the mobilization rally. Since that event, campus
Chicanos have never been able to get the same level of unquali-
fied and sustained support from that source.

The Chicano movement exemplifies the potential force within
Mexican American society to improve itself and its position in

the larger society. While many of the protests have been born of emotional desperation, and the revolts have been short-lived, the movement demonstrates that the people are eager to gain quality and justice—and the image of a lazy, complacent, humiliated people without pride or leadership has been effectively destroyed.

The decreasing emphasis on anti-Establishment rhetoric is not an indication that Chicanismo is dying, but rather an indication that Mexican Americans have firmly established a positive group identity and no longer feel threatened by stereotypes. This shift in strategy from the short-run gains of the activist period to a long-range strategy of consolidating these gains for future, viable planning, indicates the maturity and leadership potential within the movement. Without losing the ultimate objective of ethnic pride and autonomy, the Chicano movement has adopted a strategy consistent with its environment and with its stage of development. It remains to be seen whether this present thrust of Chicanismo can provide enough visible evidence of progress to prevent its radical elements from again assuming leadership of the movement.

Notes

[1] Two Mexican American scholars, Alvarez (1971:24–25) and Cuellar (1970) have used cultural eras and political periods to describe the changing shift from ethnic dependency to ethnic autonomy. However, their analyses explicitly select the 1848 period of "Anglo invasion" of the Southwest as *the single factor* that led to present-day Mexican American political and economic impotency, a highly questionable assumption.

[2] Though this factionalism centered on an organization's name, it was symbolic of differences in historical development in the area (Moore, 1970b) and the degree of ethnic autonomy demanded.

[3] Most prominent among Mexican American leaders of the organized protest era, excluding the three mentioned, is José Angel Guittierez. His dynamic leadership was a crucial factor in obtaining the election victories in Crystal City, Texas, thus demonstrating the ballot box as a legitimate alternative to Chicano power. From that localized beginning, a viable political organiza-

tion, La Raza Unida, has emerged, which held its first national convention in El Paso, Texas, in August 1972. The Texas governorship is the only statewide office for which La Raza Unida has furnished a party office seeker—Ramsey Munez. Guittierez was selected as the first La Raza Unida party chairman, over Corky Gonzales of Denver, and can legitimately be counted as one of the more important ethnic leaders of the emerging strategic penetration era.

David Sanchez, leader of the Brown Berets, is symbolic of the early Chicano militancy. Although he is prominently displayed, he has steadily lost power and support to less radical leaders within the Chicano movement. Bert Corono, head of MAPA, was a driving force in politicizing the Mexican Americans of West Coast states, principally California. His pioneering efforts and support for Guittierez and others have demonstrated his early contribution to organization and coordination of Mexican American groups in the political arena.

The late Ruben Salazar, the "Voice of La Causa" in Los Angeles, is another significant name during that period.

[4] Gonzales' "spiritual plan for Aztlán" was a dream of Chicano unity and power, a hope of regaining the glories of the past. However, as Moore comments: "Whatever the sentimental attractions of a completely separate community, such a community never has actually worked. . . . But the romantic ideal of the separate community persists perhaps only because it is romantic, and simple [1970a:96]."

Chapter 8 ◉ Joiners and Clients: Mexican Americans and Formal Organizations

The lack of involvement in organizations—both bureaucratic and less formal, voluntary types—on the part of Mexican Americans has been attributed entirely to their ethnic background. Actually, many factors such as generation, place of residence, and social-class levels, as well as external barriers of racial and religious intolerance contribute heavily to the situation.

PARTICIPATION IN BUREAUCRATIC STRUCTURES

Mexican immigrants come from the lower socioeconomic strata and have had little experience participating in formal organizations in their native land. Moreover, political and social structures in Mexico differ markedly from those in the United States. Cárdenas (1963) outlines the dependent power arrangement of the Mexican municipio, which acts as an extended organ of the state political structure through the relationship between the local mayor and the governor. The state power structure is likewise tied to the national government through the relationship between the governor and the president. D'Antonio and Form (1965) compared power structures in Ciudad Juárez, Chihuahau, and El Paso, Texas, and found the Mexican structure to be more monolithic and centrally controlled than the one in the United States. No successful civic program is initiated or legitimized in Mexico without support from higher authorities through personal channels of power. In this country, formal governmental agencies and voluntary associations work independently on community projects.

Immigrants maintain personal attachment patterns, obtaining services from Mexico, becoming dependent upon barrio patróns or family members, and avoiding formal organizations, which they perceive as the means employed by Anglos to dominate and manipulate them. Second-generation Mexican Americans often exhibit similar attitudes toward formal organizations, and a study in San Antonio noted that even among third-generation families residing in that city, few Mexican Americans joined anything other than school-related associations (Francesca, 1958:30).

To increase the resources directed to the barrio, the barrio leader must have some knowledge of the workings of an impersonal bureaucracy. Even his personal contacts require some behavior modifications, such as adopting middle-class forms of dress, speech, and etiquette, to achieve maximum cooperation from sympathetic individuals in positions of power in the larger society. But the barrio representative, in making these adaptations from lower-class to middle-class behavior patterns, fears he will lose the trust of his constituents because dissident barrio factions will use this opportunity to brand him as a cultural sellout at the very time when he might maximize his personal contacts for the good of his minority group.

The younger and partially Anglicized Mexican Americans with more education and some experience with bureaucratic structures outside the barrio are currently the most effective leaders. Philip Montez, a program director for the U.S. Commission on Civil Rights, comments on youth leadership and effective activist movements:

> Up 'til now the Mexican-American community hasn't had the sophistication for organization or movements. But things are different now. The kids are close to being anglicized and middle class—which is apparently what it takes to bring them closer to being able to work a system. That's why they're the leaders [Torgerson, 1968:283–284].

The existence of a rapidly expanding cadre of educated, competent Mexican American youth contradicts the stereotype that ethnic background is the factor which makes Mexican Americans unequal to the task of bureaucratic leadership. With experience, they compete well.

VOLUNTARY ASSOCIATION MEMBERSHIP

Americans have been described as a "nation of joiners." According to the recent scientific investigations of Hyman and Wright (1971:195), this is mainly a middle-class phenomenon. The factors associated with segregation and population concentrations influence organizational involvement greatly. The highest rates of political and social participation are in census tracts with higher socioeconomic indexes. Literacy skills and participation patterns of neighborhood residents and colleagues are similarly related influences. More than 1,000 formal voluntary associations were studied by Officer (1964) in Tucson, Arizona. Although Mexican American participation in these associations was far below what it should have been in terms of population ratios, the basis for participation in Anglo-dominated associations was a function of neighborhood propinquity rather than direct ethnic discrimination. Similarly, Browning and McLemore (1964:65) claim that the level of education and income of the minority group, as contrasted with the dominant group, varies according to population concentrations. Thus, the pressure to preserve the barrio intact for purposes of identity and cultural unity will deter barrio residents from participating in nonethnic voluntary associations.

Among all ethnic groups, physical mobility is inversely related to organizational participation. The large number of Mexican Americans in the migrant stream has done little to encourage participation in associations. Whereas voluntary associations and formal structures are often manned by the more permanent community citizens as a means of maintaining their achieved status perquisites, the mass exodus of rural Mexican Americans to urban barrios has not produced the kind of ownership or status interests that demand protection by elaborate organizational machinery. Only neighborhood concerns have been paramount, and ethnic organizations that deal with neighborhood problems have emerged. Membership in these does not require membership or participation in existing voluntary associations within the larger, middle-class society.

Although it has been shown that there are significantly fewer Catholics in voluntary associations than there are Protestants (Scott, J., 1957), this may represent more a methodological bias in studying associations than a function of religion. Scholars studying voluntary associations have generally excluded church-related associations as well as labor unions from these analyses. This results in a double bias against Mexican Americans because they are heavily concentrated in blue-collar occupations and are thus potential union members, and they also have a traditional liking for fellowship-type organizations, many of which are church sponsored.

Two major changes are apparent today in Mexican American attitudes toward joining organizations. First, an increasing number of families are moving to middle-class neighborhoods or attaining white-collar positions that encourage them to join existing associations. (This corresponds to a decrease in ethnic discrimination on the part of members from the dominant society.) A second major change is the increasing number of new community organizations (especially in the barrios) that are using formal means to voice their wants and thus solve their economic and social problems. In El Paso, there are seventeen organizations presently operating in the southside barrio. Only four of these were in existence before 1965. Nationally, this same trend is evident.

MEXICAN AMERICANS AS CLIENTS

The delivery of social services involves many things. There must be an agency to provide the services, and information about it must be conveyed to the potential clientele. The client must diagnose his own needs and decide whether the agency or representative can furnish him with help. How the aid is offered, the threat to self-determination reflected in accepting external aid, and the stigma of dependency and lost pride complicate the delivery process.

Unfortunately, where programs are needed most, they are generally unavailable. The Civil Rights Commission in a mimeographed staff report noted that although more than one-half of all Mexican American families living in Texas in 1969 were in the poverty category, only 149 of the 254 counties in Texas had either Commodity Distribution or Food Stamp programs and these served only 15.3 percent of the needs in those counties.

In Denver, Colorado, many migrant families arrive in dire need of economic or social services. Often, Anglo professionals operate voluntarily as "gatekeepers" to locate aid sources, but a central clearinghouse of available services is lacking (Kurtz, 1968).

Speech or hearing impediments and birth defects frequently go untreated in the barrio. Residents seldom know of their legal rights or privileges as citizens to obtain various social services without cost. In slum areas, disease, child mortality, and even births may go unrecorded. First, residents must be educated to recognize health and social problems and made aware of the facilities available to remedy some of these problems. Once this is accomplished, the crucial phase of cross-cultural and cross-class training arises for those delivering these services.

Many social workers from the middle-class world seek to change the barrio into a mirror image of their world. When Mexican Americans display behavior patterns typical of lower-class families throughout America, these are seen as cultural impediments to, or a lack of motivation for bettering present circumstances. Although many administrators and field workers of OEO, HEW, HUD, and the Office of Education and Public Health have been drawn from Mexican American ranks, these advisers, like their middle-class coworkers, will emphasize long-range planning and ignore the short-term economic crises faced by barrio heads of household.

Moreover, external aid to barrio residents is openly opposed by ethnic barrio leaders. These patrons correctly perceive that accepting aid from external agencies will eventually lead to loss of self-determination. While they are aware of the need for better health services, adequate housing facilities, and improved recreational outlets, they also know that improving the barrio will diminish it as a political power base. Government

officials are often surprised to find that radical barrio spokesmen who have demanded better facilities for the barrio will
violently reject these when they are furnished without consult-
ing the barrio leaders themselves.

In the helping agencies the belief prevails that poor and uneducated Mexican American barrio residents are incapable of
helping themselves. Any signs of internal organization for
solving barrio problems are seen as a sinister threat to the
custodial-oriented welfare operations. Spicer, working with a
social action program in Arizona, described the problem as
follows:

> Those persons in the higher income levels who became
> interested at all took it for granted that the people of
> Navidad [the Mexican-American barrio] were incapable
> of doing anything for themselves. The idea that they
> might have initiated efforts to improve their housing
> seemed incredible. It was even less believable that they
> might have taken part in initiating and planning a full-
> scale improvement project. Evidence showing that they
> had indeed participated over a period of many months
> prior to the OEO funding was too incredible to be ac-
> cepted. . . . If something was actually happening it must
> be the work of behind-the-scene manipulators . . . pawns
> in the hands of others [1970:16].

Professionals working on their own to help Mexican Americans often have these same misguided notions. Doctors, lawyers, engineers, and relief experts are well trained in the technical aspects of their profession, but they often have meager
knowledge of cross-cultural differences.

Medical experts forget that the cases they see are selective
and not representative of entire populations. A Texas physi-
cian, reporting on the unusually high incidence of tuberculosis
among Mexican Americans, soberly proclaimed them to be "a
diseased race." He failed to associate the high incidence of tuberculosis among Mexican Americans with the equally high
rate of poverty in this group—that is, with slum conditions.
Another medically trained professional came to some similarly
distorted conclusions about Mexican American folk medicine

on the basis of a limited number of Mexican American cases in a public clinic and supplementary interviews with four folk healers (*curanderos*) (Kiev, 1968). A more intensive investigation of randomly selected Mexican American families in the same region (Nall and Speilberg, 1967) concluded that entrenched beliefs about folk medicine were not the major reasons for the use of *curanderos*, but rather that economic resources, availability, and expediency were of greater importance. Scientific medical assistance, when offered, was readily accepted.

Anglo professionals dispensing aid in the lower valley of Texas after the 1958 flood revealed the same inability to perceive reluctance on the part of Mexican Americans to accept such aid. This reluctance was caused by the superordinate-subordinate social relationships existing between the two groups before the emergency. Even during periods of extreme stress, neither group forgot the traditional patterns of ethnic discrimination. How the aid was administered, not the quality or quantity of aid furnished, became the criterion by which disaster victims evaluated the aid organizations. Publicity given to a full trainload of relief supplies bound from Louisiana to the Tarahumara Indians in 1966 was enough to threaten the dignity of Mexican officials, who refused to accept the assistance.

The legal and law enforcement professions have a similar record of failure to perceive the differences between lower-class norms and distinctly Mexican American cultural beliefs. Moreover, the negative stereotypes applied to Mexican Americans in the courts are inexcusable on the part of professionals who claim to be objective. In the classic "Sleepy Lagoon" case, arising from the Zoot Suit Riots of 1943, a Lieutenant Ayers of the Los Angeles sheriff's office explained to a grand jury that "crime is a matter of race." Furthermore, he continued, since Mexican Americans are part Aztec and the Aztecs believed in human sacrifice "this total disregard for human life has always been universal through the Americas among the Indian populations, which of course is well known to everyone [Scott, R., 1970:110]." Legal decisions also indicate bias against Mexican Americans on the part of judges. Garza (1972) found that this was especially true in the earlier stages of bail setting, entry of pleas, and so forth. Racism in the courts has been documented by Koeninger (1968) in a comprehensive analysis of convictions and sentences for rape in Texas from 1924 through 1967. Similar discrepancies are documented in a recent publication of the Commission on Civil Rights. The support of legal institutions arises from mutual trust and respect—it is a two-way street—that deteriorates when one is forced to walk a discriminatory path.

GOVERNMENTAL STRUCTURES AND POLICIES

Mexican Americans have traditionally been treated like foreigners in their own land. It is no surprise therefore that federal policies toward Latin America have reflected similar attitudes. Although official pronouncements have been cordial, friendly, and seemingly sincere, the government, in practice, has alternately been dictatorial, neglectful, and exploitative.

Under the Monroe Doctrine in the nineteenth century, Latin America was sealed off from European domination and placed in a politically and economically servile position to the more powerful United States. Following America's participation in World War I, interaction with foreign nations forced us to develop a different type of diplomacy, and our paternalism toward Latin America eased superficially with President Roosevelt's Good Neighbor Policy. "Friendly" relations continued until World War II, when informal sanctions were exerted against some Latin American governments to support the Allied cause. Upon the conclusion of hostilities, our policy became one of "specific crisis diplomacy," handling each crisis as it arose and ignoring Latin American pleas for help when to help was not in our own interest.

President Kennedy announced the Alliance for Progress in March 1961, making money and scientific expertise available to help developing nations take a "giant step forward." The program's accomplishments during the next decade were mostly failures. Not only did it fail to accelerate the economic progress of the countries concerned, but it contributed indirectly to the rate of social, economic, and political deterioration within existing institutional structures. It was completely ineffective in containing the steadily growing culture of poverty in Latin America.

Policies pertaining to the United States–Mexico borderland region have paralleled the disregard for the worth and dignity of Latin American peoples, deprecating the Mexican language and lack of technological or industrial development. After nearly half a century of disputes over the international boundary line and haggling over trade regulations and immigration irregularities, a bilateral agreement between President Johnson and President Díaz Ordaz was signed in April 1966. This set up a joint independent Committee on Development and Friendship (CODAF) to increase harmony along the border. CODAF followed the pattern of grandiose pronouncements but little action, and it was phased out after three years. In view of past history, President Nixon's declaration about assisting Latin America to attain self-determination calls for a "wait and see" attitude. It is obvious, however, that since market and trade relations with the Middle East, Europe, and the Far East have allowed Latin America to become economically less dependent upon the United States, less dictatorial methods must be employed in future inter-American negotiations.

Any concentrated interest in this nation's second largest minority has a short history indeed. In May 1967, the Inter-Agency Committee on Mexican American Affairs was established as a coordinating body for cabinet-level programs directed specifically at Mexican Americans. To acquaint various cabinet-level officials with the special types of programs needed by this minority, two days of public hearings were held in El Paso during October. The first chairman of the committee, Vicente T. Ximenes, was pleased to have the higher administrative officials actually listening to barrio residents and leaders. However, many grass-roots Chicano leaders wished to use these hearings as a forum for airing their demands and grievances, and, under the political banner of La Raza Unida (later to develop into a full-fledged political party), they held their own conference on the other side of the city.

As Puerto Rican problems gained national prominence, minority demands for government representation required the services of a body more diffuse than the Inter-Agency Committee. A permanent cabinet-level organization, the Cabinet Committee on Opportunity for Spanish-Speaking People (CCOSSP) was inaugurated in January 1970, with a California attorney, Martin G. Castillo, serving a one-year appointment as chairman. CCOSSP operated without a permanent chairman from January to August 1971, during which time many top Mexican American staff members relocated to other governmental agencies. Henry Ramirez, a staff member from the Civil Rights Commission, is the present chairman of CCOSSP. The committee serves principally as a forum for Spanish-speaking peoples through a monthly newsletter, *Hoy* ("Today"), and through guest appearances by committee members. Its 1970 budget of $750,000 was raised by only $100,000 in 1971, however, indicating its low priority on the roster of government programs. Moreover, the recent appointments of Puerto Ricans as members now give that ethnic group a majority in the committee. At the same time, the Civil Rights Commission is extending its investigatory powers into Mexican American affairs and its survey of education of Spanish-speaking Americans in the Southwest is an example of such involvement.

Perhaps individual Spanish-surnamed congressmen and government appointees have made the most effective contributions to the cause of the Spanish-speaking Americans. Such men as Senator Joseph Montoya of New Mexico, Congressmen Henry B. Gonzalez and Eligio "Kika" de la Garza of Texas, Edward Roybal of California, and Manuel Lujan, Jr., of New Mexico, have sponsored important legislation for the betterment of Mexican Americans. The appointments of Hilary Sandoval, Jr., head of the Small Business Administration until January 1971, and Phillip Sanchez, the present director of OEO, are particularly noteworthy, although many other Spanish-surnamed Americans now work on staffs or boards of the Civil Rights Commission, OEO, the Equal Employment Opportunity Commission, HUD, HEW, and other such organizations. But perhaps the most visible appointment is that of Ramona Banuelos as Treasurer of the United States. Her Spanish surname will be indelibly printed on each piece of paper currency produced during her term of office. If money talks, it may do so in Spanish!

The notable shift in attitudes toward Mexican Americans on the part of United States officials means that the rights and desires of Mexican Americans can be more fully realized through formal governmental and political channels than they have been. And indeed, only when *all* Americans have equal access to public office, a share in determining who represents them, a channel through which their organized power can be exercised, and equal services and rewards for their efforts, only then can Mexican Americans point to this country as one "with liberty and justice for all" and know that includes full citizenship for Mexican Americans.

Chapter 9 ◉ Summary

The largest bloc of Spanish-speaking people in the United States today is the Mexican American population, composed of more than 6 million people who are principally located within the boundaries of the five southwestern states: California, Arizona, New Mexico, Colorado, and Texas. The ancestors of the many Spanish-surnamed, Spanish-speaking, or brown-skinned residents (Spanish Americans) of those states settled in New Mexico and Colorado nearly a hundred years prior to the establishment of the Republic of Mexico. Hence these people are "Mexican" in a very limited sense, yet they are still subsumed under the category of Mexican American. They were subjugated by "foreigners," Anglo Americans, who arrived after them and took over the Southwest through conquest. Their land grants were taken from them through legal chicanery and fraud, which left them in a subservient economic state.

The bulk of present-day Mexican Americans are descendants of Mexicans who emigrated to the United States during the twentieth century, especially during the Mexican Revolution. Due to cyclical economic factors in Mexico and the United States that have pushed Mexicans from their own country or pulled them here, there have been periods of heavy legal and illegal immigration (the latter being prevalent now). It is ludicrous indeed that Anglo American citizens throughout the Southwest should lump together as "foreigners" these later immigrants and Spanish Americans who were here long before Anglos had settled in the land.

The "Mexican American" is merely a label, but it erroneously implies ethnic homogeneity in a population bloc containing many diverse and distinct groups whose members have in common a language and some similar customs, traditions, and surnames. Mexican Americans use many different labels for themselves—Mexican, Chicano, Latino, Mexican American among others—on the basis of such factors as traditional usage of a name in a given region, age group, urban or rural residence, generation, and social class or economic position. Some contemporary writers search for a single term to describe this ethnic minority in the hope that the "correct" label will bring to the surface a minimum of hostility. They fail to realize that the labels themselves are not the key to these underlying resentments; rather, they are symbolic of Anglo conquest and the resulting attitude on the part of Anglos that they were superior and Mexican Americans inferior. Often, when an Anglo American applies a term such as "Mexican" or "Chicano" to a Mexican American, it conveys to him this legacy of ethnic discrimination and thus produces a negative reaction. Yet the same term used among Mexican Americans might elicit a positive reaction.

The problems associated with ethnic identity and the eventual acceptance of Mexican Americans as social equals in the larger society have two main aspects. First, the Mexican American must have a positive image of himself and be proud of his ethnic accomplishments and cultural heritage. Second, the dominant Anglo American society must relinquish its claims to ethnic superiority and cease to regard non-Anglo culture or language forms as threats to what it believes to be its superior cultural heritage. This not only requires a milieu in which past Mexican American cultural contributions are recognized, but one in which a mature Anglo population no longer feels it must write history to conform to the biases produced by Caucasian feelings of superiority. The inaccuracies in present history textbooks regarding the Mexican American's role in the development of the Southwest—both prior to and after the invasion of Anglo Americans—is probably the greatest obstacle faced by the Mexican American child in his attempt to develop pride in his ancestry and in himself. In literature a stereotype emerges of Mexican Americans as a quaint, simplistic, childlike people, with a disregard for the future or for worldly success. Epitomizing this notion is the Mexican man seated, with bowed head, in perpetual siesta, an enormous sombrero covering his head and a serape over his shoulder.

Even social scientists have created their own stereotypes by employing ethnological tools developed in isolated Mexican cultures. They have described Mexican Americans as a homogeneous folk culture or as a group with value orientations similar to those of the rural Mexican. It is doubtful if such typologies were ever an accurate picture of the Mexican American population in the Southwest. But in any case, they do not represent the vast majority of Mexican Americans today.

In 1960, 80 percent of this minority were urban residents, the bulk of them located in Los Angeles, San Antonio, San Francisco, and El Paso. With urbanization the younger generation of Mexican Americans have much more education than their parents. Unfortunately, Mexican American students are too often taught by teachers without cross-cultural training who view them as *culturally deprived* rather than *culturally different,* a factor that seriously impedes their educational development and achievement potential.

With the urbanization and increased formal education of Mexican Americans, other marked institutional changes have occurred among this minority. Not only has the patriarchal authority of non-English–speaking immigrant parents been diminished, but the once dominant extended family, a traditional characteristic of rural Mexico, has been weakened measurably. Public education, integrated neighborhoods, and social and occupational contacts between Mexican Americans and Anglo Americans of equal social standing have resulted in an increased rate of intermarriage, a trend that is expected to continue in the future. Greater education and freedom for Mexican American girls has drastically altered their traditional female roles of daughter, wife, and mother—part of the familial legacy brought from Mexico.

Mexican Americans are, for the most part, nominal Catholics. Those from a rural Mexican background have little association with the church structure beyond limited personal contact with an itinerant priest. This fragile tie with the mother church, often mistakenly described by authors as a state of complete Catholic dependency, has become increasingly strained recently. The Chicano generation sees the unyielding church as part of the Establishment rather than as an ally to assist in obtaining greater equities for minority groups. Thus many younger Mexican Americans have become alienated from even nominal Catholic identity.

The incomes of most Mexican Americans place them at poverty level. The great majority of the parents and even of the young are poorly educated and work chiefly in unskilled or lower-level blue-collar positions. Hence, they are disproportionately in the lower class. Many observers fail to realize that this class difference is a greater factor in explaining the variation between Mexican American values and those of the middle-class WASP than are existing ethnic differences. Militant Chicano leaders, who are partially Anglicized, often misinterpret lower-class norms to be those of their own Mexican heritage, and thus ridicule Mexican Americans aspiring to, or presently members of the middle-class society as cultural traitors. Yet, it might well be that Mexican American customs, language, and culture will survive in their present form in middle-class Mexican American homes, not in lower-class barrios. Because of this confusion between culture and economics, class differences have been a divisive force in attempts to organize all Mexican Americans into a single political or social movement.

The Anglo doctrine of "white superiority," originally brought from Europe to the New World by the Spanish conquistadores and enshrined in the Society of Castes, has been inflicted upon dark-skinned Mexican Americans in the Southwest in the form of a "pigmentocracy"—social ranking by virtue of skin color. Before the end of World War II, Mexican Americans tried to avoid this racial barrier by presenting themselves as Spanish. However, with the Chicano orientation of recent decades, militant Mexican Americans have overtly rejected this negative view of the dark skin of their Indian ancestors and have sought to glorify brown skin as a positive ethnic attribute.

Moreover, in a repudiation of the dominant society's right to control the criteria for establishing Mexican American identity, Mexican Americans have actively sought to choose names and labels for themselves that had negative connotations among Anglo Americans (such as the name "Chicano"). In doing so they further demonstrate their opposition to the intimidation suffered by Mexican Americans at the hands of the dominant Anglo society. But this drive for autonomy has not emerged in a vacuum.

Today's drive for ethnic autonomy, occurring at a time when many groups have become increasingly militant, is the product of a long struggle. The first of five recognizable periods comprising the history of this struggle is the 450 year period from the Spanish conquest to the Mexican Revolution of 1910. During this time, both in Mexico and the United States, Mestizos were kept in a subordinate position. The second period, the years from 1910 until World War II, was a time when most European immigrant groups living in the United States proclaimed their loyalty to their newly acquired country, the United States of America. German Americans, Italian Americans, Irish Americans, and Mexican Americans rejected their dual status and sought a true cultural blending—to become "100 percent American." Mexican Americans of that era denied their Mexican allegiances and even rejected the Spanish language for English. This period then is characterized by total acculturation to dominant WASP norms. Then, after the war, the third period began. Mexican American veterans returning to their homes in southwestern communities found that they were still barred from social clubs, veterans' organizations, and fraternal brotherhoods on the basis of their racial and ethnic characteristics. Feeling that their fathers paid too high a price for trying to become like Anglo Americans (while still being treated as subordinates), these Mexican Americans adopted a policy of *separatism* and attempted to create a culturally plural society in which the Mexican American and Spanish cultures would have a position of pride equal to that of the middle-class Anglo American culture in the Southwest. The fourth period commenced in the mid-1960s, in conjunction with the larger civil rights and radical movements. Proclaiming that Chicanos would have an equal chance to enjoy the rewards of the larger society only when existing institutional structures, with their built-in discriminatory rules and procedures, had been abolished, Mexican Americans fought for ethnic autonomy—a course of action based on self-determination. Using radical tactics modeled partially on Black Power methods, they employed threats of violence, defiance of legal statutes, public confrontations, and other more extreme tactics in order to make their demands heard and get them acted upon. Gathering increasingly strong support from liberal groups and their own ethnic members (and later from other radical elements) during the years prior to 1970, Mexican Americans instigated many programs and legislative changes that were not possible with the less militant tactics they previously employed. However, factors beyond their control such as backlash and economic slump, as well as internal dissensions, caused demands to be met with political, military, and public resistance. During the summer and fall of 1970, as the fifth and last period of strategic penetration came to the fore, a perceptible decline in the overt tactics of the Chicano movement could be noted. A more adroit and subtle strategy began to be employed—the *penetration* of existing social organizations, public agencies at all levels, and professional organizations. Individuals and groups sympathetic to the Mexican American's complaints provided support for needed legislative, judicial, and organizational reform that would bring greater equity to minority group members. At the present time, this trend appears to be the most promising long-range thrust toward realigning the larger societal structures in a way that will enable Mexican American youth to have equal access to educational and occupational rewards in America.

Failure to provide these channels may result in violence, which will recur on an irregular but cyclical basis, about twice each decade, each time gaining in intensity. This gloomy situation will be ameliorated, however, by factors such as decreased mobility and decreased population growth among Mexican Americans and others, realignment of federal budget priorities from foreign military involvements to domestic programs, increased flexibility at all levels of education, effective occupational counseling for Mexican Americans, and more openings in higher-paying executive or administrative positions for qualified Mexican Americans.

High-level governmental agencies initially defined as exclusively for Mexican Americans have now been expanded to include all Spanish-speaking peoples in America (CCOSS). This reflects an emphasis on language similarity rather than on ethnic unity. The reactions of the Mexican American leadership to this change have not been determined at this time, although in the past they have considered such agencies as their own ethnic province.

Coalitions between Mexican Americans and other ethnic or racial groups have not produced a viable and cohesive unit to advance the causes of the Mexican American minority. The abortive liaison between Black Power and Brown Power is a case in point. The black population is dedicated to reclaiming its ancient traditions and languages but has little difficulty establishing its American identity. On the other hand, Mexican Americans have their own language and a rich cultural heritage but have extreme difficulty avoiding the "foreigner" label. Thus, these two groups share only their mutual contempt for the white supremacy doctrines of the dominant society, and members of each group show little desire to be identified with members of the other. Other alliances have shown a similar absence of positive results. The hippie doctrine of "do your own thing" is repulsive to Chicano leaders, who realize that unity must be the basis for political or social action. Some journalists have even suggested a link between Chicanismo and Communism, because of the adoption by the Brown Berets of guerrilla tactics and costumes similar to those of Ché Guevarra and his followers, but Communism is described as "a white thing," and incompatible with the goals of Chicanismo. However, many police encounters only incidentally affecting Mexican Americans and arising independently of ethnic confrontations are later identified as having a "racist" genesis. These are expected to continue in the larger metropolises of the Southwest, as a result of other organizations (i.e., the New Left, MOBE) and social movements unrelated to those dedicated to Mexican Americans. Although these may be used by despotic Chicano leaders as an excuse for militancy, the desire of either ethnic faction and of participants in interethnic coalitions to "own the riot" will render any extensive coalitions untenable.

Los Angeles has the largest single concentration of Mexican Americans and thus claims to be the heart of the Chicano movement, but the United States–Mexico borderland region is the umbilical cord for nearly all Mexican Americans. The source of new Mexican immigrants (and illegal aliens as well) and of great numbers of commuting workers, this economically depressed area has an economy that has traditionally been based on a large supply of unskilled labor. Such a situation perpetuates traditional stereotypes of Mexican Americans as unskilled, uneducated, and inexperienced workers. And since legislative solutions for border problems originate in the distant capitals of Washington, D.C. and Mexico, D.F., formulated by persons unfamiliar with the symbolic dependency of the two border cultures, decisions and enforcement on the national level will do very little to ameliorate some of the basic factors producing ethnic discrimination and debasement in these areas. In fact, governmental policies may become part of the problem rather than the solution. As long as the hordes of migrant Mexican residents look across the Rio Grande at the affluent United States, and as long as American ranchers and farmers use cheap, illegal alien labor, there will be border problems, with consequences radiating out to Mexican Americans throughout not only the Southwest but the entire nation. A Good Neighbor Policy with our neighbors to the South requires goodwill on the part of each nation. Past performance has found us wanting. Present United States policies must be reevaluated and priorities reestablished to prevent future escalation of international problems along our most vulnerable border to the south.

It is hoped that an open show of force—a riot in east Los Angeles or in south San Antonio—will not be necessary to activate federal, state, and local officials to meet the needs of the Mexican American population, one of our most numerous and least remembered minorities. Procedures must be established whereby Mexican American citizens are allowed the opportunity to shoulder equal responsibility and to receive equal privileges with other citizens of the United States.

Likewise, Mexican Americans who are dedicated to the advancement of their ethnic group must avoid the temptation to exploit their fellows in order to maintain a power position based upon interethnic discontent, hostility, and suspicion. Outside resources should be accepted when they are offered in friendship and can be accepted with dignity. This is a challenge to Anglos and Mexican Americans alike. But this challenge is yet to be met, and solutions are generally unavailable at the present time. This volume proposes no panaceas, but it does define some of the obstacles that prevent the Mexican American from presently being accepted as a first-class citizen in the United States of America.

◎ Bibliography

Adams, B. N. and Meidam, M. T. 1968. Economics, Family Structure, and College Attendance. *American Journal of Sociology* 74:230–239.

Aguirre Beltrán, G. 1946. *La Poblacion negra de México, 1519–1810: Estudio etnohistórico.* México. In *Race Mixture in the History of Latin America*, p. 69. Boston: Little, Brown, 1967.

————. 1953. *Teoría y Práctica de la Educación Indígena.* México, D. F.: Instituto Nacional Indigenista.

Alba, V. 1967. *The Mexicans: The Making of a Nation.* New York: Praeger.

Álvarez, J. H. 1966. A Demographic Profile of the Mexican Immigration to the United States, 1910–1950. *Journal of Inter-American Studies* 8:471–496.

Álvarez, R. 1971. The Unique Psycho-Historical Experience of the Mexican-American People. *Social Science Quarterly* 52:15–29.

Anderson, J. G. and Johnson, W. H. 1968. *Sociocultural Determinants of Achievement among Mexican American Students.* Las Cruces: ERIC Clearinghouse on Rural and Small Schools, New Mexico State University.

Anderson, T. 1969. Bilingual Schooling: Oasis or Mirage. *Hispania* 52:69–74.

Arciniega, T. 1971a. *The Urban Mexican American: A Sociocultural Profile.* Las Cruces: ERIC Clearinghouse on Rural and Small Schools, New Mexico State University.

————. 1971b. *Public Education's Response to the Mexican American Student.* El Paso: Innovative Resources, Inc.

Barragan, M. F. 1969. Organized Religion and La Raza. In *La Raza Challenges Health and Social Welfare Practices*, pp. 49–59. Tucson: Southwest Council of La Raza and National Institute of Mental Health.

Borah, W. 1951. *New Spain's Century of Depression.* Folcroft, Pa.: Folcroft Press.

Borup, J. and Elliot, F. 1969. Relationship between Social Class and Mexican-American and Anglo-American Background as Variables Contributing to Attitudinal and Behavioral Pattern Differences of University Students. Paper read at Rocky Mountain Social Science Association, Lubbock, Texas.

Briegel, K. 1970. The Development of Mexican-American Organizations. In *The Mexican-Americans: An Awakening Minority*, pp. 160–178. Beverly Hills: Glencoe Press.

Brooks, C. K. 1968. Some Approaches to Teaching English as a Second Language. In *Educating the Disadvantaged Learner*, pp. 515–523. San Francisco: Chandler Publishing.

Broom, L. and Shevky, E. 1952. Mexicans in the United States: A Problem in Social Differentiation. *Sociology and Social Research* 36:150–158.

Browning, H. L. and McLemore, S. D. 1964. *A Statistical Profile of the Spanish-Surname Population of Texas*. Austin: Bureau of Business Research.

Burma, J. H. 1954. *Spanish-Speaking Groups in the United States*. Durham, N.C.: Duke University Press.

_____. 1970. A Comparison of the Mexican American Subculture with the Oscar Lewis Culture of Poverty Model. In *Mexican-Americans in the United States: A Reader*, pp. 17–28. New York: Schenkman.

Cabrera, Y. A. 1971. *Emerging Faces: The Mexican-Americans*. Dubuque: William C. Brown.

Cárdenas, L. 1963. The Municipality of Northern Mexico. *Southwestern Studies No. 1*. El Paso: Texas Western Press.

Carter, T. P. 1968. The Negative Self-Concept of Mexican-American Students. *School and Society* 96:217–219.

_____. 1970. *Mexican Americans in School: A History of Education Neglect*. New York: College Entrance Examination Board.

Casavantes, E. J. 1969. *A New Look at the Attributes of the Mexican-American*. Albuquerque: Southwestern Cooperative Educational Laboratory, Inc. This publication is issued pursuant to contract #OEC-4-7-062827-3078 with the Bureau of Research, Office of Education, U.S. Department of Health, Education, and Welfare.

Chandler, C. R. and Ewing, K. 1971. Urbanization and Value Change among Anglo and Mexican Americans. Paper read at Southwestern Social Science Association, Dallas, Texas.

Clark, M. 1959. *Health in the Mexican-American Culture: A Community Study*. Berkeley: University of California Press.

Cline, H. F. 1963. *Mexico: Revolution to Evolution: 1940–1960*. New York: Oxford University Press.

Cohen, A. K. and Hodges, H. M., Jr. 1963. Characteristics of the Lower Blue-Collar Class. *Social Problems* 10:303–334.

Cooper, J. G. 1972. Perception of Self and Others as Related to Ethnic Group Membership. Paper read at American Education Research Association, Chicago, Illinois.

Córdova, I. R. 1969. *The Relationship of Acculturation, Achievement, and Alienation among Spanish American Sixth Grade Students*. Las Cruces: ERIC Clearinghouse on Rural and Small Schools, New Mexico State University.

Cuellar, A. 1970. Perspective on Politics. In *Mexican Americans*. Englewood Cliffs, N.J.: Prentice-Hall.

Cumberland, C. C. 1968. *Mexico: The Struggle for Modernity*. New York: Oxford University Press.

D'Antonio, W. V. and Form, W. H. 1965. *Influentials in Two Border Cities: A Study in Community Decision-Making*. Notre Dame, Ind.: University of Notre Dame Press.

D'Antonio, W. V. and Samora, J. 1962. Occupational Stratification in Four Southwestern Communities. *Social Forces* 41:14–25.

De Blassie, R. R. and Healy, G. W. 1970. *Self Concept: A Comparison of Spanish American, Negra, and Anglo Adolescents across Ethnic, Sex, and Socioeconomic Variables*. Las Cruces: ERIC Clearinghouse on Rural and Small Schools, New Mexico State University.

Delgado, A. B. 1967. A Personal Statement. In *Proceedings of the First Texas Conference for the Mexican-American*, pp. 136–138. Austin: Southwest Educational Development Laboratory, Inter-American Education Center, Texas Education Agency.

Dotson, F. 1955. Disminución de la Población Mexicana en los Estados Unidos de Acuerdo con el Censo de 1950. *Revista Mexicana de Sociología* 17:151–169.

Dworkin, A. G. 1965. Stereotypes and Self-Images Held by Native-Born and Foreign-Born Mexican-Americans. *Sociology and Social Research* 49:214–224.

———. 1971. Patterns of Mexican American Stereotypy: A Case for Stability and Volatility. Paper read at American Sociological Association, Denver, Colorado.

Edmonson, M. S. 1957. *Los Manitos: A Study of Institutional Values.* New Orleans: Tulane University Press.

Estrada, L. F. 1972. Sociology, Social Movements, and the Chicano Sociologist. Paper read at Southwestern Sociological Association, San Antonio, Texas.

Farris, B. and Brymer, R. A. 1965. Differential Socialization of Latin and Anglo-American Youth: An Exploratory Study of the Self Concept. Paper read at the Texas Academy of Science.

Fishman, J. A. 1961. Childhood Indoctrination for Minority-Group Membership. In *Minorities in a Changing World*, pp. 177–197. New York: Knopf.

Fishman, J. A. and Hofman, J. E. 1966. Mother Tongue and Nativity in the American Population. In *Language Loyalty in the United States*, pp. 34–50. The Hague: Mouton and Company.

Fogel, W. 1965. *Education and Income of Mexican-Americans in the Southwest.* Los Angeles: Mexican American Study Project, Advance Report No. 1. Division of Research, Graduate School of Business Administration, University of California, Los Angeles.

Forbes, J. D. 1968. Race and Color in Mexican-American Problems. *Journal of Human Relations* 16:55–68.

Foster, G. M. 1953. What is Folk Culture? *American Anthropologist* 55:159–173.

Francesca, Sister M. 1958. Variations of Selected Cultural Patterns among Three Generations of Mexicans in San Antonio, Texas. *American Catholic Sociological Review* 19:24–31.

Galarza, E. 1964. *Merchants of Labor: The Mexican Bracero Story.* Santa Barbara: McNally & Loftin.

Gamio, M. 1930. *Mexican Immigration to the United States.* Chicago: University of Chicago Press.

Garcia, J. 1972. The I.Q. Conspiracy. *Psychology Today* 6:40–43, 92–4.

Garcia, R. 1969. Chicanos Get Crumbs. *The Prospector*, April 28, 1969. El Paso: University of Texas.

Gardner, R. 1970. *Grito! Reies Tijerina and the New Mexico Land Grant War of 1967.* New York: Bobbs-Merrill Company.

Garza, H. A. 1972. Administration of Justice: Chicanos in Monterey County. Paper read at the Southwestern Social Science Association, San Antonio, Texas.

Garza, R. J. 1969. Culture Contributions of the Mexican-American. In *The Role of the Mexican American in the History of the Southwest*, pp. 53–60. Edinburg: Inter-American Institute.

Goffman, I. 1959. *The Presentation of Self in Everyday Life*. Garden City, N.Y.: Doubleday.

Gonzalez, N. L. 1969. *The Spanish Americans of New Mexico: A Heritage of Pride*. Albuquerque: University of New Mexico Press.

Grebler, L. 1967. *The Schooling Gap: Signs of Progress*. Los Angeles: Division of Research, Graduate School of Business Administration, University of California.

Grebler, L., Moore, J. W., and Guzman, R. C. 1970. *The Mexican-American People*. New York: Free Press.

Greeley, A. M. 1972. Political Participation among Ethnic Groups in the United States: A Preliminary Reconnaissance. Paper read at the American Sociological Association, New Orleans, Louisiana.

Guzman, R. 1967. Ethics in Federally Subsidized Research: The Case of the Mexican American. In *The Mexican American: A New Focus on Opportunity*, pp. 245–249. Washington, D.C.: Inter-Agency on Mexican American Affairs.

Hayner, N. S. 1966. *New Patterns in Old Mexico: A Study of Town and Metropolis*. New Haven: College & University Press.

Heller, C. S. 1966. *Mexican-American Youth: Forgotten Youth at the Crossroads*. New York: Random House.

Higham, J. 1970. *Strangers in the Land*. New York: Antheneum Press.

Hoetink, H. 1967. *The Two Variants in Caribbean Race Relations: A Contribution to the Sociology of Segmented Societies*. New York: Oxford University Press.

Holland, W. R. 1962. Language Barrier as an Education Problem of Spanish-Speaking Children. In *Understanding the Educational Problems of the Disadvantaged Learner*, II, pp. 338–340. San Francisco: Chandler Publishing.

Humphrey, N. D. 1954. The Mexican Image of Americans. *The Annals* 295:116–125.

Hyman, H. H. and Wright, C. R. 1971. Trends in Voluntary Association Memberships of American Adults: Replication Based on Secondary Analysis of National Sample Surveys. *American Sociological Review* 36:191–206.

I.T.C. 1971. *The Texians and the Texans: The Mexican Texans.* San Antonio: University of Texas Institute of Texas Cultures.

Iturriaga, J. E. 1951. *La Estructura Social y Cultural de México.* Mexico: Fondo de Cultura Ecónomica.

Jensen, A. R. 1961. Learning Abilities in Mexican-American and Anglo-American Children. *California Journal of Educational Research* 12:147–159.

Johnson, B. E. 1962. Ability, Achievement and Bilingualism: A Comparative Study Involving Spanish-Speaking and English Children at the Sixth Grade Level. Unpublished Ed.D. thesis, University of Maryland.

Kennedy, W. C. 1972. The Role of Ideology in the Mexican-American Studies Programs of the California State College System. Paper read at the Southwestern Sociological Association Meetings, San Antonio, Texas.

Kiev, A. 1968. *Curanderismo: Mexican-American Folk Psychiatry.* New York: The Free Press.

Klapp, O. E. 1969. *Collective Search for Identity.* New York: Holt, Rinehart & Winston.

Kluckhohn, F. R. and Strodtbeck, F. L. 1961. *Variations in Value Orientations.* New York: Row, Peterson & Co.

Knowlton, C. S. 1967a. A Changing Pattern of Segregation and Discrimination Affecting the Mexican Americans of El Paso, Texas. Paper read at Southern Sociological Society, Atlanta, Georgia.

—————. 1967b. *Land-Grant Problems among the State's Spanish-Americans.* Albuquerque: Bureau of Business Research.

—————. 1969. Changing Spanish-American Villages of Northern New Mexico. *Sociology and Social Research* 53:455–474.

—————. 1970. Violence in New Mexico: A Sociological Perspective. *California Law Review* 58:1054–1084.

Koeninger, R. C. 1968. *The Law: Rape, Race, Time and Death in Texas.* Proceedings of the Southwest Social Science Association, Dallas, Texas.

Kurtz, N. R. 1968. Gatekeepers: Agents in Acculturation. *Rural Sociology* 33:64–70.

Kuvlesky, W. P., Wright, D. E., and Juarez, R. S. 1971. Status Projections and Ethnicity: A Comparison of Mexican American, Negro and Anglo Youth. *Journal of Vocational Behavior* 1:137–151.

Lara-Braud, J. 1970. E Pluribus Unum: La Raza. In *With All Due Respect*, pp. 9–14. Austin, Texas: Southwest Intergroup Relations Council, Inc.

Lazerwitz, B. 1961. A Comparison of Major United States Religious Groups. *Journal of the American Statistical Association* 56: 568–579.

Leeds, A. 1968. *The Anthropology of Cities: Some Methodological Issues*. Austin, Texas: Institute of Latin American Studies.

León-Portilla, M. 1960. The Concept of the State among the Ancient Aztecs. *Alpha Kappa Deltan* 30:7–13.

Lewis, O. 1951. *Tepoztlán Restudied: Life in a Mexican Village*. Urbana: University of Illinois Press.

————. 1966. The Culture of Poverty. *Scientific American* 215: 19–25.

Loomis, C. P. 1942. Wartime Migrations from Rural Spanish-Speaking Villages of New Mexico. *Rural Sociology* 7:384–395.

————. 1970. In Defense of Integration: For One Nation and For One World. *The Centennial Review* 14:125–165.

Love, J. L. 1969. La Raza: Mexican Americans in Rebellion. *Trans action* 6:35–41.

Madsen, W. 1964. *The Mexican-Americans of South Texas*. New York: Holt, Rinehart & Winston.

Manuel, H. T. 1965. *Spanish-Speaking Children of the Southwest: Their Education and the Public Welfare*. Austin, Texas: University of Texas Press.

Martinez, J. 1966. Leadership and Politics. In *La Raza: Forgotten Americans*, pp. 47–62. Notre Dame, Ind.: University of Notre Dame Press.

Matthiasson, C. W. 1968. Acculturation of Mexican-Americans in a Midwestern City. Unpublished Ph.D. dissertation, Cornell University.

Matthiessen, P. 1969. *Sal si Puedes: César Chavez and the New American Revolution*. New York: Random House.

McClelland, D. D., Atkinson, J., Clark, R., and Lowell, E. 1953. *The Achievement Motive*. New York: Appleton-Century-Crofts.

McNamara, P. H. 1968. Social Action Priests in the Mexican-American Community. *Sociological Analysis* 29:177–185.

———. n.d. Chicanos and Catholicism: A Sociological Approach. Unpublished paper.

McWilliams, C. 1933. Getting Rid of the Mexican. *The American Mercury,* March.

———. 1939. *Factories in the Field: The Story of Migratory Farm Labor in California.* Boston: Little, Brown.

———. 1969. *North from Mexico: The Spanish Speaking People of the United States.* New York: Greenwood Press.

Mead, M. 1955. The Spanish Americans of New Mexico, U.S.A. In *Cultural Patterns and Technological Change,* pp. 151–177. New York: UNESCO, Mentor Ed.

Meinig, D. W. 1971. *Southwest: Three Peoples in Geographical Change 1600–1970.* New York: Oxford University Press.

Merkx, G. W. and Griego, R. J. 1971. Crisis in New Mexico. In *Majority and Minority: The Dynamics of Racial and Ethnic Relations,* pp. 599–610. Boston: Allyn and Bacon.

Migratory Labor in American Agriculture. 1951. Washington, D.C.: U.S. Government Printing Office.

Miller, H. P. 1964: *Rich Man–Poor Man.* New York: Thomas Y. Crowell.

Mittlebach, F. G. and Marshall, G. 1966. *The Burden of Poverty.* Los Angeles: Mexican-American Study Project, Graduate School of Business Administration, University of California, Los Angeles.

Mittlebach, F. G., Moore, J. W., and McDaniel, R. 1966. *Intermarriage of Mexican-Americans.* Los Angeles: Mexican American Study Project, Advance Report No. 6. Graduate School of Business Administration, University of California, Los Angeles.

Montez, P. 1970. Will the Real Mexican American Please Stand Up? *Civil Rights Digest* 3:28–31.

Moore, Joan W. 1970a. *Mexican Americans.* Englewood Cliffs, N.J.: Prentice-Hall.

———. 1970b. Colonialism: The Case of the Mexican Americans. *Social Problems* 17:463–472.

Moquin, W., ed. 1971. A Documentary History of the Mexican Americans. New York: Praeger.

Mörner, M. 1967. *Race Mixture in the History of Latin America.* Boston: Little, Brown.

Muñoz, C. 1970. Toward a Chicano Perspective of Political Analysis. *Aztlán* 1:15–26.

Nall, F. C. II 1962. Role Expectations. A Cross-Cultural Study. *Rural Sociology* 27:28–41.

Nall, F. C. II and Speilberg, J. 1967. Social and Cultural Factors in Responses of Mexican-Americans to Medical Treatment. *Journal of Health and Social Behavior* 8:299–308.

Nogueira, O. 1959. Skin Color and Social Class. In *Plantation Systems of the New World,* pp. 164–179. Washington, D.C.: Pan American Union.

Officer, J. E. 1964. Sodalities and Systemic Linkage: The Joining Habits of Urban Mexican-Americans. Unpublished Ph.D. Dissertation, University of Arizona.

Othón de Mendizabal, M. 1968. El Origen Histórico de Nuestra Clases Medias In *Esayos Sobre las Clases en México,* pp. 9–22. México, D. F.: Editorial Nuestro Tiempo.

Palmore, E. B. 1962. Ethnophaulisms and Ethnocentrism. *American Journal of Sociology* 67:442–445.

Parsons, T. W., Jr. 1965. Ethnic Cleavage in a California School. Unpublished Ph.D. dissertation, Stanford University.

Paz, O. 1961. *The Labyrinth of Solitude: Life and Thought in Mexico.* New York: Grove Press.

Peñalosa, F. 1967. The Changing Mexican-American in Southern California. *Sociology and Social Research* 51:405–417.

————. 1968. Mexican Family Roles. *Journal of Marriage and the Family* 30:680–689.

————. 1969. Education-Income Discrepancies between Second and Later-Generation Mexican-Americans in the Southwest. *Sociology and Social Research* 53: 448–454.

Peñalosa, F. and McDonagh, E. C. 1966. Social Mobility in a Mexican-American Community. *Social Forces* 44:498–505.

Pinkney, A. 1963. Prejudice toward Mexican and Negro Americans: A Comparison. *Phylon:* 353–395.

Pitt, L. 1970. *The Decline of the Californios: A Social History of the Spanish-Speaking Californians, 1846–1890.* Berkeley: University of California Press.

Portes, A. 1969. Dilemmas of a Golden Exile: Integration of Cuban Refugee Families in Milwaukee. *American Sociological Review* 34:505–518.

Price, J. A. 1971. International Border Screens and Smuggling. In *Prostitution and Illicit Drug Traffic on the U.S.–Mexico Border,* pp. 22–42. El Paso: Border-State University Consortium for Latin America, Occasional Papers No. 2.

Ramirez, M. III 1969. *Potential Contributions by the Behavioral Sciences to Effective Preparation Programs for Teachers of Mexican-American Children.* Las Cruces: ERIC Clearinghouse on Rural and Small Schools, New Mexico State University.

Ramirez, S. 1967. *The Mexican American: A New Focus on Opportunity.* Washington, D.C.: Inter-Agency Committee on Mexican American Affairs.

Redfield, R. 1930. *Tepoztlán: A Mexican Village.* Chicago: University of Chicago Press.

————. 1941. *The Folk Culture of Yucatan.* Chicago: University of Chicago Press.

Renner, K. N. 1969. An Analysis of Acculturation of the Spanish Surname Population. Unpublished paper, Department of Sociology, University of Texas, El Paso.

Rochin, R. I. 1972. The Short and Turbulent Life of Chicano Studies. Paper read at the Southwestern Sociological Association, San Antonio, Texas.

Rodriguez, C. 1969. High School Girl Expresses Influence of Discrimination. *The Prospector* 36 (October). El Paso: University of Texas Press.

Romano-V., O. I. 1967. Minorities, History and Cultural Mystique. *El Grito: A Journal of Contemporary Mexican-American Thought* 1:5–11.

————. 1968. The Anthropology and Sociology of the Mexican-Americans: The Distortion of Mexican-American History. *El Grito: A Journal of Contemporary Mexican-American Thought* 2:13–26.

————. 1969. The Historical and Intellectual Presence of Mexican-Americans. *El Grito: A Journal of Contemporary Mexican-American Thought* 2:32–46.

Rose, P. I. 1969. The Black Experience: Issues and Images. *Social Science Quarterly* 50:286–297.

Rosen, B. C. 1959. Race, Ethnicity and the Achievement Syndrome. *American Sociological Review* 24:47–60.

Rosenthal, R. and Jacobson, L., 1968. Self-fulfilling Prophecies in the Classroom: Teaching Expectations as Unintended Determinants of Pupils' Intellectual Competence. In *Social Class, Race, and Psychological Development*. New York: Holt, Rinehart & Winston.

Rubel, A. J. 1966. *Across the Tracks: Mexican-Americans in a Texas City*. Austin: University of Texas Press.

Samora, J. and Lamanna, R. A. 1967. *Mexican-Americans in a Midwest Metropolis: A Study of East Chicago*. Mexican American Study Project, Advance Report No. 8. Los Angeles: Graduate School of Business Administration, University of California.

Sanchez, G. I. 1966. History, Culture and Education. In *La Raza: Forgotten Americans*, pp. 1–26. Notre Dame, Ind.: University of Notre Dame Press.

_____. 1967. *Forgotten People*. Albuquerque: University of New Mexico Press.

Saunders, L. 1954. *Cultural Differences and Medical Care*. New York: Russell Sage Foundation.

Schafer, W. E., Olexa, C., and Polk, K. 1970. Programmed for Social Class: Tracking in High School. *Trans action* 7:39–46, 63.

Scott, J. C., Jr. 1957. Membership and Participation in Voluntary Associations. *American Sociological Review* 22:315–326.

Scott, R. F. 1970. The Sleepy Lagoon Case and the Grand Jury Investigation. In *The Mexican-Americans: An Awakening Minority*, pp. 105–116. Beverly Hills: Glencoe Press.

Segall, M. H., Campbell, D. T., and Herskovits, M. J. 1966. *The Influence of Culture on Visual Perception*. Indianapolis: Bobbs-Merrill Company.

Sena Rivera, J. 1972. The Black and Chicano Movements—1972. Panel presentation at the Southwestern Sociological Association, San Antonio, Texas.

Servín, M. P. 1965. The Post–World War II Mexican-American, 1925–1965: A Non-Achieving Minority. Paper read at the Western History Association, Helena, Montana.

Shapiro, H. A. 1952. The Pecan Shellers of San Antonio, Texas. *The Southwestern Social Science Quarterly* 32:229–244.

Sheldon, P. M. 1966. Community Participation and the Emerging Middle Class. In *La Raza: Forgotten Americans,* pp. 125–157. Notre Dame, Ind.: University of Notre Dame Press.

Simmen, E. ed. 1971. *The Chicano: From Caricature to Self-Portrait.* New York: New American Library.

Simpson, L. B. 1964. *Many Mexicos.* Berkeley: University of California Press.

Spicer, E. H. 1970. Patrons of the Poor. *Human Organization* 29: 12–19.

Spitzer, A. 1960. Religious Structure in Mexico. *Alpha Kappa Deltan* 30:54–58.

Steglich, W. G. 1969. Availability and Usefulness of Federal Programs and Services to Elderly Mexican-Americans. *Hearings before the Special Committee on Aging.* Washington, D.C.: U.S. Government Printing Office.

Steiner, S. 1970. *La Raza: The Mexican Americans.* New York: Harper & Row.

Stoddard, E. R. 1969. The United States–Mexican Border as a Research Laboratory. *Journal of Inter-American Studies* 11:477–488.

————. 1970a. *Ethnic Identity of Urban Mexican-American Youth.* Proceedings of the Southwest Sociological Association, Dallas, Texas.

————. 1970b. The Role of Social Factors in the Successful Adjustment of Mexican-American Families to Forced Housing Relocation. *A Final Report to the Chamizal Relocation Research Project, El Paso, Texas.* El Paso: Community Renewal Program.

Swadesh, F. L. 1968. The Alianza Movement: Catalyst for Social Change in New Mexico. *Spanish-Speaking People in the United States—Proceedings of the 1968 Annual Meeting of the American Ethnological Society,* pp. 162–177.

————. 1972. The Social and Philosophical Context of Creativity in Hispanic New Mexico. *The Rocky Mountain Social Science Journal* 9:11–18.

Taylor, P. S. 1931. Crime and the Foreign Born: The Problem of the Mexican. *U.S. Commission of Law Observation and Enforcement* 10:199–243.

TenHouten, W. D., Lei, T., Kendall, F., and Gorden, C. W. 1971. School Ethnic Composition, Social Contexts, and Educational

Plans of Mexican-American and Anglo High School Students. *American Journal of Sociology* 77:89–107.

Theresita, Sister M. 1968. An Inter-class, Cross-cultural Comparison of Values. *Sociological Analysis* 29:217–223.

Torgerson, D. 1968. Brown Power Unity Seen Behind School Disorders. *Los Angeles Times*, March 17. Copyright, 1968, Los Angeles Times. Reprinted by permission.

Tuck, R. 1946. *Not with the Fist*. New York: Harcourt, Brace, & World.

Turner, R. H. and Surace, S. J. 1956. Zoot-Suiters and Mexicans: Symbols in Crowd Behavior. *American Journal of Sociology* 62:14–20.

Uhlenberg, P. 1972. Demographic Correlates of Group Achievement: Contrasting Patterns of Mexican-Americans and Japanese-Americans. *Demography* 9:119–128.

Ulibarrí, H. 1966. Social and Attitudinal Characteristics of Spanish-Speaking Migrant and Ex-Migrant Workers in the Southwest. *Sociology and Social Research* 50:361–370.

Vaca, N. C., 1970a. The Mexican-American in the Social Sciences, 1912–1970: Part I: 1912–1935. *El Grito: A Journal of Contemporary Mexican-American Thought* #3: 3–24.

_____. 1970b. The Mexican-American in the Social Sciences, 1912–1970: Part II, 1936–1970. *El Grito: A Journal of Contemporary Mexican American Thought* #4: 17–51.

Valencia, N. A. 1969. Twentieth-Century Urbanization in Latin America and a Case Study of Ciudad Juárez. Unpublished Master's thesis, University of Texas at El Paso.

Vallier, I. 1970. *Catholicism, Social Control, and Modernization in Latin America*. Englewood Cliffs, N.J.: Prentice-Hall.

Vasconcelos, J. 1926. *La Raza Cósmica*. Barcelona: Tipografía Cosmos.

Watson, J. B. and Samora, J. 1954. Subordinate Leadership in a Bi-Cultural Community. *American Sociological Review* 19:413–417.

Wiley, N. F. 1967. The Ethnic Mobility Trap and Stratification Theory. *Social Problems* 15:147–159.

Winther, S. F., Potter, E. B., and Huber, W. H. 1969. *A Longitudinal Study of the Beginning Freshman Class of 1963 at the Uni-*

versity of New Mexico: The Invisible Student. Las Cruces: ERIC Clearinghouse on Rural and Small Schools, New Mexico State University.

Yinger, J. M. 1963. Desegregation in American Society: The Record of a Generation of Change. *Sociology and Social Research* 47: 428–445.

Zurcher, L. A., Jr., Zurcher, S. L., and Meadow, A. 1965. Value Orientation, Role Conflict, and Alienation from Work: A Cross-Cultural Study. *The American Sociological Review* 30:539–548.

◎ Index

ABOUT THE AUTHOR

Ellwyn R. Stoddard is Professor of Sociology at the University of Texas at El Paso, where his area of specializiation is Mexican American studies. He also has taught at Drake University and Michigan State and he has done extensive field research in more than thirty sociological projects, among them the U.S.–Mexican Border Studies Project sponsored by the Carnegie Foundation. In addition, he has contributed to numerous sociological and anthropological journals, most notably *American Sociologist,* the *Social Science Quarterly, Human Organization,* and the *Journal of Inter-American Studies.* His articles also appear in the anthologies *Putting Sociology to Work* (1973), edited by Arthur B. Shostak, and *Social Problems Today* (1971) and *Work and Its Social Dimensions: Readings in the Sociology of Occupations and Professions* (1972), both edited by Clifton D. Bryant. Dr. Stoddard grew up in Logan, Utah, and attended schools in that state and in Michigan. He holds a Ph.D. in sociology from Michigan State University.